Adoption

Opposing Viewpoints®

Other Books of Related Interest

Opposing Viewpoints Series

Abortion
American Values
America's Children
America's Cities
Child Abuse
The Family in America
Feminism
Health Care in America
The Homeless
Homosexuality
Male/Female Roles
Population
Racism in America
Sexual Values
Teenage Sexuality

Current Controversies Series

Reproductive Technologies

Adoption

Opposing Viewpoints®

David Bender & Bruno Leone, *Series Editors*

Andrew Harnack, Professor of English,
Eastern Kentucky University, *Book Editor*

OPPOSING
VIEWPOINTS®
SERIES

Greenhaven Press, Inc., San Diego, CA

Cover photo: Rocky Thies

Greenhaven Press, Inc.
PO Box 289009
San Diego, CA 92198-9009

Library of Congress Cataloging-in-Publication Data

Adoption : opposing viewpoints / Andrew Harnack, book editor.
        p.   cm. — (Opposing viewpoints series)
    Includes bibliographical references and index.
        Summary: Debates issues concerning the adoption of children, presenting arguments both in favor of and against adopting.
        ISBN 1-56510-213-4 (lib. bdg.) — ISBN 1-56510-212-6 (pbk.)
        1. Adoption. [1. Adoption.] I. Harnack, Andrew, 1937-   .
    II. Series: Opposing viewpoints series (Unnumbered)
    HV875.A3428   1995
    362.7'34—dc20
                                                94-41043
                                                CIP

"Congress shall make no law . . . abridging the freedom of speech, or of the press."

First Amendment to the U.S. Constitution

The basic foundation of our democracy is the First Amendment guarantee of freedom of expression. The Opposing Viewpoints Series is dedicated to the concept of this basic freedom and the idea that it is more important to practice it than to enshrine it.

Contents

Why Consider Opposing Viewpoints?

"The only way in which a human being can make some approach to knowing the whole of a subject is by hearing what can be said about it by persons of every variety of opinion and studying all modes in which it can be looked at by every character of mind. No wise man ever acquired his wisdom in any mode but this."

John Stuart Mill

In our media-intensive culture it is not difficult to find differing opinions. Thousands of newspapers and magazines and dozens of radio and television talk shows resound with differing points of view. The difficulty lies in deciding which opinion to agree with and which "experts" seem the most credible. The more inundated we become with differing opinions and claims, the more essential it is to hone critical reading and thinking skills to evaluate these ideas. Opposing Viewpoints books address this problem directly by presenting stimulating debates that can be used to enhance and teach these skills. The varied opinions contained in each book examine many different aspects of a single issue. While examining these conveniently edited opposing views, readers can develop critical thinking skills such as the ability to compare and contrast authors' credibility, facts, argumentation styles, use of persuasive techniques, and other stylistic tools. In short, the Opposing Viewpoints Series is an ideal way to attain the higher-level thinking and reading skills so essential in a culture of diverse and contradictory opinions.

In addition to providing a tool for critical thinking, Opposing Viewpoints books challenge readers to question their own strongly held opinions and assumptions. Most people form their opinions on the basis of upbringing, peer pressure, and personal, cultural, or professional bias. By reading carefully balanced opposing views, readers must directly confront new ideas as well as the opinions of those with whom they disagree. This is not to simplistically argue that everyone who reads opposing views will—or should—change his or her opinion. Instead, the series enhances readers' depth of understanding of their own views by encouraging confrontation with opposing ideas. Careful examination of others' views can lead to the readers' understanding of the logical inconsistencies in their own opinions, perspective on why they hold an opinion, and the consideration of the possibility that their opinion requires further evaluation.

Evaluating Other Opinions

To ensure that this type of examination occurs, Opposing Viewpoints books present all types of opinions. Prominent spokespeople on different sides of each issue as well as well-known professionals from many disciplines challenge the reader. An additional goal of the series is to provide a forum for other, less known, or even unpopular viewpoints. The opinion of an ordinary person who has had to make the decision to cut off life support from a terminally ill relative, for example, may be just as valuable and provide just as much insight as a medical ethicist's professional opinion. The editors have two additional purposes in including these less known views. One, the editors encourage readers to respect others' opinions—even when not enhanced by professional credibility. It is only by reading or listening to and objectively evaluating others' ideas that one can determine whether they are worthy of consideration. Two, the inclusion of such viewpoints encourages the important critical thinking skill of objectively evaluating an author's credentials and bias. This evaluation will illuminate an author's reasons for taking a particular stance on an issue and will aid in readers' evaluation of the author's ideas.

As series editors of the Opposing Viewpoints Series, it is our hope that these books will give readers a deeper understanding of the issues debated and an appreciation of the complexity of even seemingly simple issues when good and honest people disagree. This awareness is particularly important in a democratic society such as ours in which people enter into public debate to determine the common good. Those with whom one disagrees should not be regarded as enemies but rather as people whose views deserve careful examination and may shed light on one's own.

Thomas Jefferson once said that "difference of opinion leads to inquiry, and inquiry to truth." Jefferson, a broadly educated man, argued that "if a nation expects to be ignorant and free . . . it expects what never was and never will be." As individuals and as a nation, it is imperative that we consider the opinions of others and examine them with skill and discernment. The Opposing Viewpoints Series is intended to help readers achieve this goal.

David L. Bender & Bruno Leone,
Series Editors

Introduction

"The basic premise of adoption in the past was that it was a viable solution to certain problem situations."

Marlou Russell, USA Today, *July 1994*

Adoption may be defined as the process of providing parents for children and children for families when birth parents are unwilling or unable to care for their offspring. Practiced throughout recorded history, only recently has adoption come to be seen as a distinct benefit to children. Ancient Romans, for example, practiced adoption primarily as a way to provide heirs for adults. Much later, in colonial America, illegitimate children were apprenticed to tradesmen, essentially a form of indentured servitude. Indentured and apprenticed children were often cared for by orphanages supported by their masters. Common law at the time, as cited by judges and courts, deemed "blood ties" necessary for legal parentage.

It was not until the late nineteenth century that legislative bodies in the United States began to grant legal status to parents of adoptive children. At the same time, new laws were passed to safeguard the welfare of children. In 1891, Michigan law required that judges investigate adoptive placements before issuing final adoption decrees. In 1917, Minnesota was the first state to require an agency or state welfare department to make written recommendations to the court after investigation. Trial periods between placement and final decree were eventually initiated, as were the sealing of original birth certificates and the issuance of new ones naming the adoptive parents in place of the birth parents. By the first quarter of the twentieth century, all states had ratified laws granting to children the right to be legally adopted if and when the criteria for such adoptions were met. In formalizing adoption as an institution, the law gave parents and children important protections. Adopted children now enjoy both the same entitlements to care and support and the same inheritance rights from their adoptive parents as biologic children do from their birth parents.

In 1970, approximately 175,000 children were adopted in the United States. Since then, however, the number of adoptions has decreased for a variety of reasons. The stigmas of out-of-wedlock childbearing and living on welfare have been significantly reduced, and more unmarried mothers are parenting their own babies. With the legalization of abortion, more women have chosen to terminate pregnancies. Both of these changes reduce the number of children, especially healthy infants, available for adoption. But the trend toward fewer adoptions is also due to legal, legislative, and bureaucratic decisions that have made adoption more complicated and adoption services more expensive, or have otherwise affected promotion of the "adoption option."

By most estimates, there are more than a half-million children eligible for adoption within the United States. From this population, Americans adopt more than 100,000 children annually. Most of the children, though, remain in some kind of foster care (more than 400,000) or in orphanages and residential communities (approximately 71,000). A large number of these children are African-Americans; many are "special needs" children with certain characteristics and conditions that make it particularly difficult to find permanent homes for them. Nevertheless, each year more than a million potential parents attempt to adopt a child. That so few are successful in adoption suggests that current policies and programs are not working efficiently or well.

While much has already been done to protect the rights of adopted children, adoptive parents, and birth parents (the so-called adoption triangle), numerous ethical issues and important legal questions affecting adoption remain unresolved. Legislatures, policy makers, adoption agencies, state welfare systems, individuals (many of whom were adopted or have adopted children), and national organizations are all involved in the debates. The issues, which often elicit highly emotional responses, include the use of open or sealed adoption records, the desirability of transracial and foreign adoptions, the rights of both birth parents, surrogate parenting, adoptions by gays and lesbians, orphanages, protections against fraudulent adoptions, search movements (attempts by adoptees to find their birth families), and the legal bias toward biological relationships.

Many voices are calling for reform. Some see the current legal partiality for biological relationships as ill-founded and urge a redefinition of society's notions of the family and of kinship. Others seek to revamp either the entire welfare system or at least society's values so that more is done to support the formation of stable families and to protect them from breaking apart. Still others want to guarantee parents and children of broken families the legal right to maintain and reestablish relationships. Some want to reinstitute orphanages. Adoption agencies, social workers, and many national organizations insist that more must be done to protect the interests of children. Politicians and law-

13

makers are being goaded into creating new funding procedures and policies. At stake is the physical, mental, social, and psychological well-being of many Americans, especially that of children.

The debate in recent years has become a matter of national interest. In 1993 and 1994 the media closely covered the "Baby Jessica" story, a contested adoption that was often a cover article or lead story, especially when the child was removed from the home of her would-be adoptive parents and returned to her biological parents. In 1995 renewed interest in the reestablishment of orphanages brought headlines to newspapers, television debates, and much animated conversation on Internet bulletin boards, in newspaper editorials, and in letters to editors.

According to national estimates, one million children in the United States live with adoptive parents. Because adoption policies will always be important to people who have been adopted, who seek to adopt, who have placed their children in adoption, and who might otherwise want to help those involved in adoptions, the viewpoints presented here are of special interest. *Adoption: Opposing Viewpoints* presents arguments about five of the most important adoption issues: Should Adoptions Be Encouraged? Whose Rights Must Be Protected in the Adoption Process? Are There Alternatives to Traditional Adoption? Are Some Adoptions More Problematic Than Others? Should Adoption Policies Be Changed?

Should Adoptions
Be Encouraged?

Adoption

Chapter Preface

Although many cultures have practiced adoption for centuries, it is only recently that the formal practice of adoption, legalized in the United States in the early twentieth century, has come under scrutiny. Critics emphasize that adoption often produces a strong sense of loss, usually first experienced by the birth mother and later by the adopted child. Some of these critics demand that adoption be abolished. While those who support the practice of adoption agree that birth parents and adoptees may experience a genuine sense of loss, they nevertheless insist that the practice of adoption is fundamentally good. Emphasizing that some parents are unable to provide appropriate care for their children, supporters of adoption believe that the benefits of new homes for many children outweigh whatever liabilities and losses birth parents and adoptees may experience.

But far more children are available for adoption than there are families available to adopt them. Thus, those who are responsible for the welfare of children—usually social workers in state agencies—are caught in a dilemma. On the one hand, they believe that many children who are abused or abandoned by their parents should be placed within other family settings—preferably by permanent adoption, perhaps by providing temporary foster-child care, perhaps by placing them within residential communities. On the other hand, they realize that the last two options—foster homes and residential communities—are frequently short-term and unsatisfactory solutions.

To manage a way through the apparent dilemma, many critics call for a renewed commitment to the preservation of families. They argue that if society relocates its resources to help troubled families overcome their difficulties, then the need for adoption as an alternative will diminish. Others, while not necessarily disagreeing with the need for family preservation, maintain that many children nevertheless need new families, new homes. To make more adoptions possible, they argue, requires an enlarged understanding and image of family. Rather than defining family as a biological unit tied to a certain culture, they urge that families be considered more as groups of individuals committed to the support of children in need of nurturing and love.

These arguments provide the bases for the discussions about adoption practices and policies in the following chapter.

"Death by adoption is the death experienced by the real mother. The baby she carried can actually die for her at either the moment of birth or as she signs 'consent.'"

Adoption Is a Violent Act

Joss Shawyer

In *Death by Adoption*, Joss Shawyer has written the first radical feminist book against adoption. Published in 1979, it contains a scathing indictment of adoption as an alternative to abortion. Although Shawyer originally directed her attack against adoption laws and customs as they were practiced in New Zealand, her wholesale condemnation of adoption has global implications. Convinced that adoption violates the rights of women to abort their fetuses or as natural mothers to keep their children in times of trouble, Shawyer attacks all policies that encourage natural mothers to turn over their children to adoptive parents.

As you read, consider the following questions:

1. According to the author, how do natural mothers suffer after they have given their children up for adoption?
2. What, as Shawyer understands it, is the special pain of adopted children?
3. What reforms does Shawyer believe are necessary?

Adoption is a violent act, a political act of aggression towards a woman who has supposedly offended the sexual mores by committing the unforgivable act of not suppressing her sexuality, and therefore not keeping it for trading purposes through traditional marriage. The crime is a grave one, for she threatens the very fabric of our society. The penalty is severe. She is stripped of her child by a variety of subtle and not so subtle maneuvers and then brutally abandoned.

No matter which social class a single woman is attached to, once she becomes obviously pregnant she takes a rapid slide to join the other "unmarried" mothers at the bottom of the social ladder. The more desperately her family are clawing their way up to the top, the more likely they are to give her a swift kick to the bottom. Specially trained state-employed personnel police her fall from grace and arrange to remove the product of her transgression to a safe and secret place.

The women who safely make it into marriage by either successfully suppressing their sexuality, or by not being caught out carrying an unplanned pregnancy to term, wait greedily with outstretched arms for their prize—her baby. They feel no guilt, for they are "good" and she is "bad" and so she has no right to enjoy the product of her sinning. Wedded, if not bedded, in the eyes of God, the married woman happily, innocently banishes all thought of the child's mother from her mind as she prepares to complete the act of making, in her own mind at least, the little stranger into her own child.

The moral implications of her part in the collusion against the voiceless child and the real mother miraculously escape her. If she has any doubts about her right to pretend to be the child's mother, the social workers, the specially trained "police," will soothe the doubts and supply the nod of approval which she gratefully accepts. If the doubts re-occur, she can banish them with thoughts of what a good mother she is going to be, of how honest she will be with the child—her child. A pretty story takes shape in her mind. Your mother didn't feel she could give you the love you needed, so you came to live with us. But the "good" act of caring for the child cannot cancel out the morally "bad" act of the adoption itself and the lies it entails. There can be nothing moral about a relationship based on lies and denials.

The very act of adoption is a denial of the right of the child to her natural heritage—her birthright—the most basic right a person has, to know who she is. People who are not adopted spend money and time trekking the world in search of their ancestral heritage, usually when they are starting to think of death, and sometimes a lot earlier than that. Family trees are pored over, endless journeys made by people who *know* who they are but still cannot resist the temptation to climb back even further into the ancestral branches. We don't think that's strange or unhealthy, and yet adopted people, clutching at nothing more than a handful of what would be to us insignificant snippets of information, mount the same intensive and seemingly hopeless search, and are treated unsympathetically, even cruelly for their efforts. They are simply people who want basic information about themselves that the rest of us take for granted. . . .

The Suffering of the Natural Mother

Used, abused, and then discarded, [the natural mother] stumbles emotionally through the years, haunted by the knowledge that her child is living somewhere, with someone, but where, and with whom? If she should try to trace the child or even try to enquire about her whereabouts, she is cruelly reminded that she has served her function and that really society couldn't care less what happens to her now. Bureaucratic doors slam in her face, "confidential" files are tauntingly kept just out of her reach, across official desks. A few are luckier than others. Presenting themselves in legal offices (where adoption consent is signed), they accidentally, sometimes, strike a sympathetic lawyer. Obviously acutely uncomfortable at the part they play in the fraud and unable to express their unease in any other way, these lawyers contrive reasons to briefly leave her alone in the office, where she gets her only glimpse of the name and address of the adoptive parents, carefully left behind on the desk. Instead of wasting energy studying the (in)stability of the single mother, social workers should instead research her extraordinary ability to read upside-down. Because of her fear of rejection, the lucky mother who knows the adoptive parents' identity cannot bring herself to actually make an approach, although she will often find comfort in looking at the house where her child lives. It is made impossible for the natural mothers of adopted children to get news of those children. The fact that many try is easily concealed and the popular traditional image of the "unmarried" mother is perpetuated. . . .

Death by adoption is the death experienced by the real mother. The baby she carried can actually die for her at either the moment of birth or as she signs "consent." It would be more bearable if the child really did die, for then she could grieve and so recover from the death. But although the child died for her, it remains very much alive for someone else. And alive for her too. *Or it would be, if it weren't dead.* Although some adopted children die in childhood, she will never know if one of them was hers and will continue to look and hope (when there is no hope) that one day her child will try to find her. From the moment her child is gone, she must hide the stretch marks and pretend she never had a baby. We do not allow her to grieve and even if we

19

did and she understood *why* she feels the way she does, the grief will always remain unresolved for the simple reason that the child is *not* dead. . . .

A Fake Child

He is a fake child.

No doubt he was born of a woman, but this origin has not been noted by the social memory.

As far as everyone and, consequently, he himself are concerned, he appeared one fine day without having been carried in any known womb: he is a synthetic product.

Since his earliest childhood, the unknown mother has been one of the chief figures of his mythology.

He both worships and hates her, smothers her with kisses and seeks to debase her.

Whenever the child tries to reach beyond the bureaucracy of which he seems an emanation to his true origins, he finds that his birth coincides with a gesture of rejection. He was driven out the very moment he was brought into the world. The child senses that a woman tore him from herself, alive, covered with blood, and sent him rolling outside the world, and he feels himself an outcast.

Jean-Paul Sartre, *Saint Genet.*

Some women recall vividly both the actual birth and the signing of "consent." Although their pain has still not diminished, by allowing themselves to feel the rage and hatred, they somehow found the strength to face it at the time. Some women suppress their pain so successfully that they cannot recollect a single detail. They know a child was born and subsequently adopted but cannot recall the date, year and sometimes even the season of the birth. No memory of either hot or cold weather; not a single event connected with the pregnancy or the birth, which is still lying dormant in her mind.

The Arrogance of Adoptive Parents

Adopted children are used to trigger ovulation, to disguise failed relationships, to complete "incomplete" family numbers (the ideal family numbers what?), to provide a child of the "other" sex, to replace dead children and generally to shore up someone's self-esteem and not least to provide relief from a boring job which is going nowhere. Some women adopt when their youngest goes to school in order to resolve the problem of what will she do with herself from 9 a.m. till 3 p.m. But mostly children are adopted because the people who have already had the icing off the cake of opportunity feel entitled to steal the crumbs they inadvertently left over for the poor—their children. Instead of asking why they have so much already while others have so little, they blissfully join the adoption queues and put in their order for the child someone else will not be able to afford to feed. . . .

When any country reaches a level of affluence when even the poorest can afford to terminate unwanted pregnancies and can afford to feed the children that they do want, they begin to look internationally for "unwanted" children. Twenty-three underdeveloped countries, mostly in Asia, are now (1976) exporting human flesh to the West. Package tours of Scandinavian mothers make regular pickups. South Korea is a good example of a society where the division between rich and poor is so great that poor babies can be had for the price of air fare and they currently (1976) export 5,000 babies a year. The Swedes, famous for their humanitarian social policies at home, are blatant offenders. In 1972 alone they imported 1,500 South East Asian babies. Swedish women enjoy a degree of equality unknown in New Zealand. They no longer expect other women in their own country to either produce "unwanted" children or to give them away at birth, but they blissfully import the children of women who are not as privileged as themselves. Apparently Scandinavian "morality" only applies to those at home, of the same color and culture. . . .

Money used to buy a child from another country would be better spent sent to agencies in that country which are working to improve conditions for the underprivileged there. . . . Ghoulish stories have emerged from the United States. Apparently many doctors and lawyers now have a get-rich-quick scheme where they find pregnant women for large sums of money, payable by the adoptive parents, with a small cut for the natural mother for medical expenses. Couples even advertise for women to have babies for them. . . . Demand contributes in no small way to the amount of pressure used to force women to give up their babies, and current demand can only be measured by the length of adoption waiting lists.

The Pain of Adopted People

Identity and self-image problems are a major cause of distress to adopted children—the people who do not know who they are. . . . Adopted children fantasize about "real" parents and are then often disappointed when confronted with the real thing, which shows adoption secrecy is unnatural and harmful. Children would accept at least their parents' physical appearance had they always known them. Although it is practically impossible to measure the shock experienced by new-born babies separated from their mothers, perhaps this shock contributes towards the high rates of psychiatric disturbances found amongst adopted children. . . .

While there is no support system for the natural family, more and more children are crowding foster homes which are experiencing identical pressures. Foster parents ideally should be capable of helping the natural family sort out its problems and the aim of foster care is to get the child back quickly to her family. Foster care can only be considered successful after the child has been happily re-united with her natural family. Too often foster parents are judgmental, non-supportive, jealous and possessive of the child they cannot bear to let go home. Instead of helping the family to re-unite, they destroy it totally. Many children would never need foster care if their own families were helped. Preventative policies are desperately needed, and natural families need relief *before* they get to the stage where collapse is inevitable. . . .

Even though they need and want desperately to know their origins, many adopted people feel guilty because they have this need, and without support usually don't attempt to search for fear of "hurting" adoptive parents. All adopted people I have met felt a deep sense of protectiveness towards their adoptive parents. They have been made to feel that to want to know about themselves will be hurtful to others. And so we have this extraordinary situation where children are forced to keep their most basic feelings about themselves hidden from their parents so the parents don't get "hurt." It is amazing how mature adopted people are (in this respect) when compared to their adoptive parents. . . .

What Can Be Done?

Prevention would obviously be a lot better for us all than these depressing cures, i.e. adoption and fostering, which certainly don't make anyone feel better. . . . We must start with ourselves so that we are capable of imparting healthy attitudes to the young. . . .

Abortion cannot compare with the trauma, illness, desperation and danger associated with unwanted pregnancies. The guilt and grief of a woman who has bashed her child because she could no longer control her resentment even though she tried to "accept" the child at birth, pales the process of abortion into insignificance. . . .

Studies show clearly that long term adverse psychological after-effects of abortion are rare, and that abortion relieves the stress which was caused by the unwanted pregnancy. Women who adopted out their babies felt much more "negative" about their experience than abortion parents did, and 20% of the mothers reported increased emotional problems after the baby was adopted. Even the women who had experienced "back street" abortions reported little or no emotional difficulties afterwards. Guilt reported by some was shortlived and emotional stress, which continued after termination, had existed before the pregnancy. . . .

Restrictive abortion laws are not only dangerous to women's health, they are insulting to the entire female population. . . .

The lack of sex education, the present abortion situation and woman's position (or lack of position) in the nuclear family obviously combine to create the situation which fosters continued oppression. Only a restructuring of society will enable women to occupy their equal place.

"We need to stress the needs of children unborn and born, and in that way become not only pro-life but fully pro-family as well."

Adoption Is an Act of Compassion

Marvin Olasky

Responding to those who denigrate adoption, especially those who advocate abortion over adoption, Marvin Olasky, a professor of journalism at the University of Texas at Austin, argues that Americans need to wage war against all anti-adoptionists. As the author of *Abortion Rites: A Social History of Abortion in America* and *The Tragedy of American Compassion*, Olasky believes that adoption works well for the vast majority of adoptive children, for birth mothers, and for those who adopt children in need.

As you read, consider the following questions:

1. What evidence does Olasky present to demonstrate that adoptions are under attack?
2. What, according to Olasky, are the needs that drive anti-adoptionists to wage war on adoption?
3. In what three ways can those who argue for adoption promote their cause, in the author's view?

Excerpted from Marvin Olasky, "The War on Adoption," *National Review*, June 7, 1993, ©1993 by National Review, Inc., 150 E. 35th St., New York, NY 10016. Reprinted by permission.

In the America of the 1990s a war has begun. Adoption, like Sarajevo, has its stout defenders, and the attempt to reduce adoption to rubble in the name of self-fulfillment and combatting "cultural genocide" may be turned back. But the attack is being pressed mightily. . . .

Winners All Around

There are problems with adoption, to be sure—exacerbated by governmental bureaucracy, trendy ideas, and tinges of racism and reverse racism—but studies show that adoption works well for the vast majority of adoptive children, whose welfare should be our first priority. It also works well for most adoptive parents and for birthmothers, who generally grieve for the departed child but are glad that they have given life and are able to get on with their own lives; as one put it, "I knew that something can hurt a lot and still be the right thing to do."

The Anti-Adoption Opposition

That's not what anti-adoption propagandists would have us believe, though. We are told that adopted children are always searching for their birthmothers—in real life, less than 5 per cent do—unless, of course, the children have already been killed by adoptive mothers. For example, Barry Siegel's *A Death in White Bear Lake* has a birthmother looking for the child she had placed for adoption two decades before, only to find that the adoptive mother (probably separated at birth from the witch in *Hansel and Gretel*) had beaten him to death. Marsha Riben's *The Dark Side of Adoption* even equates adoptive parents with the devil.

We are told that adoption is no answer in cases where the father has abandoned mother and child. In the words of feminist Letty Cottin Pogrebin, "There is no need for a big Daddy and a medium-sized Mommy to teach Baby Bear." In real life, however, Baby Bear and his medium-sized Mommy by themselves often lead lives that are solitary and poor, and sometimes nasty, brutish, and short. The economic facts are harsh: three-fifths of all illegitimate children and their mothers depend on welfare for a minimal subsistence. The social consequences are even worse: studies of families at equal economic levels show that children without fathers tend to receive lower grades, score lower on achievement tests, and get into trouble far more often than children with fathers; they are far more likely to participate in gangs, commit crimes, start fires, use drugs, or attempt suicide.

But enough unimportant details about the well-being of children: far more central, in the effort to discourage unwed mothers from considering adoption, is the psychology of birthmothers. For example, a pamphlet entitled *Adoption? Abortion?* states that mothers who choose adoption "live a life filled with pain, worry, anger, wonder, and mourning without end." The natural choice is abortion, according to the famed feminist handbook *Our Bodies, Ourselves*, which argues that "the loss of a child to adoption is a unique and unnatural one. Unlike death, which is final, adoption creates a . . . limbo loss." *The Dark Side of Adoption* uses the same term: "A limbo loss exists for mothers who do not know if the children they bore are dead or alive. . . . Birthmothers are seldom at peace." Apparently, a mother can gain peace only if she knows her child is dead. (Women in thousands of post-abortion-syndrome groups throughout the United States would argue differently.)

Another book, though, suggests the real concern is not that the adopted child may be dead; it is that the child is most likely alive and may come to visit. Marjorie and Daniel Maguire of Catholics for a Free Choice ask in *Abortion: A Guide to Making Ethical Choices*, "How will you react 21 years from now if new laws allow adopted children to be given the name of their birthmothers when they come of age, and this child arrives on your doorstep?"

Often, feminist thought police overlook fatal collisions in order to spend their time scrutinizing fender-benders. The Feminist Majority Foundation's film *Abortion Denied*, which the Turner Broadcasting System ran as a public service, examines what actress Christine Pickle termed "chilling questions" about adoption; for example, adoption-agency fees "vary widely and can range from minimal amounts for minority or special-needs babies to a high of 12 per cent of the adoptive parents' gross annual income." Viewers are told, "It would be a tragedy in this country, then, if the more money you have means the kind of child you could adopt [*sic*]. That would be very chilling." The film did not reveal how the head, arms, and legs of an unborn baby are cut off during an abortion; it concentrated on the really chilling stories.

Explaining the Rage

Why does adoption make cultural leftists rage? Three strategic needs of the pro-abortion mindset underlie the War on Adoption.

Need 1: For abortion to be legal and accepted, the unborn child has to be considered the property of the mother; if the clump of cells must die to make her free, it is a small sacrifice. Key adoption questions, therefore, must concern the mother's psychological liberty and pursuit of happiness, not the life of the child.

Need 2: For female autonomy to be affirmed, the fact that it is better for a child to live in a two-parent family than with a single parent must not be acknowledged. Therefore, the issue of adoption must be portrayed as one of class struggle (poorer birthmother *v.* middle-class adoptive parents), racial struggle (black *v.*

white), and sexual struggle (liberated *v.* confined to marriage).

Need 3: Every happy adoptee is a reminder to aborting mothers of the road not taken. Since abortion must become a guilt-free operation if women are to be psychologically as well as physically liberated, this town isn't big enough for both adoption and abortion.

Shawyer's *Death by Adoption*

Am I stating these needs and temptations too bluntly? Look at a book such as *Death by Adoption*, in which abortion counselor Joss Shawyer writes that she had compared "the traumatic results of adoptions with the comparatively simple remedy of early, safe abortion. In my view, there is no contest. . . . Adoption is a violent act, a political act of aggression toward a woman who has supposedly offended the sexual mores by committing the unforgivable act of not suppressing her sexuality." The villains are "women who safely made it into marriage by either successfully suppressing their sexuality, or by not being caught out carrying an unplanned pregnancy to term." Such women "wait greedily with outstretched arms for their prize"—babies to be adopted.

Miss Shawyer also writes about the plight of foreign-born children who come to the United States and "are whisked away in cars to arrive at strange houses full of objects they've never even imagined . . . they are popped into Western-style beds and left alone in dark rooms to sleep. Probably even teddy bears are stuffed into bed with them." The brutes!

Reactions to Pro-Adoption Ads

The few positive portrayals of adoption that make it past media gatekeepers leave pro-abortion partisans furious. Debbie McKenny, who chairs the Pittsburgh chapter of the National Abortion Rights Action League, said that when she first saw pro-adoption television ads paid for by the Arthur S. DeMoss Foundation (a Christian evangelical group), "I probably hopped out of the chair and started screaming and pacing. I was very, very angry." Pro-abortionists threatened to take away business from the advertising agency, BBDO, that produced the DeMoss ads, arguing in *Advertising Age* that the agency had linked itself with "a fringe perspective." Threats led the Lifetime and CNBC cable networks to refuse to accept the paid DeMoss ads.

For every screamer who understands that adoption is a threat to the abortion way of life, there are probably ten fellow-travelers concerned with vague questions of equity, and a hundred "useful idiots."

Government officials who will not clear abandoned children for adoption are among the useful idiots. Some, using Orwellian language such as "family preservation," will not acknowledge that a mother who has for years proffered crack to her kids should relinquish her right to ruin their lives further by keeping them trapped in foster homes. Others turn adoptable two-year-olds into ravaged and virtually unadoptable seven-year-olds by slowing down the process in many different ways, perhaps to keep their budgets alive but usually to make sure no tragedies appear on their watch.

Reprinted by permission: Tribune Media Services.

How much precaution is enough? Counseling, home studies, and a few regulations are helpful, but many adoption officials are like the football coach so afraid his team will give up touchdowns that he spends every minute of the team's practice on defense and develops an ultra-conservative playbook for the offense. When his team loses 3-0 he speaks proudly of not giving up a touchdown; had he taken some calculated risks, his team might have won 49-7. In life, the decisions are harder: we never want to see any child placed with abusive parents. And yet, a look at the abuse that tens of thousands of children face in foster care makes the urgency of relieving their suffering apparent.

Other Anti-Adoption Ideas

Practitioners of reverse racism also have joined the War on Adoption. There is no shortage of adoptive parents for black babies, as long as some can be placed in white homes; many white couples have been willing, and research has shown that black children generally do well in trans-racial adoptions. Yet, the National Association of Black Social Workers for two decades has called trans-racial adoption "cultural genocide" and demanded its elimination. The NABSW's assertion that no parents are better than white parents has ruined the lives of thousands of black children, including the over 80,000 black children now in foster care. Furthermore, a study done for the Ounce of Prevention Fund showed that young mothers, aware of the difficulty of finding adoptive homes for black and mixed-race babies, reject adoption out of fear that their children would be consigned to years in foster care.

Now that courts have decided that racism in child placement is a violation of civil rights, the practice in its overt forms may be on the way out. Another battle in the War on Adoption, however, is growing more intense: the "open adoption." This includes continued contacts between birthmother and child, with adoptive parents becoming long-term foster caregivers. Theoreticians of "open adoption" talk like proselytizers for "open marriage": Why settle for one relationship? But just as thoroughly modern marriage trades the rings that symbolize commitment and responsibility for ruinous flings, so with-it adoption destabilizes children's lives and creates conflicts between birthmothers and adoptive parents that, if the practice continues, will surely lead to real disaster stories.

The cultural Left's battalions have some unlikely allies. Most evangelical Christians are pro-adoption, but a few have expressed the view that young women should *have* to raise their out-of-wedlock children as a way of living with the consequences of sin. Others, such as popular speaker Bill Gothard, have argued that Christians should not adopt because the sins of the birthparents will inevitably pop out among their children. Popular writer Mary Pride has attacked those would-be adoptive parents who are infertile because of sexually transmitted diseases or previous abortions and "are simply seeking to escape the consequences of their previous choices. . . . These people were just not meant by God to have children." But God has compassion for the least of His little ones, and so should we.

These anti-adoption ideas have consequences. Family-planning clinics rarely mention adoption as a realistic option for unwed pregnant women; some pro-life crisis-pregnancy centers are not much better. B.J. Williams, a pro-life adoption director in California, tells of young women saying, "I have never failed at anything. I feel adoption is failing," and pro-life counselors believing that "only someone who doesn't love the child will place for adoption."

Taking a Stand for Adoption

How can we battle powerful anti-adoption forces? On an individual level, we need to recapture the original understanding of compassion—personal involvement, not passing a bill or sending a check—and be willing ourselves to adopt minority or hard-to-place children. On a public-policy level, we need to push for a streamlining of the foster-care system so that children can be freed quickly for placement in permanent adoptive homes. On a cultural level, we need to stress the needs of children unborn and born, and in that way become not only pro-life but fully pro-family as well.

The number of teenage out-of-wedlock pregnancies continues to grow, but the single-parenting craze may be peaking; it has become clear to even the enemies of Dan Quayle that the self-absorbed developmental stage that is adolescence, and the stage of total dependency that is infancy, do not go well together. Successful abstinence programs could reduce some of the pressure, but the choice increasingly will be abortion or adoption. There is no neutrality in this war.

"*I want to record the debits and credits of the orphanage I knew and draw some conclusions about the care and nurture of children without parents.*"

The Orphanage System Should Be Reestablished

Charles D. Aring

Charles D. Aring is a physician and professor emeritus of neurology at the University of Cincinnati. As the author of *The Understanding Physician*, he has published extensively in the fields of medical education, philosophy, psychiatry, and neurology. In the following viewpoint, Aring reflects upon his personal experiences in a Lutheran orphanage and contends that orphanages still offer distinct benefits for children who might otherwise be required to live in numerous foster homes.

As you read, consider the following questions:

1. How, according to Aring, might the advantages of orphanage life outweigh the disadvantages?
2. In Aring's opinion, why does Girard's program provide a good model for the development of new orphanages?
3. In addition to the Girard orphanage program, what other possibilities does the author envision?

Charles D. Aring, "In Defense of Orphanages," *The American Scholar*, vol. 60, no. 4, Autumn 1991. Copyright ©1991 by the author. Reprinted with permission.

I took up residence in an orphanage a few days before my seventh birthday and remained there until the age of fifteen and a half, a total of eight and a half years. I was a full orphan by reason of my father's desertion before my birth and my mother's death in her forty-ninth year. I have no memory of having seen my father. During the year after my mother's death, I was assigned to two foster homes seriatim, which involved my attending four primary schools during my sixth and seventh years. I was tolerated at these homes until I could be moved along. I can recall little in the way of masculine influence during my first six years until I got to the orphanage, which may account for my slow acclimatization there. It was a rough, tough existence after the totally feminine environment of my earliest years.

It has not been considered particularly advantageous to spend one's formative years in an orphanage. The immediate experience made me actively dislike almost everything about it. Nowadays, the phasing out of orphanages has thinned the ranks of the alumni.

Orphanages have fallen into desuetude after struggling along under a Dickensian cloud. The foster home has largely replaced the orphanage. The social service attitude routinely supports the primacy of the nuclear family, no matter how disorganized it may be. Social problems these days are dealt with less on principle than on the basis of cost. But I doubt whether orphanages were more expensive per capita than other modes of child care.

Before all witnesses and memories disappear, I want to record the debits and credits of the orphanage I knew and draw some conclusions about the care and nurture of children without parents. My experience was garnered in the second decade of this century. A long career in teaching enables me to know how disconcerting to some people this ancient history may be; I have in mind those who always trust what is new and feel contempt for what is old. But history has its uses nonetheless—if only the satisfaction of curiosity.

Orphanages Provide the Basics

To begin with fundamentals, the orphanage food was simple, coarse, and, as I recall, insufficient. Meals were closer to feeding than to dining. Our meager fare can be inferred from the invariable Christmas gift: an apple or an orange; the child who got an orange was considered lucky. But I recall no obesity in this population in children or staff. This was surely an advantage owing to what might otherwise be construed as a debit. Food limitation in childhood may indeed have something to do with setting the "appestat" (by analogy with thermostat) control.

Clothing was likewise plain. The boys' uniform included blue overalls, suggesting in its way our minority status. A blue short-trousered, serge suit was the emblem of confirmation in Sunday school at the age of fourteen; I do not remember what happened to it after the ceremony—very likely it wore out. But I do remember attending high school in the cast-off trousers of a mailman's uniform, and that did not help me to be self-confident. . . .

Discipline was strict, as I suppose it had to be with a hundred charges, six to fourteen years of age, about equally divided between girls and boys. Much of the work of the institution fell to the children under the supervision of the caretakers, the superintendent, and the matron. It was mainly drudgery, although some of the older children became adept at such things as shoe repairing, sewing, and mechanic's work. . . .

It can be imagined that education was not a priority in the establishment. There were bound to be some exceptional children among the lot, but intellectual achievement was neither stressed nor rewarded. The children knew who the achievers were without help or sign from the administration.

Religious training, which was wholly rote learning, occupied almost the whole of Sunday. The children were marched to the neighboring German Evangelical Lutheran Church in a long line, just as they were marched to school. It was there that I was fortunate enough to be assigned to the best teacher of my early years. Somehow she led me to appreciate the Bible as literature. But the appalling sermons in English or German, like the other religious exercises routinely performed at the orphanage, guaranteed my agnostic outlook as an adult. The vaccination, so to speak, took. Perhaps this perfunctory religious training had the benefit of preventing prejudice, religious or social.

Many Benefits

From these various defects it should not be inferred that I was unappreciative of the home I was given, and I turn now to the credits. The shelter was secure, and the environment neat and clean, owing mainly to our own efforts under steady supervision. No task was considered too menial for us to take on and be held responsible for. "Goofing off" was unknown and malingering unthought of. Discipline was strict, and we strove to keep out of trouble's way. Punishment in the form of work could be prolonged until a replacement arrived by virtue of another's misdeed. There were no really bad guys among us, which reminds me that I know nothing about the admissions policy. Whatever it was, it seems to have excluded the problem child. It also seems to me that disturbed children were much less common than today. I do not recall any such children in the eight grades of a very mixed elementary school.

The business of childhood is play; at the orphanage it was of course limited by all the work that had to be done about the place. At the same time it was an advantage to have so many playmates at hand for every kind of game. And we played every kind, without much equipment—we simply made do. Exciting ball games were had with an old rubber ball and a broomstick (it sharpened the batting eye). I became adept at constructing hard baseballs by winding the unravelings of a worn-out stocking over a rubber core, such as a ball used for playing jacks. Leather covers were salvaged from old baseballs, and these I knew how to stitch. Later, I had no trouble making the baseball team since I could always hit, thanks to this stickball training. My poliomyelitic lower limb was a handicap, to be sure, but not enough to keep me off the team.

We also made up games, such as the competitive stalking and catching of cicadas. We termed them locusts and garnered considerable lore about the habits and life cycle of this beautiful insect, to say nothing of its facility for tree climbing, which, like so much else, was forbidden.

Another plus was the brass band. Though quite young, I was given the cymbals to play, then moved to the alto horn as soon as I could manage it, and finally to the slide trombone. The younger children were instructed mainly by the older, although there was a bandmaster—a member of the orchestra in one of the local picture houses. Musical engagements away from the orphanage compound afforded us a respite from the routines and chores. We marched in parades, including the one for the Liberty Loan of the First World War, and we played at flag raisings as well as at other festivals. Eventually I became deeply interested in classical music, most likely as a result of this early haphazard musical experience.

The orphanage had a bit of a library, and I believe I read all that was in it. I had begun reading at the age of three or four, perhaps at my invalid mother's knee, and the taste for books may have been fostered by the physical limitations that followed the poliomyelitis that I contracted at the age of one year. The orphanage library was composed of books of the Frank Merriwell, Tom Swift, Rover Boys, and Horatio Alger genre. My experience leads me to recommend any sort of reading for young children; they will choose as they develop. Once begun, reading becomes a habit. When I got to high school, some use of the public library was possible, on the way to or from school, though nobody at the orphanage showed interest in whether we read or not.

Perhaps the most useful feature of the place was the camaraderie amongst the children and the variety of older boys. This was not part of the program; rather, it was a natural development in that setting. Not long after my joining the institution, one of the older boys "took my part," as it was termed. Up to that time I had lived under feminine influence, and I was lame to boot, which tended to attract the unfavorable attention of other children. It made a difference to those tempted to torment if they had to deal with one of the larger boys of the "family.". . . .

The superlative merit of the institution was the great good health that prevailed among us during my entire tenure. This was the major benefit conferred by my life in an orphanage; it set a pattern and perhaps influenced my eventual choice of occupation as well. I had come from an unhealthy environment: my mother had been an invalid practically since my birth. Her mother, who was also ill, died during my second or third year. She and my mother's younger sister, both subject to repeated depressions, often required hospital care.

Spend Lavishly on Orphanages

Some small proportion of infants and larger proportion of older children will not be adopted. For them, the government should spend lavishly on orphanages. I am not recommending Dickensian barracks. In 1993, we know a lot about how to provide a warm, nurturing environment for children, and getting rid of the welfare system [would free] up lots of money to do it. Those who find the word "orphanages" objectionable may think of them as 24-hour-a-day preschools. Those who prattle about the importance of keeping children with their biological mothers may wish to spend some time in a patrol car or with a social worker seeing what the reality of life with welfare-dependent biological mothers can be like.

Charles Murray, *The Wall Street Journal*, October 29, 1993.

At the orphanage, everyone was *expected* to be healthy—and usually we were. There was a sick room and a "nurse" on the premises, but aside from contagious diseases and some cuts and bruises, there was little illness. I myself had chicken pox, sustained a lacerated scalp in a fall owing to my own foolishness, sprained my ankle while sledding, and that was all. During my more than eight years of residence, there were no deaths. I remained healthy thereafter, except for a few iatrogenic [inadvertently medically induced] ills. . . .

Once out of the orphanage, which was located in the suburbs, the youngster often found himself living in one of the slums of the city, and suddenly exposed to the dangers that he had been shielded from by walls and regulations. All too often this devastating pressure in mid-adolescence—Shakespeare's "the ambush of young days"—was more than the child could overcome. I was lucky to find myself domiciled and in the shadow of another large institution (the Cincinnati General Hospital), which brought into my ken a whole host of behavior models.

The Orphanage in Modern Times: Girard's Program

What about orphan children today? For the orphan, like the poor, is always with us. Having seen so many of my fellows fall by the wayside, my main concern is, How can opportunity be provided for the child to fulfill his potential? Considering the problem historically, I know of no better scheme than that of Girard College in Philadelphia. It is no doubt the outstanding orphanage in the United States. There the primary goal has been the education and training of the children to the full extent of their talents. Plainly, orphans everywhere should, after primary and secondary schooling, receive vocational training if not interested or equipped for a college education.

The Girard program was drafted well over a century and a half ago by Stephen Girard (1750–1831), a self-made international trader who was reputed to be the wealthiest man in the American colonies. He put his mind to the care of orphans when drawing up his last will and testament at the age of seventy-six, and revised it in his eightieth year. The college opened on January 1, 1848.

To achieve his purposes, Girard gave a generous endowment and left little to chance in its use. The details of his plan were clearly spelled out. It needs little in the way of modernization, save for conforming to changes in the law of the land, as has been pointed out by John Keats in "The Legend of Stephen Girard," an article first published in 1978 in *American Heritage*. Girard's philosophy of nurture for orphaned children is as valid today as it was in 1827.

Girard College accepts normal children, whole-orphans or half-orphans, between the ages of six and eleven. The college consists of seventeen buildings on forty-three acres. There are more than five hundred children there, a third of whom are girls. The school maintains high educational credentials. Mental and physical health are evaluated carefully before admission. Girard's non-denominational chapel is held twice weekly. The students may attend religious congregations of their choice off campus. There are courses in comparative religion in the curriculum.

Every opportunity is afforded by a large enthusiastic faculty for students to develop to the extent of their capacity. From the day of admission, it is expected that the student will go on to a university, and practically all of them do go on scholarships underwritten by Girard. Similar arrangements are made for graduate school.

The program directs orphans toward what should be a gratifying life. Girard has graduated a host of successful persons. One development is an enthusiastic and vigorous alumni association. Girard is a happy ship for those who have had the exceptional good fortune of boarding and partaking in Mr. Girard's great concept. But what of those who for any reason cannot partake in a legacy according to Mr. Girard's grand design?

Another Possibility

Looking forward, I, too, have dreamed of an institution for the future. I can imagine a facility for housing not only orphan children but also a limited number of healthy elders who might be interested in their own development after retiring. It should be a facility modeled on the extended family of bygone years, particularly as it existed in rural areas. The administration would represent the middle generation, the children being the younger generation. In my scheme, the opportunity for communication between the generations should be always available. Some elders would want none of it. This is quite understandable. By definition my retreat would select naturally the sort of clientele that would foster its program. From the standpoint of mental health, the availability of younger generations to older and vice versa is useful and beyond dispute. Children and the elderly are natural allies.

To keep the extended family going, incentive programs could be set up in which the children and the retired folk would participate under the supervision of the middle generation serving as the administrators. The elders, expert by reason of experience in one or another discipline or technique, would be ready-made personnel for instruction and recreation. Not only literacy but art and music could be taught and practiced under their tutelage. Members of such an extended family would form friendships and groupings, by free choice and affinity, which would be lasting, a family unit in the best sense.

The pattern of an extended family "home" would resemble the real world more than the usual modern concentration of a single generation. Its clientele would be exposed to the quirks, vagaries, pleasures, ills, and interests of persons of all varieties of age, personality development, competence, and health. It goes without saying that such an establishment would require wise administration. That of the usual immuring institutions as we know them would not fill the bill. The best administrative talent has not gravitated to orphanages and retirement homes. The prevalent oppressive social philosophy of economism, which views human life in terms of production, acquisition, and distribution of wealth, has not dealt kindly with persons at the extremes of the age scale. But there they are and will always be. They deserve better than our heedless age has managed to organize for their well-being.

"Fifty years of research reconfirms the same findings: long-term institutionalization in early childhood leads to recurrent problems . . . later in life."

The Orphanage System Should Not Be Reestablished

The North American Council on Adoptable Children

The North American Council on Adoptable Children (NACAC) is a nonprofit, broad-based coalition of volunteer adoptive parent support and citizen advocacy groups, individuals, and agencies committed to helping adoptable children. As an advocate for adoptable children, the council has long argued that every child deserves a family. In the following viewpoint, NACAC contends that institutionalization of children in orphanages is not an acceptable substitute for a family, and that many important, more cost-effective, and humane options exist that have not yet been vigorously explored.

As you read, consider the following questions:

1. According to NACAC, how do children institutionalized in orphanages differ from children brought up in foster care and/or adoptive homes?
2. In lieu of placing children in orphanages, what does NACAC recommend as alternatives?
3. What fiscal evidence does NACAC present to justify its objections to orphanages?

Excerpted from the North American Council on Adoptable Children's *Research Brief #1*, "Challenges to Child Welfare: Countering the Call for a Return to Orphanages," November 1990. Reprinted with permission.

The recent deluge of very young children into the child welfare system—especially children of color and medically fragile children—prompted calls for the return of orphanages. Joyce Ladner in a *Washington Post* editorial wrote, "What these children need is permanency, but the chances are that it will continue to be difficult to find adoptive families for these so-called high-risk youngsters. I advocate that we bring back the orphanage—not the huge, depersonalized warehouses of old, but small-scale caring institutions that can offer children, and their siblings, a place that they can count on to nurture them." Recently, Sally Provence, author of *Infants in Institutions* in 1962, cautiously recommended the revival of institutions under certain conditions: for medically fragile infants who require specialized care, and for healthy infants until stable, long-term living arrangements can be assured. Provence added that intensive services for biological parents should be integrated into residential care of infants with the aim of family reunification whenever possible.

What the Research Shows

What is the history of institutional care of children? Is there a difference between large and small institutions and their effect on children's development? Early studies by researchers documented institutions' long-term, adverse effects on children's emotional, social, and cognitive development. Children exhibited retarded language development, poor concentration, attention-seeking behavior that hindered social maturity, and an inability to form emotional relationships with others. Children reared in large institutions scored significantly lower on intelligence tests than other children. . . .

More recent studies examine smaller institutions for children. Barbara Tizard studied small residential nurseries that were the result of child care deinstitutionalization efforts in England in the 1960's and 70's. Fifteen to 25 children lived in residential nurseries which were divided into small, mixed-age "family" groups of six children each attended by two staff. The children's regime emphasized personalized care and intellectual stimulation. Despite multiple caretakers (no male caretakers) and the absence of close relationships, children aged two to five developed average and above average language skills. The author points out that institutions that differ in their hierarchical social organization and level of staff autonomy influence language development in institutionalized children. Children's higher language scores were associated with rearing by autonomous staff who talked more to children and provided children with more explanations, compared to children reared by non-autonomous, highly supervised staff. . . .

In [a] recent follow-up of ex-institutionalized children, J.

39

Hodges and B. Tizard found that "children who had spent at least the first two years of their life in residential care were likely at age 16 to have more social and emotional problems than other children, and more disruptions in their lives." At this age, adolescents showed more problems at school than at home. In fact, many ex-institutionalized adolescents had good attachments to their adoptive parents, demonstrating that some children who are deprived of consistent, nurturing relationships early in life can make such attachments later. In contrast, many ex-institutionalized children who were restored to their birth parents exhibited problems both at home and at school. Hodges and Tizard hypothesize that birth parents and adoptive parents differed in how much they wanted the child and how much time and effort they were able to put into the parent-child relationship. Birth parents often had fewer resources, more other children, and higher ambivalence about reunification compared to adoptive parents who very much wanted a child and devoted effort to building a relationship with the adopted child. Hodges and Tizard state that the "prime aim should be to keep children in a family where they are wanted.". . .

Long-Term Effects

Perhaps some of the most striking research is on the long-term effects of institutionalization on psychosocial functioning and parenting of 81 adult women who were institutionalized before the age of five. Ninety percent spent at least four years in a residential nursery. The comparison group was a quasi-random sample of 41 women never admitted into care. Results reveal that institutionally reared women showed a higher rate of poor psychosocial functioning and severe parenting difficulties in adult life. Twenty-five percent exhibited a personality disorder, compared to none of the control group. Serious failures in parenting (children removed from the home or transient or permanent parenting breakdown) were evident only in the institutionally reared sample. Early institutionalization predisposed women to experience poor social circumstances (living in a dwelling without a kitchen, toilet, bathroom, or telephone, or over-crowded living situation). According to D. Quinton, M. Rutter, and C. Liddle, "Only a minority of women with a stable harmonious pattern of upbringing exhibited poor parenting when subjected to chronic stress and disadvantage in adult life, but the majority of those who lacked good rearing in childhood did so." Institutionalization appeared to leave women "less well prepared to deal with adult adversities."

Teenagers with a history of multiple placements continue to comprise a substantial proportion of out-of-home placements nationally. However, numbers of adolescents institutionalized due to foster care breakdown is overestimated, according to a study by M. Colton. Colton's study compares care practices in treatment foster and congregate care settings for adolescents. Foster care breakdown preceded institutionalization for only 13 percent of adolescents in one study cited by Colton. One might assume that institutionalized adolescents would exhibit more behavior problems and disruption compared with adolescents living in treatment foster care. However, no behavioral differences existed between institutionalized adolescents and fostered adolescents; on the contrary, fostered adolescents seemed to have more traumatic pasts. Random luck seemed to be the deciding factor when placing adolescents in treatment foster care or in institutions. Predictably, treatment foster homes were found to be more "child-oriented" compared to institutions, which were more "institutionally oriented." In treatment foster care adolescents had their own wardrobe (versus shared clothing in institutions), and decorated their bedrooms and displayed personal belongings in their foster home bedrooms. Decorations, posters, and personal effects were not in evidence in adolescents' institutional rooms.

Table 1. Estimated Daily Rates for Costs of Out-of-Home Care, 1990

Categories of Care	Daily Rate
Basic Family Foster Care	$8–15
Specialized Foster Care (Supplemental payments for care of children with physical or mental disabilities)	$15–30
LIFE Foster Home (Michigan) (Does not include AFDC transfer)	$36
Therapeutic Foster Care	$40
Residential Foster Care	$100
Hospital Placement	$300

Source: Testimony of Joe Kroll, NACAC, before U.S. Ways and Means Committee, 1990.

Staff in institutions tended to use more inappropriate or ineffective methods of control compared to treatment foster parents who displayed more effective methods of controlling adolescents. Inappropriate methods included public disapproval, threatening to discharge the adolescent, and limiting the adolescent's access to the outside world. In contrast, foster parents used rewards, sanctions, encouragement and voiced disappointment to gain an adolescent's compliance. Disapproving and controlling speech comprised the greater proportion of directives given by institutional staff, whereas foster parents used informative speech containing "approving" language. Fostered adolescents participated in household rule-making and chores while institutionalized adolescents did not.

While the kitchen and living room were the focus of household interaction in treatment foster homes, the office absorbed the majority of institutional staff's attention. Staff–resident discussions were of shorter duration than those of foster parents and fostered adolescents. Familiarity, reciprocity, and social closeness existed between foster parents and adolescents but were notably absent in staff–resident relationships. Fostered adolescents behaved in more socially acceptable ways towards their foster parents, while institutionalized adolescents interacted more deviantly with staff members. Finally, while it is possible for both institutionalized and fostered adolescents to show improvement in areas of physical violence, school truancy, court appearances, and educational performance, gains can be made in similar adolescent populations without resorting to institutional care.

A number of researchers compared the developmental outcomes of children reared in institutions with those reared in foster care and adoption. P. Roy found increased rates of inattention and poorly modulated social behavior and task performance among children reared in institutions. J. Berry found higher levels of psychiatric referral and current problems in personal and social adjustment among institutionally reared children compared with foster and adoptive children. Prolonged institutionalization in early life was the factor most likely to lead to foster care failure in G. Trassler's study of children in foster care.

A study by J. Triseliotis and M. Hill of 124 adults reared in adoptive, foster, and residential care reveals that "those who were adopted and, to a somewhat lesser extent, those formerly fostered experienced more intimate, consistent, caring, and closer attachments to their caregivers compared with those who grew up in residential establishments" [and] "Both the adoption and foster care sample, but particularly the former, demonstrated that the impact of early adverse experience can 'fade away' with the opportunity to form new positive attachments."

Better Options

A return to orphanages is in clear violation of Public Law 96-272, the federal Adoption Assistance and Child Welfare Act of 1980, which seeks to provide permanent homes for children caught in the child welfare system, either through reunification with their biological family or placement for adoption. A plethora of less restrictive options exist to institutionalization. Treatment foster care is far less restrictive and less expensive than institutionalization or residential care. Model programs exist that utilize intensive case management for biological parents, recruitment of foster-adoptive parents, and state programs that train specialized foster parents and license "non-traditional" foster families.

Institutions: The Edsels of Children's Services

Child-caring institutions are the "Edsels" of children's services. They are costly, ineffective, and will never live up to the expectations of their proponents. There are a small number of young people (in delinquent, mental health, and substance-abuse cases) who cannot be managed in less secure environments and need to be institutionalized. However, we can and should close the overwhelming majority of children's institutions in the child-welfare, mental-health, and juvenile-justice system and redirect their operating funds into the financing of preventive and other less intrusive options.

Ira M. Schwartz, in *Controversial Issues in Child Welfare*, Eileen Gambrill and Theodore Stein, eds., 1994.

B.A. Stroul states that, "Given society's belief that family life is the best environment for a child, therapeutic foster care asserts that emotionally disturbed children should not be denied the experience of family and community life by virtue of their specialized treatment needs." Nor should infants and small children—free from emotional disturbance but affected by drug exposure—be denied the chance to bond with consistent and loving parents. In a national survey of 48 treatment foster care agencies conducted by R. Snodgrass and B. Bryant, the majority were operated by voluntary, non-profit agencies. Twenty-five percent were operated by public agencies. Features of treatment foster care often include intensive work with each child and foster family, individualized case plans for children, training and other supports for foster families, small caseloads for staff working with foster families, and an immediate staff response to crisis.

The Example of a New Jersey Program

The New Jersey Department of Human Services, Division of Youth and Family Services (DYFS), teaches specially recruited foster families how to care for medically fragile children. The Special Home Services Provider Program emerged as a response to the alarming rise in the number of infants with severe medical problems, including AIDS infection and crack addiction, whose families were unable to care for them. In a survey of area hospitals DYFS found that almost half the babies awaiting placement were born drug-addicted. In a nine-month period in 1989, 71 percent of 603 infant referrals to DYFS needed specialized care. Sixty-five percent of that number were substance addicted, 26 percent had other medical conditions, and 9 percent were HIV positive. Reflecting the dwindling number of foster homes available on a national level, New Jersey needed to seek and train substitute care providers willing to undergo intensive training and abide by certain conditions curtailing work outside the home. The Special Home Services Provider Program provides foster families with financial support that reflects the difficulty of caring for medically fragile infants and the special training it requires. Foster parents receive intensive training and counseling, in-home support services, and placement of one or two infants maximum. Foster families are paid $500 per month for three months to guarantee space availability for special needs infants. Once an infant is placed, the foster family receives $900–$1200 per month, depending on the severity of the child's medical needs. The Special Home Services Provider Program emphasizes the need for a consistent primary caregiver; in two-parent families, only one parent may work outside the home. In a single-parent family, the caregiver may work only ten hours a week outside the home. . . .

An Analysis of Cost

The fiscal impact of decisions concerning children's living arrangements while in foster care can be staggering. For example, in 1990 the foster care population [increased] by an estimated 20,000. Using estimates from Table 1, if all 20,000 new children coming into care were placed in residential settings, the cost to the taxpayer would be $730 million per year. If these same children were placed in some combination of family, specialized, and therapeutic foster care at an average of $25 per day, the cost to the taxpayer for these children would be $182 million per year. Though the costs of caring for these children in foster homes is great, it is significantly less than if the children were placed in institutions.

What Needs to Be Done

The extent of the problems is new and the solutions are tentative; however, the literature seems to point in these directions:
The Need for Universal Public Health Services and Prenatal Care:
1. All women should have access to public health services and prenatal care. Public leaders must make a commitment to this area or risk losing future generations of productive

Americans to the ravages of drugs and poverty.

2. Successful programs tailor their organizational practices to meet the needs of the consumer. Saturday appointments, assistance with transportation, child care, and increased cultural sensitivity (e.g., bilingual staff) characterized successful programs.

3. Programs with an ecological approach identify both the client and the client's family as recipients of services to be delivered in the client's home and neighborhood. Home visiting by professionals yields favorable outcomes for mother and child.

4. Integration of key services can only be accomplished by scrapping the present categorical delivery of the Women, Infants, and Children Program (WIC), Maternal and Infant Care, family planning and Early Periodic Screening Developmental Testing (EPSDT) services and blending programs to efficiently meet the needs of consumers.

Fifty years of research reconfirms the same findings: long-term institutionalization in early childhood leads to recurrent problems in interpersonal relationships, high rates of personality disorders, and severe parenting difficulties later in life. Even a small residential facility is ultimately a public institution, and we know the state to be a poor parent.

Alternative Models of Child Welfare Practice:

1. More intensive and longer lasting services to children at home are needed to maintain families in times of stress.

2. Vigorous foster family recruitment should focus on families who are willing to become the child's adoptive family if reunification fails.

3. Case management practice should use a two-pronged approach in which reunification, termination of parental rights, and adoption are discussed simultaneously with biological parents in order to resolve the question of permanency in a timely manner.

4. Non-traditional families (e.g., single-parent families, families who receive public assistance and others) should be recruited and specially trained to care for medically fragile children. Remuneration should be commensurate with the conditions of fostering special needs children and the training it requires.

Finally, a comprehensive approach to treating high-risk children will be implemented on a large scale only if legislators and the public dedicate robust support to this end. We must answer the question: How much do we value our future generation?

> "A compassionate response to children must include an equally compassionate response to their parents."

Preserving Biological Families Should Be Encouraged

Nanette Schorr

Nanette Schorr, an attorney specializing in family law at New York City's Bronx Legal Services, argues in the following viewpoint that the present child welfare system needs to become more pro-family. Rather than taking at-risk children from poor families and transferring them to middle-class homes, she urges, the system should focus on family preservation programs before children are removed to foster care situations that, all too often, become permanent. Poor and working parents need publicly funded day care, health insurance, and community support systems that will help struggling families stay together, she concludes.

As you read, consider the following questions:

1. What, according to Schorr, is wrong with the present child-protective system?
2. What policy changes does the author recommend?
3. How, in Schorr's view, will the promotion of family preservation help children?

Excerpted from Nanette Schorr, "Foster Care and the Politics of Compassion," TIKKUN, May/June 1992. Reprinted from TIKKUN MAGAZINE: A BIMONTHLY JEWISH CRITIQUE OF POLITICS, CULTURE, AND SOCIETY. Subscriptions are $31 per year from TIKKUN, 251 W. 100th St., 5th Fl., New York, NY 10025.

In 1910, a single mother wrote a poignant appeal to the *Bintel Brief* (letters) section of the *Jewish Daily Forward*. The social supports in her community had failed her, and she had nowhere else to turn.

> My husband deserted me and our three small children, leaving us in desperate need. . . . I am young and healthy, I am able and willing to work in order to support my children, but unfortunately I am tied down because my baby is only six months old. I looked for an institution which would take care of my baby but my friends advise against it. The local Jewish Welfare Agencies are allowing me and my children to die of hunger. . . . It breaks my heart but I have come to the conclusion that in order to save my innocent children from hunger and cold I have to give them away. . . .

The dilemma this woman faced is hardly different from that of many working mothers today. But the editor of the *Forward*, in response to the letter, looked beyond the responsibility of the Jewish social welfare agencies to that of the larger social order that forced parents to consider such desperate measures. The *Forward* editor replied: "What kind of society are we living in that there is no other way out than to sell her three children for a piece of bread? Isn't this enough to kindle a hellish fire of hatred in every human heart for such a system?" The *Forward*'s passionate and righteous anger is unequivocal; the enemy is the capitalist system. . . .

A Typical Case of a Family in Need

The case of L.H. is striking in its ordinariness. A mother living in the Bronx in 1987, L.H. was in a position not unlike the mother who wrote to the *Bintel Brief*. She had recently separated from a husband who had abused her and was now alone with three young children, without money or job skills, in a house with broken windows. She sought help from child-welfare authorities—money to fix her windows and someone to watch over her children while she looked for work—but they responded by charging her with neglect for leaving her younger children in the care of her older ones and for causing them emotional distress by arguing with her husband in front of them. As a result, the child-protective system removed L.H.'s children from her care and insisted her problems could be solved with psychology. The institutional foster care providers ignored L.H.'s concerns for the safety of her boys, whom they deemed "fragile," and placed them in separate group homes as a way of treating "parentification" syndrome (older siblings protecting younger ones). L.H. found no justice in the family courts, either. Her court-appointed counsel was inaccessible and unresponsive, and the court itself did not have time to hear her case. L.H. was finally reunited with her children, but only after taking extraordinary legal action. The wounds of the utterly unnecessary separation have yet to fully heal.

I work as a lawyer representing parents who are trying to regain or maintain custody of their children and I see cases like L.H.'s all the time. Most of the time parents don't fight back because they have already come to believe that the system is so rigged against them, and are so steeped in the belief that they are unworthy simply because they are poor, that any serious struggle seems futile. Moreover, the degradation they have suffered—which the child-protective system only compounds by its treatment of poor families—makes some parents doubt their own ability to care for their children.

Reprinted by permission of Joel Pett.

Of course horrendous things do happen to children in some families. But defining the problem this way provides everyone with an excuse to avoid confronting the way the child-protective system works. It's analogous to questions that similar professionals raised about women who acted irrationally in the days before the women's movement. On the one hand, it was certainly true that some women acted in ways that could be described as irrational—and so one could understand why, given the level of social understanding at the time, mental health workers would typically prescribe doses of therapy, or even institutionalization. On the other hand, as early feminists pointed out, much of the behavior deemed irrational or hysterical was simply a natural expression of women's frustration and rage at an oppressive system of male domination. Similarly, the child-protective system makes things worse by intervening in ways that focus on rescuing good children from bad parents, without acknowledging the adverse conditions in which families function and the debilitating frustrations that lead parents to abuse or neglect their children.

A Disaster for Children and Parents

The good child–bad parent definition works very well for those social workers, therapists, and others whose job is to keep the system working smoothly and who long ago have given up any hope of changing the larger society. But the system's very effectiveness is often a disaster for the children and parents caught in its vise. Families are torn apart and children suffer in the process. Children may be separated from their brothers and sisters, moved precipitously from foster home to foster home, or—worst of all for children in such a vulnerable position—abused or neglected in foster care. Their parents are not much better off. As overwhelmed and undertrained caseworkers make arbitrary or impossible demands on them, parents lose hope of being reunited with their children. They complete a drug treatment program only to be told they must find a job. They receive a certificate from a parental skills class, only to be told that they can get their children back only when a therapist determines they are ready. They are told they must find an apartment, but there are no apartments to be rented for what they can afford to pay. Frightened and bewildered, they go to family court hoping to find justice, but instead they are shuffled from one court appearance to the next. Months, sometimes years, pass as cases are repeatedly adjourned and professionals who sit behind closed doors determine the fate of their families.

Children in protective care, meanwhile, are forming bonds with their foster parents and foster parents are becoming attached to their foster children. The longer children live in foster care, the more the state recognizes the bond that is built between foster parent and child—a bond that will be sustained by the state against the aspirations of parents who seek to reunite the natural family. The courts are full of custody battles between foster parents and natural parents, battles in which the state throws its substantial power behind foster parents. Ask yourself to whom a child's affections will naturally turn: the foster parent who daily provides that child's needs (as well as many things above and beyond those needs), or the parent who

49

earns a paltry income or lives on public assistance and is permitted to visit for only an hour once every other week. Social engineering, not child protection, is the net result in this system, as children are taken from poor families and placed in middle-class families that can give them a "better" life. Such interference overextends the role of the state. It is not for the state to decide what constitutes an enlightened upbringing, but rather to establish threshold criteria for the care of children above which its intervention is not required. There are many types of harm from which the state is unable to protect children, such as the emotional harm they experience when their parents argue or divorce, the internalized pain and loss of self-esteem they suffer when discipline is imposed in an arbitrary manner, or the damage they live with when they are punished corporally in ways the state does not deem "excessive." Were every kind of harm subject to state intervention, all children would at some time have been removed from their parents' homes. . . .

None of this is to say that abuse and neglect do not exist, that parents are not responsible for what happens to their children, or that child protection is merely a capitalist conspiracy to make money by stealing the children of the poor. But one cannot ignore the images evoked by the vocabulary that predicates intervention: Reductive characterizations of parents as "crack mothers," for example, justify dehumanizing social policies and underwrite the state's recourse to criminal sanctions instead of remedial therapies.

Inadequate Help for Parents

Most parents who qualify for therapeutic rehabilitation find that it is administered in a compartmentalized, ineffectual, and ultimately alienating way. Beating your children? Let's talk about learning acceptable outlets for anger—not about what you're really angry about. Leaving your children alone? Go to a parental skills class. No need to consider that what you really need is some day-care assistance, or someone to watch the little ones while you take the older children out to the store or the doctor or simply for a walk. You've sexually abused your child? Go to a sex-offenders clinic, where you will get behavioral modification therapy. No need to explore the physical or emotional violence you experienced as a child or your own lack of self-esteem and sense of alienation. Abusing drugs or alcohol? Have your urine tested regularly and exercise greater self-discipline. No need to say that you feel narcotics may be the best thing going, given the conditions under which you're living. This does not mean that these behaviors should not be controlled; indeed, they must be. But in the absence of a real commitment to addressing the isolation and degradation from which abuse and neglect follow, they will only continue.

In the early days of the child-protective movement, the most common approach to "treating" the neglect of children was to preach to parents about morality. . . . However, moralizing did little to address the root causes of bad parenting. Gradually moralizing gave way to psychological labeling, and parents who were seen as shiftless and morally lax were redefined as manifesting psychopathology. Now the focus of scrutiny has turned to single parents, many of them women. When these parents criticize a social order that gives their parenting efforts little material or emotional support, social welfare experts term this an "externalization of blame." Instead of treating the crisis in meaning—the despair and emptiness born of lifelong experiences of physical or emotional violence, unemployment or meaningless work, broken families, inadequate education, loneliness, lack of stable long-term relationships, dangerous, dirty, and violence-ridden neighborhoods, decrepit housing, and lack of community—the symptoms of crisis are treated in isolation from their causes. When one is afraid to leave home for longer than necessary or to let the children go out and play because of the drug dealers in the neighborhood, a sense of social isolation closely follows and, if unrelieved, may very well lead to neglect or abuse.

What Might Be Done

If you were designing a program to assist troubled families, what are some of the elements you would intuitively include? Instead of instructing parents on how to build ideal family units, you might teach them how to reach out to neighbors and community leaders who are familiar with local resources and address the problems that led to the neglect of their children. You might assist parents in building the kind of mutual-support societies that sustained many immigrant communities, giving them financial assistance, emotional sustenance, and connection to their heritage. You might help them locate their own experiences in a historical understanding of the social and economic organization of American life and teach them how to use that knowledge to empower other parents as well. The focus must not be on individual change—ideally that follows of its own accord—but on helping people build new social institutions that can address their needs for support, community, and meaning. . . .

The question then becomes: When should children be taken from their parents? Quite simply, when their parents are abusing or neglecting them, when there is imminent risk of harm to their lives or health, or when "reasonable efforts" have been made to ameliorate the problem. While abuse cases may require long-term removal, in the majority of neglect cases a family's

51

needs may be met by limited remedial intervention such as that provided by the "family preservation" models that are being developed around the country. The cost and pain of family separation should be—but aren't—considered before a child is placed in foster care. . . .

When we focus on the neglectful and abusive behavior of individual parents, we allow ourselves to avoid recognizing how their failure reflects larger social failures for which we are all ultimately accountable, since the state—in whose operation we are all implicated—is the most neglectful parent of all. . . . When the state uses untempered intervention as a blunt instrument, and describes all parental failures of children as "child abuse"—provoking the uniform response of removing all the children from the home—we needlessly destroy otherwise viable families.

Family Support Policies

What might a profamily politics look like? Can "family" be redefined in ways that support nontraditional alignments based on feminist, gay, and cross-cultural critiques of the nuclear family and recognize extended networks of social relationships based on ties of kinship or affection? How can we support the institution of the family—for all intents and purposes the only social institution based exclusively on loving commitment—without compromising our intolerance of domestic violence and abuse? In part, the answer lies in the emergence of new kinds of households that can renew family life—but only if they are given the social acceptance and nurturance they need in order to flourish. Thus family support policies must be designed in ways that allow such households to be economically viable and create supportive communities in which they can function.

A number of factors have compromised the goals of the child-protective movement. Cynicism born of ineffectual efforts to combat domestic violence, combined with the loss of the sense of community that lent hope to the movements of the 1960s and 1970s, has led us to believe that we need to save who we can (in this case children), since we can't change the larger social and economic environment. Furthermore, the policy of massively applying state intervention to change the balance of power in families where women and children are physically and emotionally abused has often left liberals aligned against people in inner-city and poor communities, who view themselves in an adversarial relationship to an oppressive system that is destroying their neighborhoods and their culture. The source of this problem lies in the failure of liberal policymakers to address the deeper social meaning of the issue by bringing a historical perspective to the problem and by understanding and addressing the reasons for such anger.

An analysis of the child-protective system in the United States requires (for example) understanding the brutalization of African Americans, starting with the systematic breakup of their families in slavery, and continuing with the racism and class oppression that span from the Reconstruction period to the present time—a history that is distinctly different from that of other oppressed minorities in our country. Like the War on Poverty, which gave services and money to poor communities without supporting their efforts at leadership and independence, the child-protective system respects neither its clients' cultural heritage nor their humanity. Caseworkers classify angry parents as "noncooperative" clients and treat noncooperation as a reason to keep children in foster care. Professionals need to support the efforts of parents to reassert their dignity, even if that assertion challenges the child-protective system itself.

Neglect cases too often have resulted in unnecessary removal of children, often without prior notice to parents—even when the child faces no imminent danger. The state often removes children with little attention to legal process; and the judges and attorneys in the family court system rarely question the state's actions. The net effect is to ratify the caseworkers' decisions, thereby rendering child-protective intervention arbitrary and unjust.

The courts must respect the rights of parents by ensuring that caseworkers are making "reasonable efforts," both before and after they remove children. The courts can neither rectify the unequal scrutiny given to poor families nor change the social conditions that give rise to neglect. But they can make better efforts to keep families together by ordering and supplying necessary services, even if those services cost money.

Promoting Family Preservation

The consequences of the liberal approach to child protection are disturbing. The good child–bad parent dichotomy gives credibility to conservative policies that hold parents accountable for their children's criminal acts—for example, the punitive eviction of parents from public housing when their children are found possessing drugs. Such policies mete out equal punishment to parents who have abandoned the effort to influence their children's behavior and parents who simply need support in dealing with their children's rage and hopelessness. Furthermore, such responses show little understanding of the ways in which parental failures represent the defeat of parents' own deepest hopes for the future, just as they symbolically represent the defeated aspirations of the working class. . . .

Despite the child-protective bureaucracy's heavy investment in the good child–bad parent dichotomy, the struggles of parents in impoverished communities have moved into the foreground of public consciousness. Movies such as *Boyz N the Hood* reflect a growing humanization of parents' and children's struggles to survive and even flourish amid daunting conditions. Ongoing news coverage of issues such as steadily diminishing public support for single mothers and the fears of parents whose children have been involved in violent incidents in the schools has educated the public about the often tragic limitations of liberal approaches to family policy—and helped clear the way to a compassionate, morally consistent response.

The Issues Are Not Just Economic

The Left urgently needs to address the pain of poor and working parents, and we can begin to do this only by recognizing that the issues are not merely economic, although they often stem from economic privations. Liberal child-welfare experts ignore this pain at their peril since the Right will continue to fill the resulting vacuum by claiming this issue as its own. We cannot allow the language of empowerment to be co-opted by the Right, which uses it to justify a hands-off approach to state involvement in employment, education, and welfare in order to "liberate the forces of individual initiative" in the inner city. Properly defined, empowerment of parents means helping them confront racism, condescension, and inequality.

The complexity and immediacy of the issue require us to respond quickly and decisively. Many of the clients in the child-protective system do need help. The question is, what kind of help? Rather than focusing on child removal as a remedy, that help could take the form of funding "family preservation" programs that assist families before their children are removed and maintain the parent-child bond during foster care with frequent visits. "Family preservation" should be broadly defined to include support for poor and working parents in the form of publicly funded day care and health insurance. In addition to providing services, government should support community organizations and mutual-assistance societies such as those formed by many ethnic groups that share day care, provide seed money for new endeavors, and run parenting groups and advocacy efforts.

Recognizing the pain of parental struggle does not mean that all parents are good. It does require recognizing that real support for families must be linked with efforts to change the world of work and reorganize the economy. The social significance of child neglect extends beyond its current impact. Its human implication is also profound because it shapes the lens through which future generations will filter their memories, and, in turn, their hopes and dreams. A compassionate response to children must include an equally compassionate response to their parents.

"Adoption can give children the love and nurturance they need to heal any early wounds and to flourish."

Creating More Adoption Possibilities Should Be Encouraged

Elizabeth Bartholet

An expert on civil rights and family law, Elizabeth Bartholet has taught at Harvard University since 1977. In *Family Bonds: Adoption and the Politics of Parenting*, from which the following viewpoint is excerpted, Bartholet describes her experiences in adopting her two sons and her research into the world of adoption. Arguing that governmental regulations and adoption agency policies make it difficult for *all* families to adopt, she raises new questions about the meaning of fertility, parenting, and family. Bartholet challenges current policies regarding adoption and urges new understandings for adoptive possibilities.

As you read, consider the following questions:

1. In what ways, according to Bartholet, may adoptions positively transform the lives of birth parents, infertile couples, and children?
2. What new questions does Bartholet ask about the traditional "biologic" family?
3. What does the author say adoptive families can teach about the nature of prejudice and discrimination?

Adoption as we know it often arises out of situations of loss and destruction, sadness and despair. The birth parents who surrender or abandon children generally feel forced to this action by circumstances that range from problematic to devastating. The nations that send children abroad for adoption are generally Third World countries convulsed by poverty and violence. The children themselves start their lives with the loss of the parents who would normally provide essential love and nurturance. Many suffer significant deprivation in their early lives. Many are marked by disability, illegitimacy, or race as outcasts in the societies into which they are born. Many of the people who become adoptive parents have experienced the loss represented by infertility. Often they have spent years reexperiencing that loss as they pursue fruitless treatment efforts.

Transforming Lives

These tragedies, like others, hold the potential for transformation and rebirth. Adoption can give birth parents a chance to gain control over their lives. It can open up a future that might include pregnancy and parenting experiences for which they will be prepared. In the meantime, adoption enables them to provide their child with the kind of nurturing home that they are not now in a position to offer. Adoption can give the infertile the parenting opportunity they have ached for, as well as a new perspective on the meaning of their lost fertility. Adoption can give children the love and nurturance they need to heal any early wounds and to flourish.

Adoption can also stimulate some new thinking about family and community. Adoptive families are by definition families linked not by blood but by intended parenting and a social commitment that crosses bloodlines. Often these families are built across lines of racial, ethnic, and national difference as well. The law of adoption focuses on the potential negatives, building on speculation about what might go wrong in families not based on biology, but the evidence indicates that in fact adoptive families work very well. We might learn a great deal by focusing on the potential *positives* in adoption, speculating about what might go particularly *right* in these families, and why.

Raising New Questions

Since like many adoptive parents I experience unique positives in the adoptive relationship, I now look at the "normal" family from this perspective and ask questions I never used to ask. Why, for example, should biology be considered as determinative of parental rights as it now is? Why should it be so hard to remove children from abusive parents? Why should the privacy of the biologic family be so sacrosanct?

These questions occur in part because adoptive parents have to earn the chance to parent. While much in the parental screening process seems wrong, the notion that parenting is a privilege and not a right seems appropriate.

Children Who Wait

The National Adoption Center prepared the following statistics based on children registered on their network as of March 22, 1991:

- 67% of the children are black or black/white.

- 52% of the children have some emotional problems.

- 32% of the children have some degree of learning disability.

- White children have more disabilities than black, with 71% having emotional problems.

- The largest age group is between five and eleven.

- The black children are younger, with 54% under eleven, compared to 31% for white children.

- There is a predominance of boys—almost two-thirds male.

- In total, 42% of the children are members of sibling groups.

- The average age of black children on the network is 10.2 years; white children average 12.6 years.

Carole A. McKelvey and JoEllen Stevens, *Adoption Crisis: The Truth Behind Adoption and Foster Care*, 1994.

These questions occur also because adoptive relationships have a more contingent quality than the traditional biologic family. Adopters become parents to particular children as a matter of conscious choice—choice that might not have been made. By contrast, those who give birth tend to experience the parenting of their children as a given—a natural and inevitable relationship. Adoptive families know that there is another set of parents, whether they are dead or alive, whether they are known to the adoptee or not. Adoptees can choose whether or not to pursue their biologic or ethnic roots, whether and to what degree to try to relate to birth relatives or countries or cultures. In some societies [e.g., Tahitian] adoption is designed so that they can choose to return to their birth families if life in the adoptive family becomes unsatisfactory. Students of these societies say that both adoptive and biologic family relationships are conceived of as far more fluid and flexible than in our society.

My postadoption self wonders whether children in our society might not be better off if parenting relationships here were more qualified by choice and subject to change, with children encouraged to form a broader range of intimate connections and empowered to opt out of bad relationships.

Adoption separates the biologic from the nurturing part of parenting. For adoption to work for the various parties involved, the nurturing aspect has to be understood as central to the meaning of parenting. Adoption pushes us to ask questions about whether our society has structured parenting in a way that gives appropriate recognition to nurturing.

An adoption perspective stimulates other questions about parenting norms. Why do we think of it as extraordinary and not ordinary to love as "our own" children born to others? Why do we consider it "unnatural" for a woman to surrender a child for others to raise if she is not prepared to parent and they are? In some [Polynesian] societies, those who can become pregnant feel an *obligation* to consider giving the child they produce to others who want to parent but cannot produce their own. In the African American community and in many societies in other parts of the world, there are strong traditions of shared parenting within an extended family group, and informal adoption is common.

Adoptive parenting by definition involves the parenting of children who are not "us" but "other." It leads us to think more deeply about how much "normal" parenting relationships suffer from assumptions that "our own" children will or should look like us or like better versions of ourselves.

Rethinking Prejudice and Discrimination

Adoptive families can teach us something about prejudice and discrimination. Many of those who seek to become adoptive parents are single, older, or disabled. Many are gay or lesbian. The adoption system discriminates against all these groups but nonetheless permits some of their members to parent children for whom no other homes are available. The studies indicate that these adoptive families function very well. We might learn to question some of our assumptions about what makes for good parenting if we took a closer look at these families. Many of the children who are available for adoption are from racial minority groups, and many have severe mental or physical disabilities. Large numbers of these children are adopted by white middle-class couples, who make up the vast majority of the waiting adoptive parent pool in the United States. The studies indicate that these families function very well also. We might learn something about our capacity for community if we took a closer look at these families, whose members seem to be successfully transcending racial and other differences.

We could structure our laws to recognize adoption's positive potential as a family form and to make it work to expand life's potential for birth parents, their children, and the people who want to parent. At present we seem to be doing just the opposite.

The Failure of the Present "As If" Model

Our society's current laws signal adoption's inferiority to the biologic family and proclaim the dangers allegedly inherent in raising children apart from their birth families. Almost all the rules are designed either to ensure that a child is not improperly removed from the biologic family or that a child is not placed with an inadequate adoptive family. There are no rules, or at least none with any teeth, that give children a right to a nurturing home or that limit how long they can be held in limbo.

Our laws design adoptive families in imitation of biology. The central symbolic event is the issuance of a new birth certificate for the child and the sealing of the old certificate, together with other adoption records. The goal is to ensure that the birth parents, the child, and the adoptive parents can all proceed with their new lives as if the child had never been born to the original parents. The clear implication of this "as if" model of adoption is that adoption is an inferior and not quite real form of family which can at best aspire to look like the real thing.

The central legal event in adoption is issuance of the adoption decree, which completely severs the legal relationship between the child and the birth family, transferring to the adoptive family all rights and responsibilities. Legally as well as symbolically, it is as if the child were born to the adoptive parents. This promotes a rigid separation of the birth from the adoptive family, reinforcing notions that the true family is the closed nuclear family and warding off as much as possible any sense that adoptive relationships might be more contingent and less proprietary than traditional parenting relationships.

The "as if" adoption model produces parental screening policies that confirm traditional prejudices. The home study process favors married couples who look as if they could have produced the child they will adopt. It tends to screen out prospective parents who do not fit traditional notions of what parents should look like; among those disqualified or ranked at the bottom of eligibility lists are singles, older parents, gays and lesbians, and people with disabilities. The rules for matching waiting children with prospective parents are designed to maximize sameness and avoid what is seen as dangerous diversity within families. Originally the goal was literally to match—to give prospective parents children with similar physical features and similar mental characteristics, so that the parents could pretend to the world and even to the child that this was their biologic child. In addition, the idea was (and to a great degree still is) that adoption has the best chance of working if the child is as much like the parent as possible. After all, how can you expect a smart parent to relate to a not-so-smart child, or a musical parent to relate to a baby jock? What would happen to the talented child in a family of pedestrian minds? In today's adoption world, the matching ideal has given way significantly to reality: there are relatively few healthy babies in this country to match with the mass of eager prospective parents. But interestingly, traditional matching principles are very much alive with respect to race. Powerful policies in force throughout the nation restrict adoption across racial lines, reinforcing notions of the importance of racial barriers.

Our adoption system has failed to live up even to its own limited vision. The promise to serve children's best interests and to provide them with at least a rough imitation of a biologic family has never been taken seriously. Laws and policies that are supposed to protect children have created barriers to adoption that function effectively to prevent children from getting the kind of protection they most need—a loving, nurturing, and permanent home. Scratch the surface of the system and it becomes obvious that adults' interests regularly trump children's. The system's rules proclaim that parents must be screened for fitness and that money cannot be used to obtain children, because children should not be treated as property to be sold to the highest bidder. But the reality is that prospective parents with money can and do bypass the screening system to obtain the children who are thought to be most desirable. The reality is that children are treated as property, owned by their biologic parents and their racial, ethnic, and national communities. Many children grow up in foster and institutional care because we are reluctant to cut the biologic cord so as to free them for adoption, even in situations where there is little hope for a viable life with their birth family. And children abandoned by their biologic parents are claimed as the property of particular adult communities and openly spoken of as national or community "resources," to be disposed of in ways deemed to serve the community interest. . . .

Toward a New Vision

Adoption works, and works well, both for children in need of homes and for the infertile who want to parent. Why structure it in ways that drive prospective parents away from the existing children in need? Why structure the new worlds of infertility treatment and child production in ways that encourage the infertile and others interested in parenting to produce new children, or to spend their lives trying? There may be some inborn need to procreate, but there are also inborn needs to nurture.

Why does organized society seem to want to encourage its members to obsess over the former at the expense of the latter? With my postadoption eyes I find it so obvious that we have it all backward now, so obvious that we should instead be encouraging the nurturing instinct so as to favor the care of existing children over the production of new ones. The directions for change seem similarly obvious.

Eliminating Barriers

We need to *deregulate* adoption. The current regulatory framework creates obstacles on both a pragmatic and a psychological level: it makes the adoption process costly and unpleasant, and it simultaneously degrades and demeans this form of family. Indeed, it is clear that the essential *point* of the current framework is to maintain barriers to adoption so as to ensure that this form of family arrangement can be kept in its place as a last resort. We need new policies that focus on the positive rather than the negative potential of adoption. For example, we need meaningful guarantees that children will receive nurturing homes and will not be held in limbo for longer than absolutely necessary. We need new systems providing financial reimbursement for some of the costs involved in adoption, so that more of those who are interested in this form of parenting are able to pursue it. Deregulation would make adoption less costly, but expenses would still be involved. At present we make adoptive parents pay all such expenses, except in the case of certain special-needs adoptions. By contrast, we provide significant subsidies to those who pursue procreation. We should revise our state and federal tax systems to provide credits for the costs of all adoptions, and we should revise insurance plans and employer benefit plans so that those who parent through adoption receive at least the same benefits as those who parent through procreation.

At the same time, we need to *regulate* infertility treatment and the new child production methods. The goal should be not simply to protect the rights of parties engaged in these arrangements but to discourage certain practices, such as egg and embryo sale and commercial surrogacy, altogether.

Rethinking Critical Definitions

Most of all, we need to think about how to begin to *rethink* the meaning of fertility, parenting, and family.

In my postadoption state, I find all this so obvious that I am left with a genuine sense of puzzlement as to why society is now organizing things the way it is, why it is such an uphill battle to argue the case for adoption. Maybe it is too threatening to think what might happen to the family if it was *not* defined and confined by biology and marriage. Maybe it is too threatening to think what might happen if people were *not* understood to belong to their racial, ethnic, national, or other groups of origin, if they were free to merge across group lines, if they were free *not* to reproduce more of the group's "own."

Living life as an adoptive parent forces a person to think about these issues. It provides no easy answers. It represents freedom from some constraining concepts of family, but it hardly brings instant liberation. Single women and infertile women may see adoption as opening up new opportunities for parenting, without men and free of the ministrations of the high-tech fertility doctors. But this society does not make single parenting, whether adoptive or biologic, an easy ride. Until and unless such parenting becomes financially viable, it will be oppressive both for the women involved and for their children. Adoptive families can be models for the families of the future or they can be poor imitations of the families of the past. Adoptive parents and children have to figure out whether to break the old molds, and if so, what to salvage.

Periodical Bibliography

The following articles have been selected to supplement the diverse views presented in this chapter.

Christine Allison — "Kate's Choice," *Reader's Digest*, April 1992.

Christine Bachrach et al. — "On the Path to Adoption: Adoption Seeking in the United States," *Journal of Marriage and the Family*, August 1991.

Janet Bodnar — "Adoption: The Long and Costly Road," *Kiplinger's Personal Finance Magazine*, August 1992.

Edd Doerr — "What's Wrong with the Adoption Option?" *The Humanist*, March/April 1994.

Lorraine Dusky — "The Daughter I Gave Away," *Newsweek*, March 30, 1992.

Victor Flango and Carol Flango — "Adoption Statistics by State," *Child Welfare*, May/June 1993.

The Future of Children — Special issue on adoption, Spring 1993. Available from 300 Second St., Suite 102, Los Altos, CA 94022.

Sarah Glazer — "Adoption: Do Current Policies Punish Kids Awaiting Adoption?" *CQ Researcher*, November 26, 1993. Available from 1414 22nd St. NW, Washington, DC 20037.

Lisa Gubernick — "How Much Is That Baby in the Window?" *Forbes*, October 14, 1991.

Karima Haynes — "The Adoption Option," *Ebony*, August 1993.

Sharon Johnson — "Girls: Easier to Give Up—and Adopt," *Ms.*, November/December 1992.

Kenneth Jost — "Foster Care Crisis," *CQ Researcher*, September 27, 1991.

Maria McFadden — "Rapping Adoption," *The Human Life Review*, Summer 1993.

Tom Morganthau — "The Orphanage," *Newsweek*, December 12, 1994.

Stephen Post — "The Moral Meaning of Relinquishing an Infant: Reflections on Adoption," *Thought*, (67) 1992. Available from Fordham University Press, University Box L, Bronx, NY 10458.

Joseph Shapiro	"Bonds That Blood and Birth Cannot Assure," *U.S. News & World Report*, August 9, 1993.
Dede Slingluff	"Pushing the Adoption Option Hard Enough?" *Christianity Today*, March 5, 1990.
Utne Reader	"A Child at Any Cost? Eight Views on the Adoption Question," November/December 1991.
Steve Waldman and Lincoln Caplan	"The Politics of Adoption," *Newsweek*, March 21, 1994.

Whose Rights Must Be Protected in the Adoption Process?

Adoption

Chapter Preface

An adoption significantly affects the lives of at least three parties—those of the adoption triangle: the adoptee, the birth parents, and the adoptive family. Much has been written about the rights of each party in the triangle. Yet in spite of the serious thought given to the rights of each party, no fundamental agreement has been achieved that clearly weighs and spells out how the rights of all three parties are to be fairly handled. Take, for example, the rights of children in an adoption proceeding. Legal, moral, and ethical guidelines agree that all proceedings concerning child welfare should make "the best interests of the child" the primary consideration. One would think that, by now, the rights of children in adoption proceedings would have been clearly articulated and agreed upon. But that is not the case. In 1973, Joseph Goldstein, Anna Freud, and Albert Solnit wrote what many consider the classic text on the rights of children. In *Beyond the Best Interests of the Child*, Goldstein and his colleagues argued that the child's interests should "be paramount in cases involving adoption, fostering, custody, and neglect, irrespective of the rights and wrongs of the adults concerned." In particular, they recommended that the child should be represented by independent counsel; that cases involving children should be treated as emergencies and heard without delay; that adoption orders should be irreversible from the day of placement; that custody decisions should be final; and that a temporary placement made for whatever reason should not be disturbed after a certain time had elapsed.

At first, adoption professionals received *Beyond the Best Interests of the Child* enthusiastically. Its thesis, that the child's so-called psychological parents (whoever they might be) would best satisfy the ongoing psychological needs of a child, seemed theoretically helpful, even commonsensical. Later reviews of the book, however, demonstrated that it is difficult—often impossible—to apply the book's principles to real-world situations. Sol Nichtern states the basic problem:

> There is built into this book an assumption of the ability of the professional always to recognize and choose correctly. Experience with medical jurisprudence suggests that it is almost always possible to obtain diametrically opposite professional opinions, leaving the judicial process with the responsibility of making the choice.

In other words, in court the experts will not agree on what is best for the child. For this and other reasons, *Beyond the Best Interests of the Child* has faded as an authoritative statement championing the rights of children. Although the book is interesting historically, it does not effectively describe how to satisfy the best interests of children.

The recent legal battle over "Baby Jessica" proves the point. In 1993, Baby Jessica became the center of national attention. Her face filled magazine covers; the story of her life was featured as a movie of the week. As a two-and-a-half-year-old toddler, she was caught in a court battle between two sets of parents. On the one hand, her birth parents, Dan and Cara Schmidt, wanted her back; on the other hand, Jan and Roberta DeBoer had reared her and wanted to finalize her adoption. After a lengthy legal process, the courts ultimately decided that she should be returned to her birth parents. Today she is no longer known as Baby Jessica; her name is Anna Schmidt.

The Baby Jessica case, focusing attention on the rights of everyone in the adoption triangle, raised important questions. For example, if a choice must be made between sets of parents, what determines which set of parents is better suited to make sure that the best interests of the child are satisfied? Should those who have provided ongoing care, creating a psychological bond between a child and parents, have the stronger claim? Or does the stronger claim lie with the biological parents, whose association with the child is founded on a genetic bond?

The case of Baby Jessica also highlighted the dilemma and rights of birth parents—the birth mother in particular. Faced with the need to make choices without adequate counsel, birth mothers have sometimes decided to place their children for adoption and later regretted their decisions. The question then arises as to how best to protect the legal rights of birth parents.

Finally, the Baby Jessica case raised important questions about the rights of those who seek to adopt children: Do they not also have the right to adopt and love children without fearing that someday the child will be taken away?

While most would agree that, in theory, the best interests of the child should prevail, the Baby Jessica case underscores the need to examine further the various viewpoints offered by the other members of the adoption triangle—a discussion undertaken by the authors in the following chapter.

"[A birthmother] will always be a parent even if she does not raise her child."

The Rights of Birth Mothers Must Be Protected

Concerned United Birthparents

Concerned United Birthparents (CUB) is a national nonprofit organization founded by birth parents who had surrendered their children for adoption. The organization focuses on the needs and rights of parents whose children have already been adopted or who may be considering the adoption of their children. In the following viewpoint, CUB argues that traditional adoption practices do serious harm to all involved: birth parents, adoptive parents, and adoptees. In order to ameliorate the suffering, CUB contends, strong measures must be undertaken to prevent unnecessary family separations. Birth parents must be informed of their rights and all options and alternatives to adoption, CUB maintains. If adoption is ultimately necessary, the organization urges that all parties openly work together to form mutual bonds of love and respect.

As you read, consider the following questions:

1. What, according to CUB, are the consequences of a birth parent's surrendering a child to another family?
2. What objections does CUB have to much of the usual terminology used in adoptive circles?
3. What, in CUB's estimate, must be done to correct an adoptive process that causes so much pain?

Excerpted from *The Birthparents' Perspective on Adoption*, a publication of Concerned United Birthparents, 2000 Walker St., Des Moines, IA 50317. Reprinted with permission.

We believe that families are important and that they should be assisted to remain together whenever possible. We know first hand that each family member's thoughts about the birthfamily profoundly influence him or her, and that people who have been separated through adoption, divorce or personal misfortune often feel rootless, rejected, guilty or incomplete. We know the pain of separation experienced by birthparents, their surrendered children, other children who lose the opportunity to grow up with or know their siblings and extended family members. In those very rare circumstances when adoption is necessary because a family's remaining together is impossible even with temporary assistance, we recognize that the family of origin remains important and believe that adoptions should be arranged with mutual respect, cooperation and concern for the present and future needs of all involved. Because we view adoption as the blending of two families, we believe that truthfulness and cooperation are essential so that all parties can respect each other and appreciate the place that each parent occupies in the child's life.

The Consequences of Birthparents' Surrendering Children

[Why do we use the term "surrender" the child?] "Surrender" best fits the experience. Few parents want to be separated from their children, but their temporary circumstances, combined with pressure tactics and lack of support from family members, society or adoption professionals, may leave them no alternative. Our research among members indicates that the factors leading to the surrender of a child are generally a lack of extended family support, lack of financial resources and pressure by social workers or others who arrange adoptions.

When birthparents' lack of resources necessitates allowing adoptive couples the privilege of raising their child, birthparents are generally allowed no options. They are not legally entitled to know anything about those who will adopt their child, nor to know anything about their child's subsequent health or welfare. They have no legal right to an attorney's counsel, to be informed of alternatives, to receive or even be informed of services that would enable them to raise their child themselves. They have no right to their child's original birth certificate, nor to the falsified version that will later be substituted to state that the adoptive parents gave birth. Often they have no right to know the name of the court that handles their child's adoption nor to know the legal process involved in adoption. They have no right to copies of any information that agencies write about them, nor to receive a copy of the document that separates their child from them. They have no right to choose any of the terms of their child's adoption or to have their identities known to their child.

A surrender is not a legal contract setting forth the respective rights and responsibilities of each of the parties. It is not a contract at all, but a very real surrender of all rights and choices. Without providing guarantees of any kind for the child or birthparents, the surrender document permits the child to be adopted and denies birthparents any form of compensation, not even the knowledge of their child's welfare. . . .

Problems with Terminology

We find the terms "biological parent" and "bio-parent" offensive, since they are descriptive of a mechanical incubator or unfeeling baby machine. Birthparents are neither; we continue to love and feel concerned for our children just as other parents do. Terms like "woman who gave birth," that strip us even of the term "parent" and deny our continuing relationship, are degrading, dehumanizing, punitive and insensitive to our ongoing love for our children. We have no objection to the term "natural parent," but we choose not to use it out of consideration for the feelings of some adoptive parents who feel the term implies they are "unnatural parents." Although we recognize that there is no ideal term for parents who are separated by adoption from the child they created and continue to love, we feel the term "birthparent," one word, analogous to terms like "grandparent," "grandmother," and "grandfather," accurately reflects birthparents' place as their children's progenitors without the punitive connotations associated with so many other terms.

The Experience of Birthparents

The popular myth about adoption is that traditional closed adoption offers single parents the chance to go on with their lives as if they had never "sinned" and had babies, infertile couples the babies they want just as if they had given birth to them and "unwanted" babies "better lives" in two-parent homes. In this tidy formula, adoption is presented as equally beneficial for everyone involved in it. Unfortunately, the true experience of adoption is often far different than this rosy fantasy.

That a *pregnancy* was unplanned or unwanted does not mean the *child* is unwanted. There is no closer human relationship than that shared by a mother and her unborn child. A mother's body and deepest emotions are intimately involved with the child she shelters within her, an involvement that progresses with every flutter and kick she feels. By the time her baby is born, she is no longer the same person. Any woman who elects to complete her pregnancy becomes a mother. No matter how disastrous the timing of her child's birth may be, she is irrevocably a mother. Like any other mother, she has a basic, biologically based need to love and nurture her infant. Like any other

70

mother, she has been raised to believe that mothers and babies belong together, and to expect to raise any babies she may bear. Mothers are neither biologically nor culturally prepared to surrender their children for others to raise. Surrendering a child to adoption is, for a variety of reasons, sometimes necessary, but it assuredly is not easy. Signing a document cannot erase the most profound experience and emotions of a mother's life, nor does it mean "postponing" parenthood until she is ready. She will always be a parent even if she does not raise her child.

Perception of Why Birthparents Chose Adoption

Adopted teens believe their birthparents chose adoption because . . .

76% Birthparents wanted them to have a better life.

72% Birthparents were not ready to take care of a child.

70% Birthparents cared deeply for them and wanted the best for them.

61% Birthparents did not have enough money to take care of them.

8% Birthparents didn't want them.

Adoptive Families, July/August 1994.

Every adoptee has a birthfather. A majority of adoptees were conceived in a long-term, loving relationship. About 17% of CUB members married the other birthparent subsequent to the surrender. Birthfathers' love for their children can be as real, as deep and as permanent as any other parent's, yet birthfathers are seldom acknowledged. Often the birthmother or her parents made all of the decisions regarding the child, with the birthfather having no options about his child's fate. Some were not told of the child until after the surrender. In addition to sharing many of the same experiences and feelings as birthmothers, birthfathers suffer from society's negative perception of them and insensitivity to their commitment and caring for their children.

It is a myth that time heals all wounds and that eventually birthparents go on to make new lives for themselves and forget their surrendered children. The fact is that birthparents have only one life, and that life is permanently affected by the parents' unnatural separation from their child. In a meticulous study of birthmothers by noted Australian researcher Robin Winkler, it was found that for half of birthmothers, the pain of losing a child to adoption either worsened or never improved over the years. He also found that even forty years later, birth-mothers regarded the surrender of a child as the most stressful part of their lives. We have had members who were searching for children surrendered over sixty years earlier. The loss of a child to adoption is not a one-time event; the losses continue as each new day is yet another day of knowing, loving and nurturing the child that is lost to the birthparents.

The losses involved for birthparents are staggering. Birthparents have described adoption as a wound that never stops bleeding, as an emptiness inside, as empty arms eternally aching to hold the lost baby, as a limbo loss, as similar to the pain experienced by the families of soldiers missing in action.

Birthparents' losses and grief have typically been denied or ignored by our society. So have the fears birthparents suffer when the adoption is "closed." When they lack information about their child's welfare, birthparents worry about whether their child is happy, healthy or even alive. Birthparenthood can profoundly affect birthparents' feelings about themselves. It can affect other areas of life too, including relationships, marriage, subsequent children and religion, to name only a few. Different pains and problems stemming from birthparenthood may arise at different stages of the birthparents' lives.

The Experience of Adoptive Parents

Adoption does not cure infertility and adopting a child is not the same as having a child by birth. Adoption gives adoptive parents the wonderful opportunity to raise and love a child, but adoptive parents can never be their child's only parents. No matter how much they love him, they cannot change the fact that they did not create their child. Their child's life, body, talents, and many of his personality traits were given to him not by them, but by his birthparents. Other parents recognize themselves and their families in their children. They know that an uncle or brother or sibling "went through a stage of that and look at him now." Adoptive parents cannot recognize their own families in this child they love but whose genes they do not share. Their child is at least partially a mystery to them. He is usually medically a mystery too, because they are typically given only sketchy medical information available at the time of the adoption separation. They know nothing of any medical conditions arising in the birthfamily in the years following the surrender.

Even though adoption is not the same as raising a child by birth, adoptive parents are given the impossible task of pretending it is the same. In traditional closed adoptions, adoptive parents are often given little information about the child's background and no understanding of birthparents' feelings. They are

72

encouraged to deny birthparents' humanity and continuing concern and to forget their existence, even though they see the birthparents reflected in their children's faces, bodies and personalities every day. Feelings of anger and resentment, common in infertility patients even after they adopt, may be displaced to the birthparents. Lacking knowledge of the birthparents, adoptive parents may fantasize about them, fostering unrealistic fears. Adoptive parents who feel a kinship with their child's birthparents and want to know them may find little support or understanding for their feelings in their communities.

The Experience of Adoptees

Adoption has given adoptees the parents they grew up with and love. Most people see that as a happy circumstance for adoptees and have difficulty understanding that in addition to the gains in adoption, adoptees also experience losses. Adoptees have two sets of parents, not just one. Like children of divorce and remarriage, they do not live in complete, intact families as they do not live with all of their parents. Even adoptees who cannot imagine what it would be like to live in a complete family may mourn its loss.

Adoptees are not, for their adoptive parents, the link with both past and future that nonadopted people are, for they are neither. The adoptive parents did not give the adoptee their own parents' twinkling eyes, curve of eyebrow, shape of toes or tiny waist, nor will they see these traits in the adoptee's children and grandchildren no matter how much love they share. The adoptee grows up cut off from his own generational line. An adoptee has seen, all her life, people who have the same narrow noses, cleft chins, sloped shoulders, hairy arms or webbed toes as their parents. The adoptee has heard, all his life, people talking casually, as if it were the most natural thing in the world, about sharing such similarities with their relatives. Yet the adoptee usually does not know facts as basic, as taken for granted, as her name at birth and whether her mother loved her and sang to her. The adoptee does not know whether his father is bald or whether he likes liver and onions. He does not know whether his forebears are Swedish, Irish or Lebanese.

Lacking the opportunity to know for himself, with his own senses, the adoptee is, in essence, forced to float always in the present, unconnected to past or future. Coming from nowhere, how can you go somewhere? It is natural and understandable that learning the answer to "where do I come from?" can become essential to knowing "who am I now?" and deciding "where am I going?"

Most adoptees are not looking for love or for a "Mommy" or "Daddy" but for a sense of connection with all humanity through being a part of the generational line. They are looking for the missing parts of themselves from which adoption has separated them. . . .

What Must Be Done

We cannot support a system in which loving families are not informed of alternatives to help them stay together and in which those who must choose adoption are forced to accept secrecy. Our members therefore encourage social policy and legislative changes in the present system.

We believe it is important to prevent unnecessary family separations and promote good parenting by providing temporary support and assistance for families at risk. The circumstances leading to the surrender of a child are most often temporary and can be overcome with caring support for a time. A temporary lack of finances or support should not require a loving parent and child to be separated. To prevent unnecessary separations, some of our members have welcomed young mothers and their children into their homes. They have been moved to see these mothers and children beaming at each other with love, and often have proudly attended the mothers' weddings and graduations. By providing temporary support, we have been able to help vulnerable young families overcome their temporary difficulties so they could be strong, healthy, positive families. Often members assist by sharing their own situations and feelings with young parents-to-be and their families. . . .

We think it is important that parents considering surrender of a child be informed *in writing* of all services and alternatives prior to surrender. Because we believe that no child should be treated as a commodity, we feel that when children must be separated from their families, adoptive placements should be arranged on the basis of the child's needs, rather than on the wishes of those who seek to adopt. The ability to love, accept, guide and nurture a child born to others should be more important criteria than infertility or finances. Under no circumstances should any person, agency or entity be permitted to make a profit from the placement of a child.

We believe preparation for adoption is important for the psychological health of all involved. A decision to surrender a child should never be made prior to birth. Birthparents should be encouraged to see, hold, feed and care for their children so that if separation becomes necessary, the birthparents will be dealing with the reality of their child and their situation, not with a fantasy that they will someday forget. If separation is proved necessary, they should be encouraged to participate in the selection of those who will adopt their child and to meet those they have selected before they sign a surrender of parental rights. The birth-

74

parents and prospective adoptive parents should be assisted to determine the terms of the adoption, such as who will name the child and how often the birthparents will visit. Prior to an adoption, the parties should be assisted to thoroughly understand what adoption will and will not do for each of the people and families involved.

We view adoption as a blended family situation in which the birth and adoptive families each contribute to and love the child. Each family should be respected and acknowledged for their contributions and love. Adoption should be used as a method of adding to a child's life, not of taking away. We believe that blended families work best when all members communicate with one another, the child has access to everyone who loves him, and all parents cooperate in the child's best interest.

*"Social workers must reorient their attitudes and
practice vis-à-vis birth fathers and energetically
seek their involvement in the adoptive proceedings."*

The Rights of Birth
Fathers Must Be Protected

Paul Sachdev

In the following viewpoint, Paul Sachdev challenges much of
what he says is the stereotypical thinking of social workers
about biological fathers whose offspring are available for adoption. Recent evidence, he contends, indicates that many of these
birth fathers want to participate in the adoptive processes.
Social agencies, Sachdev argues, should reach out to birth fathers to help them deal with their anxiety, remorse, and emotional trauma. Sachdev is a professor at the School of Social
Work in the Memorial University of Newfoundland in Canada.

As you read, consider the following questions:

1. According to Sachdev, why have the biological fathers of
   adopted children usually played no significant role in the
   adoption process?
2. What group, in Sachdev's analysis, most strongly opposes
   disclosing the adult adoptee's whereabouts to the birth
   father? Why?
3. Why and how should the prevailing views about adoptees'
   birth fathers be changed, in the author's opinion?

Excerpted from Paul Sachdev, "The Birth Father: A Neglected Element in the Adoption
Equation," *Families in Society*, March 1991. Reprinted by permission of Families
International, Inc.

Although it takes two to conceive a child, the birth father of an adopted child is not accorded the same recognition in the literature as is the birth mother. Usually, he is not involved in the decision regarding the disposition of the pregnancy and the placement of the child because he is often seen by the birth mother as irresponsible and exploitive. Although a principal protagonist in the existence of the adopted child, the birth father is often viewed as an illusory entity whose only link with this child is his involvement in the biological event. Adoption agencies reinforce this attitude by not seeking his active involvement in planning for the baby. It is convenient for agencies to deal with the birth mother only and disregard the existence of the birth father, who simply "complicates" the situation. The negative attitudes of both the birth mother and adoption agencies have historically justified birth fathers' simply fading away. Since the early 1970s, court cases in the United States and Canada acknowledging the right of birth fathers to be involved in the custody and adoption proceedings have refocused the attention of child-care agencies on the birth father's role in adoption plans. Moreover, the sheer number of teenage fathers (they are responsible for an estimated 1.1 million unintended pregnancies each year) has also caught the attention of professionals. More than half (55%) of adolescent pregnancies end in live births, and many of the infants are relinquished for adoption. As a result of these developments, adoption agencies in Canada and the United States are increasingly recognizing the need for active involvement of birth fathers in contraceptive, abortion, or adoption counseling as well as planning for the baby.

Birth Fathers Want to Be Involved

Recent research studies show that contrary to prevailing beliefs, a large majority of adolescent unwed fathers do care about the child and remain committed psychologically or physically to both the mother and the baby during pregnancy and after childbirth. Studies of male partners of women who have an abortion show that many men feel guilt and remorse about the pregnancy, feel isolated and removed from the decision-making process, and care about the trauma and turmoil their partners experience. In one of the few major studies involving 1,000 males who accompanied their pregnant partner to an abortion clinic, A.B. Shostak and G. McLouth noted that 94% of single men wanted to be actively involved in the decision, 72% offered to marry or provide financial child-rearing support, and 66% were prepared to support the female's decision. Only 7% denied paternity or terminated relationships. M.A. Redmond studied 25 adolescent expectant fathers in Ontario and achieved similar results. Whether in a casual or serious dating relationship, all of the men wanted to be told of the pregnancy and wanted to participate in the decision-making process, and most (95%) would accompany their partner for an abortion and provide emotional support after the abortion. Less than 8% said that they would break off the relationship. That teenage fathers do not generally abandon their female partners during the trying period of pregnancy and childbirth is confirmed by other studies as well. Many of these studies show that prospective fathers would like to participate in childbirth and child rearing. S. Panzarine and A.B. Elster interviewed a convenience sample of 20 adolescent fathers; more than 17 fathers accompanied their pregnant partners for clinic visits or participated in antenatal classes. E.P. Rivara, P.J. Sweeny, and B.F. Henderson studied 81 black teenage expectant fathers and found that two-thirds attended clinics while the mother was in labor, one-fourth were present during delivery, and more than four-fifths visited their children in the nursery. In another study of predominantly black teenage unwed fathers, R.L. Barrett and B.E. Robinson noted that a large majority (92%) expressed desire to participate actively in the fathering experience.

Not only do a sizeable proportion of unwed fathers remain committed to the child's birth mother, an increasing number of them are also searching for children relinquished for adoption. In a convenience sample of 125 birth fathers drawn from the national support and advocacy group of birth fathers (NOBAR), E.Y. Deykin, P. Patti, and J. Ryan noted that nearly half of the fathers had had some involvement in the adoption proceedings and two-thirds had been searching for the child at the time of the study.

Attitudes Toward Birth Fathers

Despite the judicial recognition of paternal rights of birth fathers and their interest in the birth mother and her child, however, little attention has been focused on how members of the adoption triad—adoptive parents, birth mothers, and adopted persons—view the birth father and his role as a parent. This viewpoint presents study findings that examined the attitudes of the adoption triangle toward birth fathers. . . .

Data reveal that members of the triad were either opposed or divided in their views on disclosure of the adopted adult's whereabouts to the birth father. The strongest disapproval was voiced by adoptive parents, with 8 of 10 parents opposing such a policy. The 1958 and 1968 adoptive parents were slightly more opposed (89%) than were their younger (1978) cohorts (74.1%). Birth mothers were almost evenly divided, with 49% in favor of this policy measure and 51% rejecting it. Like birth mothers, adoptees were split in their opinion whether the birth father should be granted right of access to information about adult adoptees' whereabouts. . . .

The study indicates that birth mothers who were opposed to releasing identifying information to the birth father resented the birth father because he deserted the young mother and the child. They disagreed with the principle of coterminous rights [i.e., the same rights for both birth parents] because the birth father voluntarily abdicated responsibility for the care of the child and thus lost his right to learn the child's identity or to establish contact. Birth mothers' indignation is epitomized in the following excerpt:

> It takes two to tango. When he gave up his responsibility to marry me and care for the child, he gave up all rights as father. As far as I'm concerned there is no such thing as a birth father.

These birth mothers also questioned whether the father would be interested in the child in that he didn't show interest when the child was born.

> If the birth father was not interested in the beginning, there is no sense in him coming around years later looking for information about the child. I'd just tell him to get lost. The guy left me and didn't care enough to stay around. So why should he care now?

A few birth mothers doubted whether birth fathers would seek information, citing the fathers' potential fear that they might be faced with paying child support. A 1968 birth mother stated:

> There are probably millions of fathers walking around who have dozens of kids. I'm sure these men don't want to go to the department and tell them they have a child; otherwise they might end up providing support for a lot of children.

The birth mothers who favored release of the adoptee's identity to the father acknowledged that the father had failed to meet his responsibility to the child and did not share decision-making tasks. However, some birth mothers justified their support for releasing information by the fact that the child might want to meet the father despite the father's evident lack of parental feelings. A 1968 birth mother stated:

> I feel I'm the mother, but probably he doesn't feel he is the father because he never went through the pain of signing any paper. But I don't see why it should be any different from the birth mother as far as the child is concerned. Besides, the child would like to know both the mother and the father.

Opposition from Adoptive Parents

Adoptive parents disapproved of sharing identifying information with the birth father for many of the same reasons as did birth mothers. They felt he did not show concern for the predicament of the young mother or share responsibility for plan-

"So! Who's the father?"

ning and care of the child. One 1968 adoptive mother said that the birth father "washed his hands" of the whole affair and allowed the mother to put the child up for adoption. Some adoptive parents argued that the father was not a principal party to the adoption agreement.

Opposition from Adoptees

In the minds of most adoptees, the birth father was merely a biological entity. He was referred to as "that person," "that man," "biological father." The study shows that more than 77.4% of adoptees felt indifferent toward the birth father when they were growing up. By contrast, less than one third, 30.2%, felt this way about the birth mother. Their genealogical past was generally symbolized by the birth mother and her family:

> I have never ever thought of a birth father. I know that sounds crazy. It's as though that person never existed. I know there

must have been one. But I'm concerned only with my natural mother and I have no feelings toward that person.

Interestingly, adoptees were virtually amnesic about the birth father and reacted with near astonishment when he was mentioned. Their characteristic response was: "I never really thought of him. I don't know why." A female adoptee felt embarrassed: "I didn't ever think there was a father involved; it tells you something about my sex education." Similarly, a male adoptee stated: "I never thought I had a birth father. I know you have to have one in order to conceive."

Adoptees who supported the birth father's right to information were motivated by a sense of fairness, because they had endorsed the right of the birth mother to such information. A recurring sentiment was voiced by a male adoptee who was working as a correctional officer: "Although I have no feeling toward that man, I have to be fair to him. I think the same law should apply to him as does to the natural mother." To the question of whether the birth father should be given such information, these adoptees responded laconically, "Same as the birth mother, no distinction" or "whatever applies to the birth mother, the same applies to the birth father."

But Attitudes Often Change

Significantly, the study points out that with the passage of time and age, the adoptees' feelings toward both birth parents changed in a positive direction. Several adoptees got married and had their own children, which gave them a different perspective on being a parent and making difficult choices. As adults, they felt considerably more positive (55.1%) and less indifferent (16.9%) toward the birth father than they did when they were growing up. However, for adoptees, the birth mother remained the preferred link with their past. For example, more adoptees (66.3%) had positive feelings toward the birth mother than for the father (55.1%). Similarly, more adoptees were unconcerned about the father (16.9%) or had negative feelings toward him (16.2%) than they did for the birth mother (9.9%).

The adoptees' most predominant positive feelings were expressed as understanding and empathy for the birth mother's decision and a nonjudgmental attitude toward the birth father. They tended to appreciate the predicament of the birth mother, who as a young girl was compelled to surrender the child to escape the stigma of illegitimacy. They were convinced that the decision she made was not an easy one and felt she was driven to do what was best for the child. Adoptees felt grateful to the birth mother because her decision to relinquish them for adoption had provided them with a loving, secure, and stable home. They were convinced that given her trying circumstances and meager resources, the birth mother could not have provided them with a stable and financially secure home.

> When I was young I used to wonder how this woman could not want me. Any woman could have a baby and give it up. Over the years, I understood a bit more and realized that it was the best thing for her to do under her circumstances. Being a parent, I realize now that in order for her to give me up, it must have been hard for her. You must have some kind of feeling after having a baby. However, I'm glad that she had the sense to give me up. I'm grateful that she did this and gave me a chance to have a great home. If I was with her now, I would probably be God knows where.

> When I gave birth to my kid, the girl across from me was having a baby. She had [completed] Grade 8 or 9, had no money and means of support for the child. But she was determined that the best thing to do for the child was to give it up for adoption. I now have sympathy for my birth mother to the extent I now realize how difficult it must have been for a mother to give up a baby for adoption.

Though these adoptees were more appreciative of the circumstances of the birth mother, they also became, as adults, less judgmental about the birth father. They said that because they did not know the circumstances of the birth father and the reasons why he did not remain committed to the birth mother, it would be unfair to blame him.

> It's difficult to make judgment when you don't know the situation. I don't know anything about him; so really it's hard to judge him. Unless you sit and talk with him, I can't really pass judgment.

From the above explanation it appears that the chief reason for the triad's opposition to releasing information to the birth father was the negative feelings they had toward him. They felt resentment that he deserted the birth mother and the child. They argued that the birth father voluntarily abdicated responsibility for care of the child and therefore lost his right to learn the child's identity or to establish contact. Birth mothers felt victimized because they got pregnant and had to make difficult decisions without the birth father's support. Adoptees tended not to consider the birth father in the adoption configuration.

Re-Orienting Stereotypical Beliefs

Adoptees who supported the birth father's right of access to information were motivated by a sense of fairness; they felt that because they supported similar rights for the birth mother it was only just. Birth mothers' support was due largely to their consideration of his biological participation. But respondents who supported the birth father's right to information felt as much resentment toward the birth father as did the respondents who opposed access to information.

Clearly these data indicate that members of the adoption triad shared the prevailing stereotypical view of the birth father as being a "Don Juan" (i.e., he sexually exploited a young, innocent girl) and "phantom father" (i.e., evading responsibility for the support and care of the mother and child). Such images of the birth father are not helpful in view of the emerging trend toward releasing information about birth parents to adopted persons. This measure is supported on the grounds that adoptees need such information and that contact with birth parents will help them complete their identity and personality development. An adoptee's negative image of the birth father may interfere with the identity-formation process. An adoptee's identity formation and self-image begin at an early age; adoptive parents contribute to this process by sharing information regarding the child's birth parents. Agencies can better serve adoptive couples by providing them with more and better information about the parents.

Learning About Birthparents

Among adopted teens . . .

65% would like to meet their birthparents, but haven't.

65% think about their birthmother once a month or less.

77% think about their birthfather once a month or less.

52% wish they knew more about their birthmother.

45% wish they knew more about their birthfather.

1% have met at least one birthparent.

Adoptive Families, July/August 1994.

Influenced by the stigma surrounding unwed parenthood, adoptive parents, like the professional community, have often trusted the stereotypical images of teenage fathers. In the absence of scientific information, adoption agencies reinforce these stereotypes and biases. In light of the latest research findings, social workers must reorient their attitudes and practice vis-à-vis birth fathers and energetically seek their involvement in the adoptive proceedings. Studies have shown that the birth father is more likely to become involved if the birth mother agrees to his involvement. Thus, the logical place to begin is with the birth mother, who should be encouraged to permit the birth father to participate in the decision-making process. Because of the punitive attitudes of the past, social agencies need to reach out to birth fathers. Agencies must be assertive in their approach, stressing constructive attitudes that inspire trusting relationships. The birth mother may not recognize that the young father also needs support and therapeutic help in dealing with his anxiety, remorse, and emotional trauma. Programs that exclude birth fathers deprive mothers of vital support. Studies have demonstrated that once they become involved, many young fathers become caring and understanding of the birth mother's anguish and continue their support after the child has been relinquished.

Agencies should ensure that the adoption records contain as much information about the birth father as possible. Most adoptees search for the birth father after they have met the mother. The birth mother who has been positively influenced by the father's caring attitude and behavior is most likely to project a positive image to the adoptee. Similarly, a social worker who has reoriented his or her stereotypical beliefs regarding teen fathers may be less likely to project negative attitudes when discussing the adoptive child's genealogy with the adoptive parents. Given a positive image, birth fathers are likely to gain support of the adoption triad for equal access rights to information about adoptees and possible contact with them.

"The treatment accorded adoptive parents and prospective adoptive parents . . . has been no less troubling than the treatment traditionally accorded birth parents."

The Rights of Adoptive Parents Must Be Protected

Hal Aigner

As the author of *Faint Trails*, a handbook for adult adoptees searching for their birth parents, Hal Aigner is known for his advocacy in all areas of adoption reform. His book *Adoption in America Coming of Age* (1992), from which the following viewpoint is taken, examines legal cases from state and national courts as well as numerous law review essays. Studying all involved in adoption policy making, Aigner lays blame where institutions fail and advocates reforms that he believes will help protect the rights of everyone involved: birth parents, adoptees, and adoptive parents. Concerning those who want to adopt children, Aigner traces the history of their legal disappointments and makes clear that they too need greater protections.

As you read, consider the following questions:

1. How does Aigner define "wrongful adoption"? What two common factors he does associate with wrongful adoption?
2. How did the *Adoption of Runyon* and *In re Haun* courts differ in their responses to adoption agencies' authority to place children for adoption, as described by the author?
3. In Aigner's view, what do prospective adoptive parents need to benefit from judicial review of adoption agency actions?

Critical scrutiny of the agency system of child placement should be undertaken in an effort to understand why, in the early 1970s, a number of legal commentators were moved to such conclusions as "[t]he interests of the child and the interests of those who care about the child's welfare are often ignored in the attempt to preserve this system and the authority of the licensed placement agencies" [Jane A. Restani] and "[t]his case [that of California's 1969 *Adoption of Runyon*, discussed below] demonstrates the helplessness of the judiciary in the face of the almost unlimited power of adoption agencies to dispose of children relinquished to them in any manner they see fit" [Brigitte M. Bodenheimer].

The Marginalization of Adoptive Parents' Rights

Some attention is required here, however, for the adoptive-parent presence in the mounting dissatisfactions currently being expressed with the practices that have traditionally governed child relinquishments and placements. For once it is recognized that so-called relinquishment procedures have been profoundly influenced by poorly founded policies, coercive pressures, and a lack of legal safeguards for the principals involved, then it would be naive to imagine that those very same forces have not exerted a troubling influence on adoptive placements as well. And the written record indisputably shows that over the years, the treatment accorded adoptive parents and prospective adoptive parents by the institutionalized processes of adoption has been no less troubling than the treatment traditionally accorded birth parents.

But perhaps most strikingly, a review of the record further reveals that, in the greater scheme of American adoption, the legal interests of adoptive parents have been marginalized. Unwed mothers have had their advocates, whose support over the long run has contributed substantially to the marked improvement of their lot. The challenges faced by unwed fathers have at least become the subject of intense discussion. The termination of parental rights proceeding has at least received detailed scrutiny in legal journals. Yet, the open dialogue on matters of concern to adoptive parents has barely been raised above a whisper. True, it is possible to locate a very few essays addressing one aspect or another of adoptive parents' rights scattered here and there in several decades of law journals. But, in fact, adoptive parents have had to wait until recently for in-depth examinations of their interests to appear with the publication of such writings as John Maley's exposition on adoption fraud in the 1987 *Indiana Law Review* or Janet Hopkins Dickson's pathbreaking essay, "The Emerging Rights of Adoptive Parents: Substance or Specter?" in the 1991 *University of California Los*

Angeles Law Review.

Nonetheless, important issues have existed all along, a circumstance no more vividly illustrated than by the rise of wrongful adoption litigation. As a legal phrase, the term "wrongful adoption" first arose in the mid 1980s with the Ohio case of *Burr v. Board of County Com'rs of Stark Cty* and connotes the presence of fraudulent conduct in adoptive placements. The concern central to wrongful adoption, however, had surfaced many years before. Will placement agencies ever lie to prospective adoptive parents regarding the health of the child being placed with them? Apparently, yes. In 1958, for example, the Appellate Court of Indiana affirmed a lower court decision to annul an adoption after it was established that the County Department of Public Welfare of St. Joseph County had "falsely represented to (the parents) that the child was of good health mentally and physically" and that the parents "would not have adopted this child if they had known the true facts."

It was in the 1980s, however, that this concern began to receive the attention it was due. In 1984, awareness of the problem of fraud in adoption prompted the introduction into the United States Senate of a bill that, had it been enacted, would have provided legal protections in the form of civil and criminal penalties for adoptive parents and natural mothers who fell victim to fraudulent adoption practices. (The measure failed to pass, partly because of opposition from the United States Justice Department.) Meanwhile, in California, a compilation of news reports and formal studies both revealed something of the scope of the problem and began to interpret wrongful adoption in terms of two common factors associated with fraudulent conduct, that of affirmative misrepresentation (or in plain talk, "lying") and that of failure to disclose what is known. As summarized by Janet Hopkins Dickson:

> Between 1983 and 1987, sixty-nine adoptions in California were reportedly annulled because county agencies had fraudulently misrepresented a child's background or mental or physical health. Nondisclosure seems to be even more prevalent than fraudulent misrepresentation. A recent Berkeley study found that more than one-half of parents who had adopted sexually abused children were not informed about the abuse; one-third who had adopted a physically abused child were similarly unaware, and one-third who had adopted children with learning disabilities were likewise uninformed. A significant number of others did not know of physical, developmental, emotional, or behavioral problems.

To place the impact of this absence of information in actual perspective, it should be recognized that the consequences of this fraud or nondisclosure can be so extreme as to border on the fatal. As Dickson noted: ". . . one couple was never in-

formed that their adopted daughter had been diagnosed as need-
ing long-term psychiatric care, with a recommendation of immediate admission to a psychiatric hospital; the adoptors discovered her background only after she tried to burn down the family house and poison her adoptive father with Lysol-laced soup."

The *Burr* Decision

And then there was the 1986 *Burr* decision. What made *Burr*
significant was that it was the first reported case to sustain an
award of "damages," that legal term signifying a monetary
award for injuries incurred. In brief, the facts of *Burr* are these.
The Burrs first approached the Stark County Welfare Department hoping to adopt a male child up to the age of six months.
A few days after the initial contact, an employee of the Department telephoned them, advising that a seventeen-month-old boy
was available for adoption. The Burrs then met with a Department caseworker who presented them with a highly fabricated
description of the child's health and genetic history, while omit-
ting such details as the history of mental illness in the child's familial background, his fever at birth and subsequent slow development, and his susceptibility to Huntington's Disease, a hereditary ailment that manifests through destruction of the central
nervous system. Over the following years, the boy then exhibited physical twitching, speech impediment, poor motor skills,
and learning disabilities. By high school, he suffered hallucinations. He was eventually diagnosed as having contracted Huntington's Disease. While the boy was undergoing treatment, the
Burrs went to court, obtained an order opening the boy's sealed
adoption records, and then discovered what the Ohio Supreme
Court itself concluded was a "complex scheme of deception."

In affirming the appropriateness of a damages award for this
deception, the majority here observed:

> Just as couples must weigh the risks of becoming natural par-
> ents, taking into consideration a host of factors, so too should
> adoptive parents be allowed to make their decision in an intel-
> ligent manner. It is not the mere failure to disclose the risks
> inherent in this child's background which we hold to be ac-
> tionable. Rather, it is the deliberate act of misinforming this
> couple which deprived them of their right to make a sound
> parenting decision and which led to the compensable injuries.

Other Trend-Setting Court Cases

Ohio's *Burr* decision could easily have marked an important
milestone in the development of procedural protections for the
interests of adoptive parents. In 1988, California joined Ohio in
recognizing the validity of wrongful adoption proceedings, this
time on the basis both of intentional misrepresentation and
fraudulent concealment. In 1989, Wisconsin joined the fold on

the basis of negligent misrepresentation. In October 1991, Massachusetts entered the ranks with a decision that was noteworthy not so much for its cause of action, but rather for the $3.8 million award given by the jury where evidence showed that a municipal placement agency had concealed from prospective adoptive parents the medical history of an eight-year-old girl who was being placed in their home, alleging that no medical records existed as to the girl when in fact she had been examined and diagnosed as retarded. The direction of the trend was clear. Yet . . . promising beginnings are just that. They are not guarantors of final outcomes. And, in the pro-institution mix of statutes and ordinances that is American adoption law, what the legal consequences are to be as regards what is said, or not said, to adoptive parents on the occasion of a placement of a child in their home still has yet to be determined. . . .

The fate of wrongful adoption litigation, however, is far from the only issue of continuing concern to adoptive parents. . . . Adoptive parents are no more immune to the abuses of traditional American adoption practices than are any other groups of individuals whose lives are touched by adoption. For them also, there are matters of arbitrariness in procedure, of being stereotyped, and of fair treatment that have proven to be of enduring concern.

Arbitrary Decisions and Procedures

And through such scant materials as are available, it is possible to catch a glimpse of where additional remedial attention is needed on adoptive parents' behalf, beginning here with a review of two judicial case reports of actions taken to set aside objections raised by placement agencies against an adoption's finalization, California's January 1969 *Adoption of Runyon* and Ohio's December 1971 *In re Haun*.

As a ruling, *Adoption of Runyon* is brief, to the point, and contains not a whisper of sympathy for the couple who had served for more than seven years as the parents of a child with exceptional needs. According to the opinion, James Runyon was born on August 17, 1959, in Sacramento, California. His custody was almost immediately assigned to the county Social Welfare Department. Three days later, the Department placed the boy in a private home as a foster child. Three weeks later, the foster parents were advised that the child would require surgery to remedy a major heart defect. They were then given the option of returning him to the Department or continuing to provide for his care. They were also told that he was not available for adoption.

He was, at least, not available to them. The foster parents elected to nurture and raise the afflicted child through his surgery and continued in their roles as his mother and father until an unreported date in 1967. The youth was then removed from their custody and placed for adoption in another home.

Soon thereafter, the foster parents presented a petition to the Sacramento County Superior Court, asking to adopt the boy. The petition was denied. The judgment was appealed to California's Third District Appellate Court. The plea was denied there also, with the Justices deferring to a narrow reading of a state statute prohibiting anyone but "prospective adoptive parents selected by the adoption agency from adopting a child relinquished to such agency." No mention was made of the "best interests of the child," or of the importance of the relationship that had developed between the boy and the couple who had served as his parents since he was three days old. Only procedure mattered.

In re Haun had a happier ending. The child whose future was decided upon in this action was a baby born in Cuyahoga County, Ohio; December 1968. For reasons not alluded to in the case report, she was given into the temporary custody of a local social welfare agency referred to as Children's Services. She was described as premature at birth and as possibly suffering from slight brain damage incurred during a difficult delivery. Fifteen days later, she was placed with the Haun family specifically "because of their previously demonstrated expertise in the care of premature babies." The following April, permanent relinquishment of the infant was made to Children's Services.

In December 1971, the county probate court observed of the child's stay with the Hauns:

> Until about a year ago Julie was slow in achieving normal accomplishments such as crawling and pushing. Although a child is customarily left by Children's Services with foster parents not more than six months, rather than risk regression from the steady progress manifested, Julie, by concord of the Hauns and Children's Services, was allowed to remain with the Hauns. Presently Julie is happily characterized as a normal child having an IQ of 112. Without doubt the improvement over somewhat cloudy beginnings is due to the care, affection, attention and love accorded by petitioners. In turn love and affection are exhibited by Julie toward the Hauns. On this all are agreed.

Mr. Haun was 68 years old at the time of the petition; his wife, 55. Both were described as in excellent health. They owned their home outright and were otherwise very secure financially. They were the parents of four children, one adopted, and had served as foster parents to an additional 34. The most recent foster child was Julie, who, again for unmentioned reasons, was also referred to as Sheila Smith.

In spring 1971, the Hauns expressed their desire to adopt Julie to Children's Services. As Mrs. Haun later testified: "There was something special about Sheila from the very first when she first came to our home, there was just something about her that we just fell in love with. When all these problems came up we just poured out all our love and we began to love her more and more and felt that this was a child that really needed us."

Children's Services responded by contending that, solely on the basis of their ages, the Hauns were not suitable to assume permanent familial custody of the child. The agency then proposed that the girl should be moved from the home in which she had so prospered, for eventual placement with new prospective adoptive parents.

The Hauns subsequently petitioned the court to grant an adoption over the Children's Services objections. Their plea received the support of a pediatrician and assistant professor of neurology associated with the University Hospitals of Cleveland Neurology Clinic where Julie has regularly received medical attention. In an evidentiary memorandum, he wrote:

> Her medical observers, including myself, were very impressed with the excellent care and interest shown by her foster mother, Mrs. Haun. It is my opinion that the child's satisfactory development has to a large extent been a credit to the care she received in this home. While it is not in our power to wish to dictate any policy to the agency, we would respectfully submit that continuation of the care received from Mrs. Haun would be highly desirable for this delightful child.

Additional testimony referred to another physician who, in reacting to the proposed transfer of Julie to new prospective adoptive parents, ". . . just threw his hands up in the air and . . . said 'what the hell is the matter with those people downtown, don't they know they can't move this baby?'"

Over the objections of those people downtown, the petition was granted and the Hauns permitted to adopt.

But where, from the placement agency's position, were the best interests of the child in both of these actions? Where was the regard for the familial bonds supposedly forged by the onset of psychological parenthood? Or in the *Runyon* decision, where was the august judicial power of *parens patriae* [the state as parent] that has loomed so formidably when moves have been made to remove children from their birth parents' custody? In light of American adoption's general history, consistency alone would seem to dictate that such highly touted mainstays of relinquishment and termination procedure, if they are to be endorsed as valid at all, should not conveniently be suspended solely because prospective adoptive parents find themselves in conflict with placement agency powers.

And continuing on with the *Haun* decision, the objection raised therein to the proposed adoption merely on the basis of the applicants' advanced age provides a clear indication that prospective adoptive parents have been as vulnerable as birth parents to evaluation by adoption caseworkers in terms of stereotypes rather than realities.

Stereotyping on the Basis of Age

Of all the stereotypes to which prospective adoptive parents have been subjected, that based on age is the most conspicuous. In the appendixes of the 1957 advice book *If You Adopt A Child*, for example, a directory of placement agencies throughout the country, accompanied by a summary of their eligibility requirements, repeatedly reveals a preference for parents no older than their early forties, and for wives to be younger than husbands. This posture was later rationalized in the 1974 *Adoption and After*, as follows:

> Anyone nearing middle age who is considering the adoption of a very young child should remember: It is an inescapable fact that emotional and physical resiliency *does* start to decline in the middle years. Wrestling off four muddy snow suits from your squirming child and three of his playmates is just another chore when you're twenty or twenty-five; if you're pushing forty-five this and the hundred other daily chores that a toddler creates may so deplete your energy and frazzle your nerves that you just can't be the warm, sunny, unruffled mother he is entitled to have.

This is a openly bigoted statement, presented without a semblance of documentation and made noteworthy by all the wrong reasons. How, for one, does such an outlook account for the Hauns and their exemplary work with an infant with special needs? Why should any parents be burdened with the expectation of agencies that don't know that maturation requires experience with a greater range of human emotions? Is it an inescapable fact that emotional resiliency declines with age? The truth may lie in quite the opposite direction, given that normal stresses of early adulthood are so often alleviated in the passage of time. For one, people who have reached middle age and above can be expected to be more financially stable—the Hauns owned their home outright. Likewise, they are more likely to have stabilized their professional lives and secured their marriages. This last concern is of special importance as among the tales frequently told at search support groups are those describing divorces occurring two to four years after an adoption, perhaps a result of too many placements with parents in the 20- to 25-year-old age bracket. A case could be made, then, that older prospective adoptive parents are preferable.

Yet, taking exception to the conventional thinking found in advice books does nothing to erase the fact of a long-standing procedural bias against prospective adoptive parents of middle age or older.

The Issue of Fair Treatment

"Child care agencies have been criticized for requiring unnecessarily strict and sometimes arbitrary qualifications of adoptive parents," noted an essay in the December 1971 *St. John's Law Review*, and, in addition to capricious age requirements, the list of considerations raised over the years by placement agencies in opposition to adoptions has grown to include the decisiveness of subjective responses of agency personnel, meaning that the mere feeling of a placement's unsuitability has been presented as sufficient reason to deny an adoption; differing religious affiliations between prospective parents and the children they hoped to adopt; the untimely death of one prospective parent; previous status as a foster parent; unverified accusations anonymously made against a prospective parent; the parents' weight exceeding limits established by unwritten guidelines; and, in what is perhaps the most outlandish instance of agency arbitrariness on record, the prospective father's high intelligence and sound education.

Further, in efforts to preserve their own authority, agencies have also contested prospective adoption by asserting that, so far as their placements were concerned, courts were powerless to finalize the legal union of parents and children where an agency had not given its consent to such an action. (To be fair, however, a number of judicial case reports also provide clear evidence of agency assistance commendably given to prospective parents in efforts to overcome various state statutes that once prohibited mixed racial adoptions. The picture here is not entirely bleak.)

A Possible Healthy Trend

Much to the benefit of prospective adoptive parents, however, throughout the 1970s, most of the obstacles placed by agencies in the path of an adoption's finalization were disallowed by the courts on those occasions when prospective parents appealed to the judiciary for relief. Despite occasional hesitations, courts have responded with little enthusiasm to the idea that their authority must yield to that of placement institutions. Indeed, the California judiciary eventually so repudiated the conclusion of judicial deference to placement agencies reached in *Adoption of Runyon* that by 1979, an appellate court was moved to comment that recent cases in the state had established "a trend of increased attention to adoption agency decisions. . . . [W]e believe that this trend is a healthy one."

And as was pointed out with compelling simplicity in the Golden State's 1973 *C. v. Superior Court for County of Sacramento*:

> The objective of *de novo* judicial review [a review of the facts in their entirety] is not to supplant the adoption agency or to

denigrate the expertise of trained social workers. Their decisions and their expert opinions should be received with respect. Rather, the objective is to prevent arbitrary judgments; to guard against placement terminations generated by the subjective inclinations of case workers and supervisors untaught in the analysis of evidence and not doctrinated in the concept of fair hearing; to promote fairness by interposing a law-trained judge between the agency and prospective parents; to insure that the ultimate decision is firmly hinged in the only permissible criterion—the welfare of the child.

But, as is a running theme in adoption reform, gains must be appraised carefully. True, it is of clear advantage to prospective adoptive parents that the courts have disapproved of many of the objections raised by placement agencies to pending adoptions. And true, the judicial insistence on reserving to the courts the final word in adoption proceedings does represent a major victory for prospective parents whose interests clash with agency arbitrariness and subjectivity.

The Importance of Due Process of Law

Yet, such developments may be of only passing value to many prospective adoptive parents unless an overriding problem they share in common with birth parents, married and unmarried, is effectively resolved. For judicial review of agency actions to mean anything, parents must have access to the law, which includes some working knowledge of their options, an ability to finance litigation, and some timely forewarning of pending changes in their status. And taken together, these considerations once again raise the issue of due process of law.

Whether prospective adoptive parents are entitled to due process of law when their familial interests are in jeopardy is a question that has received only scant attention from legislatures, courts, and legal commentators. The available record of such an entitlement reveals only isolated instances of specific legal protections having been granted to the emerging familial status that characterizes the early stages of adoptive placement. For example, in winter 1975, an essay appearing in the *Missouri Law Review* bluntly stated: "Whether prospective adoptive parents have a due process right to notice and a hearing before their legal custody of the child may be terminated has never been litigated in Missouri." The author evidently could have been speaking of the situation present in most other jurisdictions as well. Judging from the paucity of legislation, litigation, and commentary bearing on this issue, the idea that a protectable interest might accrue to preadoptive parents while an adoption's finalization is pending appears to have entirely eluded the greater segment of this country's legal community. . . .

Other Problems

There are, of course, many other areas of overlapping interest. For one, the practice of secrecy in adoption has also likely interfered on a grand scale with the opportunity of birth parents and prospective adoptive parents to act as joint participants in the adoption process. That this option is viable is clearly demonstrated in a very few judicial case reports of actions in which birth parents have appeared in court to support pending adoptions, against the opposition of outside parties. In the best of all possible worlds, it is important for relinquishing birth parents to have the opportunity to find and work with their equivalent of the Hauns.

For another, adoptive parents are placed in a particularly vulnerable position when faulty relinquishment procedures may, quite necessarily, result in the return of a child to its birth parents. For yet another, there is the baby black market. In September 1985, an undisclosed number of adoptive parents became subject to investigation as part of a probe into a black market scandal involving an estimated sale of some 150 Mexican infants for as much as $10,000 each. According to news reports of the incident, the operation further involved forgery of birth certificates and the illegal entry of the children into the country, though the complicity of adoptive parents in the traffic remained an open question. Relinquishment and placement are opposite ends of a continuum, and irregularities at the beginning of the adoption process may well complicate its finalization.

Finally, the ultimate bond shared by adoptive parents and birth parents is that of care and affection for the children who are the true center of adoption. For, in general, adoptive parents are the very people on whom whatever successes can be claimed by American adoption have always depended. No other possibility presents itself. The history of American adoption reveals a string of failures on the part of those professionals normally considered responsible for the effective operation of the adoptive system. The many state legislatures have done a poor job of formulating procedure. The behavioral sciences have consistently been unable to produce findings substantial enough to survive criticism from within their own ranks. Some unknown number of physicians, attorneys, and on occasion even placement agency personnel, have been shown to be so lacking in integrity as to engage in the thinly disguised sale of infants. The courts have been confused in their stewardship over procedure. To a disturbing degree, social service personnel have been appraised as poorly educated and trained. Placement agencies have been charged with often subordinating the interests of parents and children alike to the interest of maintaining their own authority. Overall, the system has not been one to inspire confidence.

A Final Reminder

There remain adoptive parents who, outside the incidents of abused adoptees, have not failed in their trust. And where adoption becomes a necessary alternative for birth parents who, for whatever reasons, are unable to retain custody of their children, it is to adoptive parents that they must ultimately look for help. Without the adoptive parents' capacity to serve as mothers and fathers, all the laws and regulations and court opinions by which relinquishment and placement are supposedly guided would amount to so much wishful thinking. More than a hundred years of failure to adequately shield adoptive parents' interests against the inevitability of institutional error, then, stands as further testimony to the insensitivity to human needs and dignity that has haunted American adoption practice and procedure during the nineteenth and twentieth century.

"Anna . . . was finally safe with her very own parents."

In the "Baby Jessica" Case, the Court Was Right

Carole Anderson

Carole Anderson, an attorney and a birth mother, is the vice president of Concerned United Birthparents (CUB) and editor of the *CUB Communicator*; she has authored numerous articles on adoption from the birth parent perspective. In the following viewpoint, Anderson sets forth the history of the Baby Jessica case from the birth parents' perspective and comments on what she perceives as media exploitation and bias. In contrasting the actions of the birth parents with those of the couple who tried to adopt the child, Anderson concludes that the court's final decision has been vindicated.

As you read, consider the following questions:

1. What, in Anderson's view, is the value of retelling the story about Anna Schmidt?
2. How does Anderson evaluate Robert and Jan DeBoer, the couple who fought to adopt "Baby Jessica" [Anna] during the first two years of her life?
3. According to the author, how and to what extent were the media responsible for shaping the public's perceptions of events as they unfolded?

Carole Anderson, "Editor's Comments," *CUB Communicator*, August 1993. Reprinted by permission of Concerned United Birthparents, 2000 Walker St., Des Moines, IA 50317.

[The 1992–93 events labeled by the media the "Baby Jessica case"] upset many birthparents watching media coverage of the DeBoers' struggle to keep Anna Schmidt [also known as "Baby Jessica"] away from her parents, Dan and Cara Schmidt. Many have bled for the pain we know the Schmidts have had to endure, and that their daughter would have to endure if she were not returned to them. . . .

The case has taught us much more than we wanted to know about how media treat and ignore facts. Most articles and television reports discussed the anguish of the "adoptive parents" as they faced efforts by the "biological" parents to take "Jessica" away from them more than two years after her "adoption." The facts are very different. Only in [the summer of 1993] have the media bothered to admit that this child's parents have been fighting since she was less than a month old for their daughter's return.

What Happened Initially

The facts in brief: Neither of Anna's parents ever signed a legal surrender of their parental rights. The DeBoers' attorney had Cara sign a surrender only 40 hours after birth, which is before Iowa law allows, while Dan never surrendered. Within a month of Anna's birth her parents had filed court documents seeking her return. Both scrupulously followed all court orders throughout the long ordeal of getting their daughter home. There was never an adoption, there never could be, and adoption was not even an issue in the Michigan action in which the DeBoers, who were acting in open defiance of court orders and without legal custody of Anna, sought to be made Anna's legal custodians.

Jan and Roberta DeBoer, a Michigan couple, cannot have children because Mrs. DeBoer has had a hysterectomy. Michigan allows only agency adoptions. The DeBoers were unable to adopt through an agency in Michigan, perhaps because of Jan DeBoer's arrest record or perhaps because they lacked the confidence or patience to wait. But they had friends in Iowa, and through them they learned of Cara Clausen.

Cara Clausen and Dan Schmidt, Iowa residents who weren't married at the time, had split up during Cara's pregnancy and Cara didn't tell Dan he was to be a father. Unfortunately, Iowa is one of the states that allows non-agency (also called attorney or independent) adoptions, which means that there is no requirement of counseling mothers about their rights, their alternatives, the meaning or process or consequences of an adoption surrender. This has made Iowa a popular place for would-be adopters on both coasts to seek drug-free, healthy white infants from young mothers who won't know their rights or alternatives until it is too late to exercise them. In small town Iowa the pregnancy of a single woman is still very much frowned upon. Confused, scared, feeling guilty for being pregnant, Cara was an easy target for non-agency adoption. No one counseled her about the dramatic difference between feelings and attitudes—of others and herself—about an unplanned pregnancy and about having her child.

While pregnant, when she could not yet realize what her baby would mean to her, she agreed to adoption. Even married couples who plan a pregnancy find that how they thought they would feel about their baby and how they do feel are a world apart. No one can know what it is like to be a parent until the baby arrives. No doubt that is why those who promote family separation also push for early surrenders. Cara's feelings began to change the instant her daughter was born. But before the new mother could fully awaken to that difference, the DeBoers' lawyer had her sign a surrender.

It was not a legal surrender; Iowa law requires a woefully inadequate minimum of 72 hours after birth before a surrender can legally be taken and the DeBoers' lawyer did not wait even that long. The same lawyer also told her that the baby's father would have to surrender his rights. With little understanding of the adoption process and no counseling, Cara, abruptly faced with this demand, did not want to give Dan's name when she had never told him she was carrying his child. She gave the name of the man she was then dating rather than immediately face Dan and tell him he was the father.

CUB's Involvement and Further Developments

Immediately after signing the illegal surrender, Cara knew she had made a mistake of gigantic proportions but didn't know where to turn for help to rectify it. The lawyer who had taken her surrender told her he was working for the DeBoers, not for her. She didn't know any other lawyers. She saw a notice of a Concerned United Birthparents (CUB) meeting in the paper. In terrible pain and desperately missing her child, she decided to attend. She asked if she could get her daughter back since the surrender was illegal. Cedar Rapids member Laurie Parker suggested she call me. I suggested an attorney in her area and talked to that attorney, Jackie Miller, who agreed to represent her. Jackie met with Cara and Dan, then prepared and filed court papers. All this took place within less than a month of Anna's birth.

Told at four weeks of age that both parents loved and wanted Anna, instead of returning her, the DeBoers fought to keep her with them in Michigan. They had been appointed temporary custodians after presenting the illegally taken surrender to the court and obtaining a termination of Cara's rights based on it. They used their status as temporary custodians to block efforts to have Anna returned. They denied Dan was Anna's father and resisted efforts to test her to prove she was Dan's child.

OHMAN—*THE OREGONIAN*. Reprinted by permission: Tribune Media Services.

At 5 months, tests showed Anna was Dan's. At 10 months, the trial court agreed Dan was Anna's father and was entitled to her custody. The DeBoers' petition to adopt this little girl who clearly did not need them had been dismissed. The DeBoers, though, still refused to return Anna. Still they refused to allow Anna's parents to even see her. They appealed to the Iowa Supreme Court. When the district court refused to issue a stay, they convinced two of a three-judge panel of the Iowa Supreme Court to order a stay while their appeal was pending. They refused to allow Anna's parents to see her during the appeal. The Schmidts married in April 1992 while the appeal was still pending. The case, thanks to the DeBoers, dragged on.

Iowa law requires that juvenile matters be kept confidential. During the many long and agonizing months that the Iowa courts took to determine Dan's paternity, a process resisted by the DeBoers every step of the way, and the lengthy period of the appeal to the Iowa Supreme Court, Cara and Dan followed instructions and kept everything about the case confidential. They wanted Anna home and did not want their daughter's privacy lost to the media. The DeBoers were quiet at first, but when it was plain they had lost in Iowa, they flagrantly disregarded the admonitions for confidentiality and turned their fight to keep this baby girl away from her family into a media circus. They allowed and encouraged the media to plaster Anna's picture on front pages and television screens, thus assuring that controversy and the curiosity of strangers would haunt Anna's life for years to come. They let the world, through legions of reporters, see Anna Schmidt, but they wouldn't let Anna's parents visit her.

The Schmidts' suffering was nearly unbearable. They repeatedly won in court: Anna was their daughter; the DeBoers could not adopt her; the Schmidts had not legally surrendered her; they had full parental rights and sole legal custody; the DeBoers had no rights at all where Anna was concerned. Yet the Schmidts still didn't have their daughter. Every time the Schmidts won, the DeBoers convinced some other court to grant a "temporary" stay allowing them to keep Anna away from her family while they engaged in more legal maneuvering. The Schmidts and their lawyers begged to at least be allowed visits with their daughter during these stays. Mrs. DeBoer always refused, apparently wanting to be able to argue to the courts that the child's parents were "strangers."

Toward the Michigan Supreme Court Decision

Finally, there were no more stays, no more reconsiderations. The Iowa courts unequivocally ordered the DeBoers to return Anna to her parents. But Mrs. DeBoer announced on national television that she would not return the child no matter what the court said. Even though they were not adoptive parents, not pre-adoptive parents, not foster parents, not custodians or guardians, and even though they were acting in defiance of the Iowa courts, the DeBoers then filed their custody action in Michigan. Many think they should have been arrested for kidnapping at that point. Instead, the media outcry, based on months of misinformation promulgated by the DeBoers and their supporters, was against the Schmidts.

At the time they filed their custody action in Michigan, the DeBoers knew they could never adopt Anna even if they won. Even if Michigan changed its laws to allow non-agency adoptions, there were no grounds for terminating the rights of Anna's loving, fit parents who had long fought so hard to recover her. The DeBoers continued to defy court orders and the Iowa courts issued warrants for their arrest. Michigan authorities refused to honor them.

Only one court, of the many courts in which they have appeared, has found in favor of the DeBoers, and that was the Michigan circuit court for Washtenaw County. Judge Agers, who refused to enforce the Iowa court orders the DeBoers were so baldly defying and instead issued a restraining order against Dan Schmidt, alarmed lawyers everywhere when he found that Michigan had jurisdiction to hold a custody trial. His later decision that the DeBoers could keep Anna was no surprise. Even before hearing evidence, he had ordered Dan and Cara to refer to the DeBoers as the "adoptive parents" even though that was absolutely untrue because there had never been and could not be an adoption. The judge also ordered Dan and Cara to refer to their daughter as "Jessica" in his courtroom, even though they were their daughter's legal parents with legal custody and had named her Anna. The only kindness he showed Anna and her parents was in ordering, at her parents' request, that the DeBoers not permit any more media photographs of her.

By this time, not surprisingly, the Schmidts' legal bills were tremendous. They could not afford to pay for legions of experts—indeed, they could not even pay the expenses of experts like Annette Baran who were willing to testify free. Even if they could, the judge's orders on how to identify the parties had made it obvious that it would not matter what experts said in favor of the natural family because he had already decided to rule in favor of the DeBoers. The DeBoers, meanwhile, had raised huge amounts of money with their appeals to public sympathy, and had also obtained free legal services for their battle to keep little Anna away from her parents.

The Michigan Supreme Court Decision

This time the Schmidts appealed. The Michigan Court of Appeals promptly ruled in their favor and ordered their daughter's return. Again, though, the DeBoers appealed. Again, the DeBoers obtained a stay. Again, they refused visits between Anna and her parents while they took their custody action to the Michigan Supreme Court. Again, they brushed aside the pleadings of the Schmidts that they work with the Schmidts and their therapist to make the transfer easier for Anna. They held press conferences, appeared on numerous talk shows, wrote letters, begged people to write to the court.

The Michigan Supreme Court agreed that the Schmidts were Anna's parents and entitled to her custody. But instead of returning Anna immediately, the court allowed a month for Anna's return. That month was supposed to be used to arrange for the transfer of custody in the best way possible. Finally, a therapist was ordered to assist with visits and the process of transfer. The transfer, of course, would have been far simpler if Anna had been allowed to know her parents all through the struggle, but the DeBoers, caring only about themselves and about being able to describe the Schmidts as strangers, had denied her that.

The Role of the Media

Roberta and Jan DeBoer took their Michigan non-parent custody case to the United States Supreme Court, which had previously turned them down on their request to review their Iowa action. Again, they took their distorted version of the case to the public, this time to magazines like *Time* and *Newsweek* and television shows like *Larry King Live*, on which Roberta DeBoer explained that she and her husband were the natural parents. Even the show's host was taken aback at that. Current photos of Anna with the DeBoers appeared in *Time* and *People*, as well as countless newspapers. More invasions of Anna's privacy. More using her as a symbol instead of respecting her as a person. More guaranteeing that people on the street will stare at her and her family. All of this was against the Schmidts' wishes that their daughter be allowed to live a normal life with her loving family. All the carefully staged pictures of their daughter with the DeBoers were taken in defiance of Anna's and the Schmidts' rights and without the Schmidts' permission. The media knew the Schmidts were Anna's legal parents and alone had the legal right to release her photographs, but they ignored that.

It's been hard for birthparents to see all of this. It's been hard to watch people treat a child like this, treat a family like this, and be rewarded for their arrogant selfishness with an outpouring of sympathy, not to mention a small fortune, for exploiting Anna. It's been hard to see how callously so many people have dismissed the continuing agony the DeBoers have put Anna's parents through. Even worse was watching the DeBoers' cruelty to Anna at the time of transfer.

One Final Media Scene

August 2, 1993, was the day scheduled for Anna's return to her parents. There had been a visit with her parents on August 1 in which Anna was very happy to see them. The DeBoers spent other portions of that day doing television interviews. The DeBoers may not have allowed her to sleep much that night, because she was very tired the day of the transfer. The Schmidts had wanted a private, positive transfer. The DeBoers, though, engineered an emotional public scene, complete with dozens of photographers and hysterical supporters witnessing Mrs. DeBoer's wailing and clutching at Anna. She had said, some time before, that Jessica would have to be torn from her arms crying, and by the way she insisted the transfer take place she made very sure her prediction would come true. The DeBoers arranged the transfer as a media event guaranteed to make Anna cry with fright at the sight of sobbing adults and the many cameras aimed at her.

The Schmidts rightly insisted on privacy, so the cameras didn't show a brainwashed public what a relief it was for Anna to reach out to the Schmidts, where she was at last safe from the cameras, safe from frenzied public scenes, safe from DeBoer supporters sobbing, safe from being used as a cause. She was finally safe with her very own parents who act like parents: patiently, privately and lovingly providing her with the normal home and family she deserves. At last, this little girl is safe with her parents, sister, grandparents, aunts, uncles, cousins. The tragedy of their unnecessary separation is over. Anna is home.

"Stability and security are more important for a child than genes and chromosomes."

In the "Baby Jessica" Case, the Court Was Wrong

Mary Beth Style

Mary Beth Style is the vice president for policy at the National Council for Adoption. In addition to coauthoring *The Adoption Option: A Training Manual for Pregnancy Counselors*, Style has contributed to the *Adoption Factbook* and *Children and Adolescents: Controversial Issues*, and is the author of numerous articles on adoption. In the following viewpoint, Style argues that in the Baby Jessica case (and others similar to it) the adoption system—most importantly, the courts—failed Baby Jessica by placing her interests below those who treat children as property, making "decisions based on the parents' desires rather than on the children's needs."

As you read, consider the following questions:

1. According to Style, what must first be done to help birth parents make informed choices?
2. In what ways does the author disagree with such organizations as Concerned United Birthparents?
3. What is wrong with such "children's rights" as the right to divorce one's parents, in Style's view?

Mary Beth Style, "Putting Children First in Child Welfare Decisions," a 1994 article originally written for *The World & I*. Reprinted by permission of the author.

The cases of Baby Jessica (the toddler returned to her biological parents after 2½ years of residing with prospective adoptive parents), Gregory K. (the 11-year-old who "divorced" his biological parents as his only means to a stable, permanent family), and, to a lesser extent, Kimberly Mays (the teen who was "switched at birth" and who sued to remain with the father who raised her) brought to the attention of the American public the current crisis in the American child welfare system, which too often treats children as property and ignores their basic emotional needs that enable them to become healthy functioning human beings. These cases have been reported from a variety of angles and have been used by many special interest groups to promote various, often opposing, agendas. Public policy changes following this new public awareness can either bring long overdue protection for children or can be a disastrous example of a bad case making bad law, depending on how deep and thorough the debate is about the very complex issues involved in parental rights and child welfare. The major public policy concerns that must be addressed are (1) informed decision making in choosing a resolution to a problem pregnancy; (2) termination of parental rights of unknown, uninvolved, abusive or negligent parents; and (3) child protection.

The Importance of Informed Decision Making

Most ethical professionals in the field of adoption believe that counseling is critical for any woman or couple facing a problem pregnancy in order to make an informed decision. In licensed adoption agencies, counseling of pregnant women is standard practice, and when possible, biological fathers of the babies are encouraged to participate in the counseling. Most ethical attorneys or other adoption intermediaries also encourage counseling for all women considering adoption.

In 1989, the National Council for Adoption (NCFA) convened a group of adoption agencies and attorneys to draft a statement of "Principles of Good Practice in Infant Adoption." In these "Principles" were recommendations to require counseling for all individuals considering adoption for their children. The guidelines include a checklist of issues that should be discussed, such as the fact that resources are available to assist women who choose to parent. Since the publication of this document, a number of states have passed legislation requiring at least one hour of counseling for every pregnant woman considering adoption. NCFA is also advocating a certification process for "Adoption Specialists" to ensure that persons providing adoption counseling and placement services are not only ethical, but competent to meet the special needs of each pregnant woman, the father of the baby, the prospective adoptive parents and the child.

While most in the adoption field recognize the need for counseling, until these current cases were exposed, legislatures and the public have not seen a reason to become involved. But benign neglect is not the only reason for a lack of statutes. Attorneys in many states have opposed mandating counseling because they see it as an attempt by licensed agencies to encroach on their private adoptions. In other places, attorneys have well-founded concerns that many social workers and other counselors are anti-adoption and will make an effort to talk women out of adoption. In some states, there has been a hesitancy on the part of legislatures to become involved in requiring informed consent legislation in adoption because of their unwillingness to require it in the abortion decision-making process.

In the Baby Jessica case, good counseling of the biological mother might have prevented much of the tragedy. Cara Clausen, although a 29-year-old woman, did not receive prenatal care until late in her third trimester of pregnancy and reportedly did not seek counseling. This is an indication that she repressed the pregnancy. In a lengthy article in the *New Yorker*, Ms. Clausen says that she chose adoption even after pressure from her parents and others to keep the baby. The very nature of a problem pregnancy will unfortunately mean that some women will regret the decisions that they make. Society and the law can only go so far in protecting citizens from making bad choices.

Organizations That Try to "Undo" Adoptions

Information revealed in the media suggests that if Ms. Clausen had had a competent counselor to discuss the option of adoption with thoroughly before making the decision and to provide her the emotional support necessary after making the difficult decision, she either would never have placed Jessica for adoption or after doing so would have left her alone. But instead of counseling after the adoption, Ms. Clausen fell prey to the anti-adoption group Concerned United Birthparents (CUB). Ms. Clausen's remarks that Baby Jessica would be emotionally scarred if she were adopted suggest that Ms. Clausen has bought into the angry, erroneous rantings of CUB completely.

CUB and other anti-adoption "support" groups like Adoptees Liberty Movement Association (ALMA) and the American Adoption Congress (AAC) state repeatedly in their newsletters and other materials that adopted persons and parents who place their children for adoption never recover. A "support" group that is stuck in the anger phase of grief can be devastating to any new members, but it is impossible to outlaw such organizations. CUB, in this case and in others, has encouraged women to try to "undo" the adoption by either trying to regain custody of the child or by attempting to locate the child and become part of the child's life. The extremism of CUB was most apparent in the case of Kimberly Mays when it encouraged Regina Twigg, who has not yet recovered from the death of Arlena, to pursue custody of Kimberly Mays against Kimberly's will. [Kimberly and Arlena were switched at birth and grew up in each other's birth families. The switch was discovered when Arlena became terminally ill and genetic tests showed she was not the biological child of the Twiggs, the family who had raised her.] A common theme in both Baby Jessica's case and Kimberly Mays's case was the belief by both biological mothers that the child's identity came from the mother as shown by their insistence on calling the children by the names that the mothers preferred.

Biological Parents Can Make Timely Decisions

While NCFA and CUB agree that counseling should be required for all women and, whenever possible, men who are considering adoption for their children, NCFA has a much more optimistic view of the capacity of women to make intelligent decisions. NCFA also insists on ensuring that the needs of children are protected in any practice or policy related to adoption. In contrast, CUB is proposing that women not be allowed to sign any consents to adoption until the child is six weeks old and the mother has a chance to get to know the child. CUB believes that women cannot make the decision any sooner. While NCFA believes that there are some women who are not ready to make the decision until six weeks, it is also likely that those same women are so conflicted that they may never feel ready to make the decision. Most women who choose adoption do so because they believe it is best for the child, even though it may be painful for the mothers. Most women agonize over the decision from the time they discover they are pregnant. Their reasons for choosing adoption generally do not change once the child is born.

Not only are most women ready to make a decision earlier than six weeks, delaying the decision will be counterproductive for most women. Human beings can only handle the emotional intensity of a crisis for a limited amount of time. If a crisis drags out, people must employ defense mechanisms such as denial and repression to get through the pain. In the end, women may be making decisions just to get the decision over with.

From a child's point of view, a delayed decision will inhibit the bonding process, which should begin as soon after birth as possible for healthy development. Because children are the most vulnerable, their needs must be paramount in any and all child welfare decisions. A poor start in the world where children are denied the opportunity to feel secure and safe can impede their future ability to form healthy relationships and become productive citizens.

States could also institute the use of a very detailed consent form stating that the biological parent has been informed of his or her rights (with a listing of the rights), has been provided counseling on all the options (with a listing of the options), and understands the finality of the decision and the permanence of adoption as terminating all rights, relationships and responsibilities of the biological parents and transferring them to the adoptive parents. Some have suggested that states should have extended periods of time for biological parents to change their mind after signing a consent to adoption. However, there is significant evidence that there are more problems in states where consents are revocable. Human nature causes us to be more cautious if there is no back door out of a decision. It is the position of the National Council for Adoption that no parent should ever sign a consent to adoption until the parent is absolutely sure of the decision. While there is no legal limit on how long a woman can take to make up her mind, any woman who is considering adoption should be encouraged to make the decision in as timely a manner as possible so that the child is not negatively affected by the delay.

Terminating the Rights of Unknown, Uninvolved, Abusive or Negligent Parents

In the Baby Jessica case and the Gregory K. case, the central issue was how far the state must go to protect the rights of uninvolved parents. Baby Jessica's biological mother and her fiancé signed consent to the adoption and subsequently had their rights terminated by a court. Later it became known that Dan Schmidt was the child's biological father and he successfully convinced the Iowa court to grant him custody. The Iowa Supreme Court decision in this case leaves it open that any man can come forward at any time and claim ignorance to undo an adoption placement. At what point does the state hold parents accountable for taking responsibility for children without being asked to do so? Many court decisions and several states require affirmative responsibility on the part of an unmarried father to establish a relationship with his child in order to be considered for custody. This means that he must find out if there is a pregnancy and make an effort to support the child. If he fails to do so, he forfeits his rights and may not interfere with the rights of the child to maintain relationships with people who have taken affirmative responsibility.

The issue of "putative (not legal) fathers' rights" has been one of the most troubling issues for women and children for more than twenty years. Until 1972, unmarried fathers had no protected parental rights. But a bad case, *Stanley v. Illinois*, has created bad law across the nation. Stanley had an established live-in relationship with his children when their mother died. Because he was not married to the mother, his children were being removed from his custody. The Supreme Court correctly ruled that even though he was an unmarried father, he should have the same rights as any other parent. Unfortunately, this case with its special circumstances has been broadly interpreted to give the same rights to men who are no more than sperm donors as to men who have provided consistent care and guidance to their children. At this point in adoption, in many states, if a man cannot be found or will not cooperate in a woman's decision to place a child for adoption, he can effectively deny the woman and child the choice of adoption. Many women are forced into abortion or single parenting because men will not consent to adoption, even when they have no intention of providing child support.

Reprinted by permission: Tribune Media Services.

The states that have most effectively dealt with the issue of "putative fathers' rights" have established a registry system where an unmarried father registers his intent to take parental responsibility for the child. All legal fathers (husbands) are automatically part of the process, but for unmarried fathers, only men who have registered their interest in the child are notified of pending adoption proceedings. This registry protects the rights of fathers who otherwise would be at the mercy of a birthmother, who may be angry, to tell the truth. The registry also shows the court that the father is serious about his interest in the child. Women and children are protected because their adoption plans are not delayed or denied because of an absent or uninterested father. NCFA has developed a model putative fathers' registry bill incorporating the best elements of the various existing statutes and will circulate the bill to every state.

In Gregory K.'s case, Gregory had not lived with either of his parents for seven years, yet the state took no steps to terminate parental rights so that Gregory could belong to a permanent family. Currently, the buzzword in child welfare circles is "family preservation." Most Americans would agree that the state should attempt to preserve families. The question is "at what point does the state recognize that there is no family to preserve and allow the children to become permanent members of a family with whom they have established strong emotional bonds?" At what point does the state decide that it will not allow a child to be returned to be abused or neglected again? The current child welfare establishment seems to believe "at no point should a decision be made to terminate parental rights." Society recognizes that it is not appropriate to send a battered wife back to "preserve her family," yet, battered, helpless children are sent back repeatedly. This brings us into another critical issue, "the best interest of the child."

The Best Interest of the Child: The Highest Priority

Who speaks for children when they cannot speak for themselves? Most people, even supporters like this writer of Gregory K.'s efforts, do not believe that "divorcing" one's parents is an appropriate action. Unfortunately, Gregory K. and the foster family who wanted to adopt him had no other recourse, so this was a very creative strategy to get the needed result. Some are troubled that had Gregory K.'s "divorce" been upheld, there would be children seeking to "divorce" their parents because of every perceived slight. This is unlikely. However, the "divorce" action and many other suggested "children's rights" are inappropriate because they require children to make adult decisions and take responsibility for themselves. A child has the right to be protected and to feel secure. He should not have to establish his own security and protect himself. When the parent abuses, neglects or abandons the child, the state has the right and responsibility to protect the child. But what happens when the state abuses, neglects or abandons the child entrusted in its care? There is a need for limited rights for the custodial parents to bring action against the state for its failure to protect the child.

The issue of terminating parental rights is serious; it should only be done because it is necessary to protect the best interest of the child—meaning preventing future harm to the child. The decision is not one to be based on material goods or socio-economic status, but on established relationships and the developmental needs of the child. But a balance that does not currently exist in America's child welfare system must be struck, with the scales tipping to the side of the child when needs and wants are in conflict. NCFA is discussing the most appropriate means of developing statutes to protect the best interest of children, while respecting the rights of parents. It appears at this point that a safe place to start may be to require all courts in custody battles to make the best interest of the child paramount whether we are talking about divorce, foster care, or adoption. Making the children's needs paramount also means giving priority to custody cases and resolving them in as short a period of time as possible.

Perhaps the most dramatic message in the public's response to these three tragic cases was a signal that enough is enough of parents' treating children as property and making decisions based on the parents' desires rather than on the children's needs. Society is rejecting the views of anti-adoption groups and others who believe that a capable parent is anyone who has sex and conceives a child. If that were so, we would not have 600,000 children coming into the foster care system each year severely abused and neglected. Society is rejecting the claim that parents should be able to put children's lives on hold while they grow up or decide whether the child fits into their plans. The segment of society that is child-focused has made it clear that stability and security are more important for a child than genes and chromosomes. The challenge now is to have the legislatures and courts catch up with the American public in abandoning the precepts of the "me generation" in which parents believe, "if it is good for me, it is good for the child."

Periodical Bibliography

The following articles have been selected to supplement the diverse views presented in this chapter.

Christine Bachrach, Kathy Stolley, and Kathryn London	"Relinquishment of Premarital Births: Evidence from National Survey Data," *Family Planning Perspectives*, January/February 1992.
Leslie Bennetts	"The Baby Jessica Story: Why the Court Was Wrong," *Parents*, September 1993.
Sara Chira	"Adoption Is Getting Some Harder Looks," *The New York Times*, April 25, 1993.
Sara Chira	"High Court Call: Father's Rights or Child's Interests," *The New York Times*, July 17, 1994.
Geoffrey Cowley	"Who's Looking After the Interests of Children?" *Newsweek*, August 16, 1993.
Linda Cushman	"Placing an Infant for Adoption: The Experience of Young Birthmothers," *Social Work*, May 1993.
Marcia Custer	"Adoption as an Option for Unmarried Pregnant Teens," *Adolescence*, Winter 1993.
Lucinda Franks	"The War for Baby Clausen," *The New Yorker*, March 22, 1993.
Nancy Gibbs, Andrea Sachs, and Sophfronia Gregory	"In Whose Best Interest?" *Time*, July 19, 1993.
Lois Gilman	"Buried Lives: Four Birthmothers Reveal the Pain of Placing Their Children for Adoption," *Adoptive Families*, July/August 1994. Available from 3333 Hwy. 100 No., Minneapolis, MN 55422.
Stephanie B. Goldberg	"Having My Baby: Unwed Fathers Score Victory in California," *ABA Journal*, May 1992.
Michele Ingrassia	"Standing Up for Fathers: The Troubling Case of Baby Jessica Focuses Attention on Paternal Rights in Adoption," *Newsweek*, May 3, 1993.
Michele Ingrassia and Karen Springen	"She's Not Baby Jessica Anymore," *Newsweek*, March 21, 1994.

David Kallen et al.   "Adolescent Mothers and Their Mothers
                             View Adoption," *Family Relations*, July 1990.

Terry O'Neill   "Special Report on Birthfather Rights,"
                             Adoptive Families, September/October 1994.

Marty Smith and   "Which Side to Take in the Adoption
Leslie Dawson   Triangle?" *Los Angeles Times*, August 11,
                             1993. Available from Times Mirror Square,
                             Los Angeles, CA 90053.

Michael Sobol and   "The Adoption Alternative for Pregnant
Kerry Daly   Adolescents: Decision Making,
                             Consequences, and Policy Implications," *The
                             Journal of Social Issues*, Fall 1992.

John Taylor   "Biological Imperative," *New York*, August
                             16, 1993.

Are There Alternatives to Traditional Adoption?

Adoption

Chapter Preface

It is estimated that there are more than 400,000 children in the United States foster care system; in 1990, there were only about 118,000 adoptions. Many of the children who remain unadopted are members of minorities or multiracial, or are "special needs" children—those who are beyond infancy or are part of a sibling group, or who have physical, mental, or emotional problems. To help these children find adoptive homes, adoption agencies now actively recruit individuals, families, and institutions that might have been previously overlooked. To help make more adoptions possible, for example, in the early 1980s George Clements founded One Church One Child, an organization that recruits and supports adoptive parents among black churches. With chapters in thirty-seven states, One Church One Child seeks to place black children (who make up about 45 percent of the adoptive population) within black families. One Church One Child makes a sustained effort to open new doors to people who were not previously given encouragement and opportunities to adopt children.

Others—single adults, gays, and lesbians—who were once neglected as possible solutions to the problem of so many waiting children have also become candidates for adopting. Single parents still often have many hurdles to overcome before they are able to adopt, but it is gays and lesbians who have become the focus of perhaps the most opposition. Until recently they were rarely considered at all as prospective adoptive parents, and the dialogue on this emerging issue is often both heated and strident.

The debates over alternatives to traditional two-parent, same-race adoptions are examined in the following chapter.

> "As long as there is love and care between the caregiver and the child, the sex of the person providing that care is irrelevant."

Gays and Lesbians Should Have the Right to Adopt Children

Carole Cullum

Carole Cullum is a partner in the San Francisco law firm of Cullum & Sena. In this viewpoint, she writes to help other attorneys promote the legal rights of gays and lesbians seeking to adopt children as same-sex adoptive parents. Noting that the rights of gays and lesbians to adopt children are "slowly being recognized in the courts," Cullum reviews legal precedents and suggests ways by which lawyers may represent both the interests of their clients and those of adoptable children.

As you read, consider the following questions:

1. According to Cullum, what are the two types of family structure within which gays and lesbians generally raise children?
2. What legal protections does the author say gays and lesbians may seek when a child's sole legal parent dies or divorces? What guarantees does she say such legal efforts provide?
3. What persuasive measures does Cullum recommend that attorneys use to convince the courts that gays and lesbians should be granted legal custody in the best interests of the child?

Excerpted from Carole Cullum, "Co-Parent Adoptions: Lesbian and Gay Parenting," *Trial*, June 1993. Reprinted with permission of *Trial*. Copyright The Association of Trial Lawyers of America.

Over the past several decades, the concept of what constitutes a family has changed, and several nontraditional types of families have been legally recognized throughout the country. For example, in an effort to meet the need for care of so-called unwanted children, many states have allowed adoptions by single adults.

Another type of adoption is emerging from the nation's lesbian and gay community. It is called by various names—"second-parent adoption," "co-parent adoption," or "same-sex adoption." This kind of adoption has been described as the desirable legal outcome to the situation that arises when "nonmarital cohabitants share parenting duties," yet only one of the partners is the child's legal parent. (A nonbiological parent becomes a child's legal parent through adoption.) In this case, the legal parent consents to the adoption by a co-parent without giving up any of his or her own parental rights. In most cases involving two legal parents, one of the legal parents must give up his or her rights. However, in some recent cases, courts allowed the two biological parents to retain their legal rights while granting rights to a third party.

Lesbian and Gay Parents

About 10 percent—or 25 million—of the nation's population is homosexual. Surveys have found that 40 percent to 70 percent of gay men and at least 45 percent to 80 percent of lesbians are involved in steady relationships at any given time and the longevity of these relationships is comparable to that of heterosexual relationships.

Because of fear of discrimination or violence and/or fear of losing custody or visitation rights, many gays and lesbians raising children are not open about their family structure. This makes it difficult to accurately measure the number of these parents in the United States. However, the number of lesbian mothers and gay fathers is estimated to be well over 2 million and the number of children being raised by them to be as high as 6 million.

This is a historically significant time for lesbians and gays seeking the same rights and protection afforded the population at large. President Clinton has moved to eliminate the ban against lesbians and gays in the military. Many cities, countries, and states are in the throes of legal battles regarding the protection of civil rights of lesbians and gays in the areas of housing, employment, health care, and hate crimes.

Lesbian and gay parents conduct their lives no differently from other families—searching out decent day care, balancing jobs with family life, getting children to school and to extracurricular activities, and offering each other guidance and support.

These parents take vacations, play games, share holidays with extended family members, and work hard to raise their children to be upstanding citizens. But the obstacles they face are different from those faced by heterosexual couples. Without co-parent adoptions, children raised by homosexual couples have no *legal* relationship with one of the caring adults they live with.

But with little fanfare, the rights of lesbians and gays and their children are slowly being recognized in the courts.

Gay and Lesbian Family Structures

There are two types of family structures in which lesbians and gays raise children:

• Lesbians and gays who parented their children in a heterosexual relationship but now raise them either on their own or with their homosexual partner, who may or may not adopt the child. (Adoption may not be possible if there is a known biological parent who would not agree to the adoption. The adoption process is much easier if lesbian couples go to sperm banks and the donor is unknown.) Many of these parents are still "closeted," fearful of losing custody and visitation rights from their former spouses.

• Lesbians and gays who parented children or adopted children outside the traditional heterosexual relationship and raise them on their own or with their partner. These parents are forging new legal paths of co-parent adoptions.

Roberta Achtenberg, Assistant U.S. Secretary for Fair Housing and Equal Opportunity, has estimated that as of 1976, there were about 300,000 to 400,000 lesbian and gay parents, many of whom were their child's sole legal parent. However, the recent "baby boom" among lesbians since the late 1980s may have easily tripled that number, mainly because of artificial insemination.

Many lesbians plan their families for years, discussing everything from which sperm bank to use to what the child will call the two women who will raise the child. These parents spend time seeking out extended family members and friends and defining their roles.

The role of the psychological parent in these families is not so different from that of the biological parent. A child forms attachments from the day-to-day attention to his or her needs—not from a biological relationship. The psychological parent can be a biological parent, an adoptive parent, or any other adult in whose care the child can feel valued and wanted. Research has shown that as long as there is love and care between the caregiver and the child, the sex of the person providing that care is irrelevant. The consistency and continuity of the love and support provided will bond a child to the adults, regardless of their sex.

New families may try a series of legal approaches to protect

119

their children in the event of the death or legal incompetence of the sole legal parent or of a split between the adults.

• *Parenting agreements.* The parties enter into contracts and outline their intent and desire to be equal parents, write out plans regarding financial and day-to-day care of the children, and agree about custody and visitation should the relationship end. Parenting agreements, while not yet tested by the appellate courts, are often ignored by lower courts. If a child's legal parent dies, only a surviving legal parent is *presumptively* entitled to guardianship.

• *Wills.* The protection wills can provide is limited. People may change their wills without beneficiaries' knowledge, and wills are often challenged by family members who do not agree with the terms of the decedent's bequests.

• *Consent for medical authorization.* A legal parent may give written authorization for his or her partner to provide medical care for a minor. However, these consents are often ignored by educational and medical institutions and by people who may not approve of the parents' life-styles.

• *Nomination of guardianships.* A guardianship proceeding is subject to investigation and approval by the court, with relatives or others having standing to contest. This process could be long and costly, and the eventual outcome is often uncertain. The child, who is already experiencing trauma, may also run the risk of losing his or her second parent merely for lack of legal status. Even after a parent is appointed, anyone may apply to the court to have the named guardian removed and revoked.

Courts May Ignore *de Facto* Parenthood

Two recent cases illustrate these issues. In Vermont, a lesbian mother died in a car accident, leaving behind her partner of 12 years, SB, and the son they had been raising together. The child had been conceived through artificial insemination and had no known father. SB was appointed as the child's guardian. But the deceased's parents, displeased with the mother's sexual orientation, challenged the appointment and sought custody. SB eventually succeeded in retaining custody of the boy, but the process traumatized the child and caused uncertainty about his future and fear that he would be removed from the psychological parent.

In a similar case in Florida, the biological mother died after a long illness, leaving behind her partner of 13 years and their 5-year-old daughter. (Here, too, the child had been conceived through artificial insemination and had no known father.) The child's biological grandparents obtained custody and later adopted the child without any notice to the psychological mother. The partner challenged the adoption based on her *de facto* parental relationship with the child and convinced the trial court to overturn it.

Even if a *de facto* parental relationship is proven to exist, it will not guarantee rights to the *de facto* parent. A court in California, ruling in a lesbian custody dispute, said that taken alone the psychological relationship between the nonlegal parent and the child did not entitle her to custody over the biological mother's objections. The court said the nonlegal parent must allege facts on which the court could determine that she is the child's legal parent or she must offer sufficient proof that awarding custody to the biological parent would be detrimental to the child and awarding custody to her would serve the "best interest of the child." The court held that the partner would qualify as a legal parent *only* if she were the child's biological or adoptive parent.

The issue the courts must decide is not whether a close, warm, and loving psychological relationship will develop between a child and an adult who is not married to the child's legal parent, but rather how to legally protect that relationship and permanently ensure the continuity and stability crucial to a child's health and well-being. Short of allowing same-sex marriages, co-parent adoption is the only way in these instances to ensure the permanence of the child's relationship with both adults.

Obtaining Protections Through Adoption

Several protections for children and parents are available through adoption. For example, in the event one parent dies or becomes incapacitated, the other would have superior right to custody. The child would be provided with continuity of relationships, surroundings, and environmental influences—crucial for normal development. Studies have shown that when parents—whether they are heterosexual or homosexual—"divorce," the child's feeling of family stability and security is threatened.

A stable custody and visitation plan, guaranteed through adoption, is necessary to alleviate psychological wounds that the dissolution of a relationship can inflict on a child. Preserving a child's emotional bonds to both parents is integral to the child's emotional health and growth.

Adoption also ensures the child's right to inherit from both parents and their respective families, providing the child with future financial stability.

Other protections guaranteed by adoption are:

• *Financial stability during minority.* In the event of the parents' separation, the children will receive child support from both parents until they complete their education.

• *Health Insurance.* Unless there is legal adoption, it is virtually impossible to obtain health insurance benefits through employment for an "unrelated" child. If the biological parent becomes unemployed and the child develops a severe or prolonged illness, the entire family could become impoverished. Some counties and companies may offer coverage through "domestic partnership" benefits, but these are few and far between.

• *Full legal status as a parent.* The child will be protected from third parties like doctors, hospitals, and schools that refuse to accept decisions made by the nonlegal parent.

• *Benefits.* These include Social Security benefits if a parent dies, pension plan benefits, and employment-related sickness and death benefits.

Only Florida and New Hampshire have specific statutes prohibiting lesbian and gay adoptions. Second-parent adoptions are being granted in other states. They have occurred where the adopting co-parents were the child's natural parent, a heterosexual partner of the parent, and a same-sex partner of the parent. Co-parent adoptions have been granted by judges in Alaska, California, Minnesota, New York, Oregon, Vermont, Washington, and the District of Columbia. Several cases have involved adoption by the mother's female partner where both the legal mother and father were allowed to retain their parental rights (Alaska, California, and Oregon).

Reprinted by permission of Kirk Anderson.

In virtually all adoption cases, the parties and their attorneys are arguing successfully to the court that co-parent adoptions meet the two basic requirements of all adoption statutes: the legal parents or guardians must formally consent to the adoption, and a finding must be made that the adoption will be in the child's best interest.

Many judges may be reluctant to grant co-parent adoptions (perhaps because of personal prejudice or lack of familiarity with lesbian and gay families). The attorney must remind the courts that the "best interest" of the child is the "hallmark of American adoption," as described by Ruth-Adene Howe, and that determining this interest is the court's sole governing factor in adoption proceedings. As most family law practitioners know, this definition is left to judges to decide case by case.

Many courts have recognized that sexual orientation alone cannot provide the basis for denying custody or visitation. Courts have also ruled that the parent's sexual orientation is not contrary to a child's best interest unless there is a proven causal connection between harm to the child and the parent's behavior, condition, or status. For courts that need more persuasive arguments, attorneys must argue that children raised by gay parents are no more likely to have psychological problems than those raised by straight parents. Research suggests that "there are no particular developmental or emotional deficits for children raised by gay or lesbian parents," as Dr. Michael E. Lamb of the National Institute of Child Health and Human Development and other researchers have found.

As mentioned above, only two states prohibit adoption by lesbian and gay parents. However, attorneys may find that there are no laws specific to this type of adoption. It is important to urge the court to examine the legislative intent of the adoption statutes and the overall purposes and structure of state adoption laws. A liberal construction is often necessary to effect the intent of the legislature: the protection and promotion of the child's best interests. As the courts stated in *Weinschel v. Strople*, "Being unusual . . . does not make it illegal, against public policy, or contrary to the best interests of the child."

Protecting Natural Parents

Traditionally, courts have required biological parents to relinquish all rights to their child before giving their child up for adoption. This protects the biological parents' privacy interests. It also releases the child from the burden of owing duties to two families. But in cases of most co-parent adoptions, specifically those where the child is conceived through artificial insemination or where the sperm donor is unknown, there is only one legal parent. There is no second family to create a conflict.

A sample consent form for independent adoption reads:

> I, (Mother's name), hereby approve and consent to the foregoing adoption, provided that this adoption shall not alter my

own legal relationship with the minor child, and that by this adoption, the minor shall have two legal parents, Petitioner and myself.

Dated: (Mother's name),
                                             Natural Mother

Once the petition is filed with the court, a state or county agency (at the county's option) must ordinarily interview and investigate potential adoptive parents and submit recommendations to the court. In some California cases, the state Department of Social Services has refused to perform the investigations, stating in form letters:

> The California Department of Social Services does not believe that this adoption is in the best interest of the minor and recommends denial of the petition because the best interest of the minor is served by fostering and maintaining a secure and stable relationship between parents and children as promoted by legal parents.

> The policy of the California Department of Social Services is that where a child is to have two parents by adoption, it will approve the petition only if the two parents are a married couple. This is true whether they petition jointly or separately. In view of the foregoing facts, as the petitioner is not legally married, the California Department of Social Services recommends denial of this petition.

This policy to deny even the investigation is not consistent. However, when the state or county agency refuses to investigate, the attorney must obtain an order compelling the agency to file a full factual report. Only then will the agency complete its report. Again, in California, once the home visit and report are completed, and the social worker determines that it is in the best interest of the child to remain with both parents, the agency will refuse to recommend the adoption due to its "policy" to approve an adoption petition only if the two parents are a married couple.

Going to Court

At that point, a hearing or trial will need to be scheduled and trial briefs presented to courts unfamiliar with co-parent adoptions. If the county has not experienced co-parent adoptions or judges are particularly opposed to this new area of law, additional information and assistance can be obtained from the National Center for Lesbian Rights.

As the San Francisco County Superior Court stated in *In re the Petition of Nancy L. and Donna J.*:

> This is not a matter which arises in a vacuum. Social fragmentation and the myriad configurations of modern families have presented us with new problems and complexities that cannot be solved by idealizing the past. Today a child who receives

proper nutrition, adequate schooling and supportive sustaining shelter is among the fortunate, whatever the source. A child who also receives the love and nurturance of even a single parent can be counted among the blessed. Here this court finds a child who has all of the above benefits and two adults dedicated to his welfare, secure in their loving partnership, and determined to raise him to the very best of their considerable abilities. [There is] no reason in law, logic or social philosophy to obstruct such a favorable situation.

"*Single-parent adoption emerged as a good plan for children.*"

Single Adults Should Be Encouraged to Adopt Children

Vic Groze

Vic Groze is an assistant professor at the School of Social Work at the University of Iowa in Iowa City. In the following viewpoint, he presents the results of numerous studies of single adoptive parents. Finding that the percentage of successful adoptions among single parents does not differ significantly from that of married adoptive parents, he urges that welfare agencies should generate policies for actively recruiting more single adults as adoptive parents.

As you read, consider the following questions:

1. How does Groze define "special needs children"? According to the research he reviews, which of these children are more likely to be adopted by single rather than dual parents?
2. What characteristics of single adoptive parents does the author cite from the studies he reviews?
3. In what situation does Groze suggest that a single-parent adoption might be better than a dual-parent adoption?

Excerpted from Vic Groze, "Adoption and Single Parents: A Review." This article was originally published in *Child Welfare*, vol. 70, no. 3 (May/June 1991), ©1991 Child Welfare League of America. Used with permission.

Adoption of special-needs children is relatively new. The Adoption Assistance and Child Welfare Act of 1980 (Public Law 96-272) was passed, in part, to encourage agencies to take prompt, decisive actions to place children permanently with other families when they cannot be returned to their biological families. However, T. Tatara estimates that of the 35,000 to 39,000 children legally free for adoption in 1985, over half were in substitute care and awaiting adoptive placement. Furthermore, almost half of the children remaining in substitute care waiting for placement have one or more special needs: they are over the age of six, have a disability, are minorities, or are a member of a sibling group. While special-needs status poses some severe obstacles to adoption, the finding that over half of these children persist in substitute care brings under scrutiny the effectiveness of current practices to place special-needs children in permanent homes.

To address this problem, attention should focus on the development of resources for permanent placement of children in adoptive homes. This viewpoint reviews the available literature on single persons who adopt and argues that agencies should increase their recognition and recruitment of this nontraditional form of the family as a resource for the adoption of children with special needs.

As used here, a single parent is one who adopts as a single mother or father; those parents who adopt as a couple and later divorce are not characterized as single parents. The former made a conscious decision to be a parent as a single adult while the latter became single parents as a result of life circumstances. This viewpoint examines what is known about those who choose to become single adoptive parents. The demographic and personal characteristics of single parents who adopt are reviewed first; then the studies that have dealt with the experiences of single parents with the children they adopt are summarized.

Single Parents Who Adopt

Table 1 presents a summary of the studies reporting family composition in adoptions that occurred between 1970 and 1988. The percent of single-parent families varied greatly. The percent of placements with single parents ranges from a low of .5% reported by E. Branham in 1970 to a high of 34% reported by T. Festinger in 1986. . . .

It is clear from Table 1 that there was an increase in the percentage of single-parent adoptions in the studies conducted in the 1980s compared to the studies in the 1970s. The studies in the 1980s indicate at least double the number of adoptions by single parents reported in the 1970s, and Festinger's study, over eight times the highest percent in the 1970s. That is not to say that twice as many single parents were adopting in the 1980s as in the 1970s; sampling strategies influence these percentages to some degree. These studies do show, however, that the number of single parents who adopted since 1970 has dramatically increased.

Table 1: Family Composition in Special-Needs Adoption Studies

Study	Year	Sample	% Single Parents	% Female
Branham	1970	----	0.5 (n = 40)	97
Grow and Shapiro	1974	125	2 (n = 3)*	100
Boneh	1979	160	4 (n = 6)*	----
McRoy and Zurcher	1983	60	8 (n = 5)*	100
Boyne et al.	1984	273	20 (n = 56)*	----
Nelson	1985	177	17 (n = 30)*	98
Urban Systems	1985	197	8 (n = 16)*	----
Festinger	1986	183	34 (n = 51)*	88
Partridge et al.	1986	230	14 (n = 32)*	----
Kagan and Reid	1986	78	23 (n = 18)*	----
Unger et al.	1988	56	11 (n = 6)*	----
Barth and Berry	1988	927**	15 (n = 137)	----
		120***	13 (n = 12)	----

*secondary analysis of data   **case records   ***interviews   ---- data not reported

Although the percent of single-parent adoptive families is variable and has increased, it is not comparable to the percent of single-parent households in the general population. In the 1970s, approximately 13% of all households were single-parent families, a number that doubled in the 1980s to approximately 26%. In three of the studies conducted in the 1980s, the percent of single adoptive parents is similar to the percent of single parents in the general population. In the other seven studies reviewed it is much lower. This may indicate that recruitment efforts focused on single adults to adopt special-needs children have not been as successful as efforts to recruit two-parent families, a deficiency that may contribute to the problem of children's remaining in foster care with no permanent adoptive home.

Like most one-parent households in the general population, most single adoptive parent households are female. Even in the studies that do not report the gender of single parents, there is some indication that a majority of single-parent adopters are women.

Several studies report on other attributes of single adoptive parents. Branham indicates that single parents have a high level of emotional maturity, have a high capacity for frustration tolerance, and are not overly influenced by other opinions. Other studies have noted single parents' enjoyment of children and the personal fulfillment they receive from interaction with their children.

Single parents tend to have lower incomes than two-parent adoptive families. The higher incomes in two-parent families are mostly the result of dual incomes. The incomes of single-parent families are lower because women are overrepresented in single-parent families and women in nearly every occupational category earn less than men performing similar functions.

In addition to a demographic profile of the adoptive parents, several studies reported on selected characteristics of the adopted children whom single parents accept into their homes. [Research] indicates that single parents wish to adopt an older child rather than an infant and that single parents are more likely than couples to adopt older children, more likely to adopt boys, and less likely to adopt siblings or to have been a foster parent who adopted their foster child. . . .

Adoption Disruptions

Disruption refers to the removal of a child from the adoptive home before legalization of the adoption. The percent of disruptions is estimated to range from less than 3% to over 50%, and to have a high positive correlation with the age of the child at placement. Current estimates indicate that approximately 10% to 13% of all adoptive placements disrupt.

Table 2 presents the disruption rate for single parents and compares it to the percent of single-parent adoptions and the disruption rate for the entire sample. In some studies the disruption rate reported in Table 2 is very high; these high percentages were due, however, to sampling strategies employed by the researchers.

Most studies found that single parents were equally represented in both disrupted and intact adoptions. Urban Systems [a Washington-based research firm] collected data from five states on the characteristics of children and their adoptive parents involved in disrupted adoptions. Their report indicates that single parents constituted 8% of the adoptive placements and 9% of the disruptions. J. Boyne et al. analyzed data on special-needs children placed for adoption by Spaulding for Children in New Jersey between 1975 and 1981. They indicate that 20% of placements involve single parents and about 26% of disruptions involve single parents, a difference that is not statistically significant, indicating that single-parent placements were no more likely to disrupt than placements with couples. Festinger used a computerized listing to generate a sample of children over the age of six in New York City, 34% of whom were placed with single parents. Of the latter, 88.5% were placed with single mothers and 11.5% with single fathers. The nonmarried status made no difference in adoption outcome.

Table 2: Disruption Rates for Single-Parent Adoptions

Study	Year	% Single Parents Adopt	% Single Parents Disrupt	% Sample Disruptions
Boneh	1979	4	83	51
Boyne et al.	1984	20	26	23*
Nelson	1985	17	----	3
Urban Systems	1985	8	9	13
Festinger	1986	34	----	8
Partridge et al.	1986	14	20	27
Kagan and Reid	1986	23	----	53
Barth and Berry	1988	15	14	10

*secondary analysis of data   ---- data not reported

R. M. Kagan and W. J. Reid collected data through interviews with social workers and child care workers who had been closely involved with adoptive families, 23% of whom were single parents. Data were collected on 78 older youths placed between 1974 and 1982 in Albany, New York. Fifty-three percent of the youths experienced a disruption before legalization in at least one adoptive placement. Although [these researchers] did not indicate the disruption rate for single parents, they report no significant difference in outcomes for single adoptive parents and for married adoptive parents. Their results, however, indicate an interaction between parent gender and child gender. Single women who adopted boys did not experience positive adoptive outcomes; only one of six boys placed with a single mother remained in adoptive placement at the time of the study. R. P. Barth and M. Berry analyzed data collected by adoption workers on 927 children placed between 1980 and 1984 in California. Single parents represented 15% of the placements and 14% of the disruptions. They found that single-parent adoptions were no more prone to disruption than adoptions by two-parent families. Overall, the results from these studies are positive about placement with single parents, indicating that marital status was unrelated to disruption. . . .

The Experiences of Single Parents

Only a few studies have focused on the experiences of single adoptive parents. V. Jordan and W. Little in 1966 were the first to report on single-parent adoptive homes. They examined the placement in California of eight children with single adoptive mothers. They report that the mothers had an "above-average child orientation," had an ability to give of themselves, were not possessive of their children, and were capable of developing a healthy relationship with their children. They had strong positive opinions about single-parent adoptive placements and the development of the adopted child, reporting steady improvement of the children in their adoptive homes.

Several years later, also in California, Branham examined the experiences of single parents by gathering data from the case records of 36 one-parent adoptive placements. Thirty-five of the parents were women and 77% were nonwhite (the one man who adopted was black). Branham indicates that most of the single parents had relationships with other children before adopting a child, either through their own families or through their employment. She concludes that the children adopted by single parents had found "familiness" and that single-parent families were one resource helping to close the gap between the number of special-needs children waiting for placement and permanency in a family.

Adoptees Adjust Well with Single Parents

W. Feigelman and A. R. Silverman in 1977 compared the adjustment of children adopted by two-parent and single-parent families through the use of a mailed questionnaire taken from a national sample (60% response rate). Fifty-eight single adoptive parents [43 females, 15 males] were compared to an unspecified subsample of couples. There were no significant differences in how single- and dual-parent families rated their child's physical or emotional health, growth, and development. There was, however, a significant relationship between single parents' positive ratings of their children and the support given to them by their extended family; 80% of the single parents whose own parents responded positively to their adoptions judged their adopted children to have excellent adjustments, as compared to only 40% among those whose parents responded with indifferent, mixed, or negative reactions. There was also some indication that friends played a role analogous to that of the extended family. Feigelman and Silverman conclude that single parents have experiences substantially similar to those of the adoptive couples in raising their children, and therefore support single-parent adoptions.

In 1981, Feigelman and Silverman recontacted 60% of their sample; 7 or 47% of the single fathers and 28 or 65% of the single mothers were in the follow-up study. Because of the limited number of single fathers, no separate subgroup analysis was conducted. Six years after the initial study, Feigelman and

Silverman reported that adoptive adjustments among the children raised by single parents were similar to the patterns of adjustment for children raised by adoptive couples.

S. Dougherty in 1978 mailed a questionnaire that contained both multiple-choice and open-ended items to 131 single women who had adopted children. Sixty-seven percent responded to the questionnaire; 82 or 63% of the questionnaires were used in her analysis. Two-thirds of the children adopted had characteristics that labeled them as being hard to place. Dougherty found that these women possessed personal maturity, were highly educated, and were successful in their individual fields. They were aware of their own needs as well as the needs of their children and had built personal support systems for themselves in the community.

As of 1991, only one longitudinal study [by J. Shireman and P. Johnson] has been conducted with single parents as the focus. Thirty-one single parents who had adopted children under three years of age were in the initial sample. Eighteen parents were interviewed when the children were four or five years old to examine the development of the children and the stresses the families had undergone. Single parents reported many problems right after placement, a difficulty attributed to anxiety made more severe because they were new parents and had to deal with the child alone. An initial concern expressed by the researchers was the extreme isolation some of the families were experiencing and the intensity of the relationship between parent and child. The researchers concluded that some of the single-parent homes demonstrated the ability to handle crisis and stress as well as provide a positive climate for a child's development, while others seemed to present risks for the child. Their judgment was one of guarded optimism.

Follow-up Studies

Four years later, when the children were eight years old, the experiences of black children placed with single parents were compared to transracial placements of black children and the placement of black children with black couples. Most parents in all three groups owned their own homes, and about one-third of the single parents had relatives in their homes who helped with child care and household responsibilities. Almost all the single parents worked full-time and were the sole wage earners in their household. The incomes of the traditional adoptive families were comparable to the incomes of the transracial families, with both being higher than the incomes of single parents. The isolation of single parents lessened with the children's entry into school. Over half of the single parents were highly involved in school activities and these activities were their major involvement in the community, compared to less than one-third of the other adoptive parents, who were involved in school activities as well as many other community activities. Overall, most of the children were doing well and were judged by the interviewers to be accomplishing the major developmental tasks appropriate to their age. About one-fifth of the children were having difficulty, with the adjustment of boys being more problematic than that of girls. Among the children of single parents, there were few problems with sexual or racial identity. Shireman and Johnson determined that single parents had skillfully managed the logistics of child care, home, and work, but expressed concern over the excessive closeness of the parent-child relationship, particularly as the child entered adolescence and needed to change the nature of the intimacy between parent and child.

At the last interview in 1988, when the adopted children were in early adolescence, only 15 single adoptive parents could be located by Shireman. Single adoptive parents were compared to single biological parents, traditional adoptive families, two-parent biological families, and transracially adopting families.

Five areas were explored in the last interview: family relatedness, peer relations, gender identity, school performance, and self-esteem. When adopted children in early adolescence were compared to a representative group of nonadopted children, there were no significant differences between them. Overall, the children were judged as doing well, and those with problems in one area showed strength in other areas.

The results of Shireman and Johnson's longitudinal study demonstrated that adoption, particularly adoption by a single person, was an appropriate strategy for these children who could not grow up with biological parents. These adoptive homes provided continuity and stability, the family systems showed strength and changed appropriately, and most adopted children did well.

Implications of the Research

In [these] studies, single-parent families were found to be as nurturing and viable as dual-parent families. In fact, single-parent adoption emerged as a good plan for children. Studies that focused only on adoptive single-parent families indicate that these families and their children function well. Singles make up a significant portion of the population, and a number of single people are raising children on their own. Single adoptive parents are not only a feasible but an untapped resource for children with special needs, a recommendation suggested by A. Kadushin in 1970. Not only are they a competent resource, but as Feigelman and Silverman indicate, waiting to be adopted may have an adverse adjustment impact on the child but being adopted by a single parent does not appear to have a detrimental effect.

Although the two-parent family is the most familiar way to rear children and is usually considered the best of all possible choices for an adoptable child, there are instances in which a two-parent family is not likely to be available or a two-parent family is not in the best interests of a child. One advantage, as Kadushin reports, is that a one-parent family is better than a temporary placement in a foster home or an institutional setting. A second benefit is the meeting of needs of some children who may be denied adoptive placement as well as the meeting of needs of some parents. It is also an advantage that a single adult, unencumbered with the demands of a marital relationship, can give the kind and amount of involvement and nurturance that some children who have had severely damaging experiences need. For children who need intense and close relationships with an adult, single-parent homes may be particularly appropriate. For some children such a close bond may meet their needs and be a step toward normal development.

Here is strong evidence that single-parent families can meet the needs of some children now denied adoption and assist the child welfare system in providing permanent homes for children waiting for adoptive placement. . . . It is time to . . . generate policies for actively recruiting single adults as adoptive parents.

> "*Most participants [in surrogate parenting transactions] have ended up happy, and 500 children have experienced a life that otherwise would never have occurred.*"

Surrogate Mothers Should Help Childless Couples Have Children

Elizabeth Hirschman

Elizabeth Hirschman is a professor of marketing in the School of Business at Rutgers University in New Brunswick, New Jersey. In the following viewpoint, Hirschman places surrogate motherhood within a larger tradition wherein commodities such as human blood and human organs are exchanged commercially. She suggests that despite its commercial involvement, surrogate motherhood is an acceptable alternative to traditional adoption because it satisfies our sense of a sacred transaction qualified by profane considerations.

As you read, consider the following questions:

1. What comparisons does the author imply should be made between objections to surrogacy for money and contemporary adoption practices?
2. What benefits of surrogate motherhood does Hirschman suggest?

From Elizabeth Hirschman, "Babies for Sale," *The Journal of Consumer Affairs*, vol. 25, no. 2 (Winter 1991); ©1991 The American Council on Consumer Interests. Reprinted with the permission of The University of Wisconsin Press.

Both historically and currently, there are several markets in which humans and human components are exchanged for money or other economically valued resources. In the past, persons were sold into slavery, and women in the United States were considered chattel property of their husbands until the 20th century. Thomas Laqueur writes that a thriving market in human cadavers and body parts for medical dissection existed in both France and England from the 1790s through the 1840s. Currently, four markets exist in which human components are exchanged for economic compensation concurrent with altruistic donations of the same components: human blood, human organs, surrogate motherhood, and human reproductive cells. Strong ethical and consumer policy issues have been raised by each of these markets. . . .

The Ethics of Marketing Human Commodities

In his seminal book, *The Gift Relationship*, Richard M. Titmuss describes in detail the ethical and economic underpinnings of two markets for human blood—that based upon the altruistic gesture of providing one's blood for transfusion (usually) to strangers and the other based upon selling one's blood to a commercial blood bank. Titmuss strongly advocates the enforcement of altruism as the only mechanism for meeting the medical demand for blood, arguing that the presence of a commercial blood supply acts to devalue the human gift of blood. To Titmuss, the value of enforced altruism in a society greatly exceeds the economic benefit for some members of that society who would choose to sell their blood. In essence, his argument rests upon maintaining a distinction between *sacred* products (such as blood) and *profane* products (such as automobiles). Sacred products, he proposes, must only be given to others, never sold, because the presence of a commercial market in sacred products could destroy the presence of altruistic donations of these same products, i.e., why should someone give away that which can be sold?

In rebuttal to Titmuss' position, Douglas E. Hough argues that there is nothing inherently unique about blood as a commodity. In his view, people sell other aspects of themselves (e.g., cognitive abilities, physical effort), hence why should human tissues and organs be exempt from commercialization? Hough maintains that "by assigning a price to blood, an efficient allocation of blood resources within the medical industry can be maintained." He further proposes that the concurrent existence of a commercial market for blood will not necessarily inhibit altruistic donations. Rather, he argues, the decline in such donations may simply reflect the breakdown of communal ties in modern society.

The ethical arguments regarding transfers of human blood

largely are reiterated within discussions of policy issues surrounding markets for human organs. . . .

An overriding ethical concern in human organ markets, as in human blood markets, is whether or not to sanction *commercial* exchanges. Currently, there are over 70 times as many persons waiting for heart, liver, and kidney transplants as there are organs available. However, commercialization of these markets has been legally prohibited in the United States, largely due to cultural norms which circumscribe sacred-for-profane exchanges. . . .

Sacred and Profane Exchanges

At the center of ethical discussions regarding the exchange of human components lies an important societal distinction between those entities deemed *sacred* and those deemed *profane*. Sacred resources, entities, or products are culturally viewed as "above" or "outside" the commercial or economic sphere. They are "set apart" from the realm of profane commerce. Roy Calne and others view blood and human body parts as typifying sacred products. Conversely, profane resources would include those for which the above attributes are lacking; that is, those resources deemed common, unexalted, and readily marketable.

Virtually any product or service could conceivably be either sacred or profane. For example, even a mass-produced child's doll may become sacred to the child who loves it; analogously, even religion may be profaned by ministers who seek only to materially enrich themselves. However, societal norms generally serve a sorting function which effectively labels goods and services as to their appropriate role as sacred and profane entities. Within anthropology, Mary Douglas, Lewis Hyde, and Edmond Leach write extensively about the significance of the sorting function which concepts such as sacred and profane serve.

Douglas in *Purity and Danger* writes persuasively of the cultural importance of identifying and classifying objects, peoples, places, and events as sacred and profane. Although in various cultures, different entities will be placed into the sacred and profane categories, the designations themselves act to enforce important societal boundaries. As Douglas states, "Holiness requires that [entities] shall conform to the class to which they belong. And holiness requires that different classes of things shall not be confused. . . . It therefore involves correct definition, discrimination and order."

This reasoning suggests that transfers of sacred-for-sacred would be socially acceptable, as would exchanges of profane-for-profane, because, essentially, entities within the same cultural meaning category are being exchanged. Transferring entities *across categories* is generally considered culturally taboo, because it creates disorder and introduces ambiguity into the schema of cultural meaning. As Douglas notes, cultural notions of pollution and inappropriateness are reactions "which condemn any object or idea likely to confuse or contradict cherished classifications." Thus, a basic cultural repugnance to the exchange of blood and human organs for money would appear to stem from the fact that such exchanges violate the taboo separating the sacred from the profane. Blood and vital organs are culturally seen as appropriately transferred to another only out of love or generosity. Conversely, money is usually seen as appropriate for obtaining those entities which are similarly viewed as profane, e.g. automobiles, detergent, lawn mowers. . . .

Transformative sacred-for-profane exchanges are among the most ethically challenging transactions in society, because they lie at the normative boundary between what society believes should and should not be bought and sold for money. . . .

Babies as Commodities

Despite prevailing cultural norms to the contrary, there are currently several markets in which human commercial transactions do occur with regularity and, at the extreme, in which people are exchanged for money. These markets are centered around the production and acquisition of *babies*—babies in the form of component sperm and eggs, babies in the form of fresh or frozen embryos, babies in the form of tissues and organs, and babies as full-term living infants. . . .

One of six married couples in the United States (2.4 million) is infertile, unable to conceive a child within a year. . . .

The one-in-six ratio of infertile couples represents a large and often emotionally desperate market that has increasingly turned to biotechnical entrepreneurs in novel areas of reproductive medicine in the quest for a child. The popular press has reported the outcomes of some of these quests in vivid detail. The national attention given to the "Baby M" surrogate mother trials (1986–1988) brought to the fore several legal, business, and moral issues that remain unresolved. . . .

Often the popular press chooses to emphasize the most socially disturbing aspects of these cases, predicting the advent of genetic engineering or establishment of a "breeder class" of minority women carrying children for the affluent. However, beneath this rhetoric lies a more basic, core question of relevance to consumer policy: Are there aspects of human life that should not be subject to commercial exchange?

Many voices in the medical, legal, judicial, and political arenas have put forward ideological statements regarding these questions; yet the business community and consumer policymakers have been largely silent. In the absence of normative guidance from policy-makers, entrepreneurs have entered the field of commercial reproductive technology with few or no standards for evaluating performance or practices. There are currently sperm banks, in vitro fertilization clinics, surrogate mother clinics, and embryo transfer clinics, as well as private medical practices specializing in sex selection, fetal reduction, and surrogate fetal carriers. . . .

The newer human reproductive markets, such as surrogate motherhood, are best understood if they are first placed in context with the traditional solution to infertility—adoption.

The Commercialization of Adoption

Traditionally, infertile couples who desired a child obtained one through adoption. Although the adopted child was not biologically linked to the parents, the parent-child union was commonly viewed as sanctified, because the parents provided a needy infant with a home, love, and nurture. Thus the family bond was secured. In the past few decades, however, the supply of adoptable children has decreased dramatically. Observers attribute this phenomenon to a variety of social factors, among them the widespread availability of birth control and abortions, and the growing cultural acceptance of single parenthood. Concurrently, the pool of persons wishing to become adoptive parents has grown dramatically. Viviana Zelizer notes that prior to the 1920s, illegitimate and orphaned babies were commonly viewed in an instrumental, economic fashion. Often such infants were sold to "baby farms," where most perished due to a lack of adoptive parents. During the 1920–1930 period, babies were culturally redefined as sacred entities, valued for their sentimental and emotional qualities. By the 1950s a severe shortage of adoptable infants resulted in black market prices of $10,000. By 1984, more than two million couples were competing for the 58,000 children placed, a ratio of 35 to 1. In 1985, two million couples sought to adopt; only 22,000 were successful. Ironically, as Zelizer observes, as children's value as labor decreased (due to a shift in cultural norms against child workhouses), "their emotional worth became increasingly monetized and commercialized."

The enormous disproportion between supply and demand in the adoption marketplace, highly reminiscent of that found for organ transplantation, has led to increased pressure for commercialization and entrepreneurism. In the process, both babies and prospective adoptive parents are often transformed into profane products. The parents-as-products phenomenon is found most commonly in the public adoption agency sector of the market. These baby suppliers establish stringent socioeconomic criteria for choosing potential parents. Cynthia Martin details the primary adopter attributes sought by suppliers:

> The primary factor the adoption agency looks for when examining potential parents is *financial* stability . . . the agency would prefer that [they] be in the best financial situation possible . . . the more money and job stability you have, the better your chances are to win a baby . . . Education in our society is highly valued, [therefore] a college background is an asset in your application. The higher the degree, the better.

Although many natural parents would not meet these criteria, as Martin notes, it is a seller's market.

Potential adoptive parents have responded to this situation in two ways. First, they have increasingly turned to private entrepreneurs who broker infants for a fee. One form of baby brokerage is the traditional "home for unwed mothers," which continues to operate in the South and Midwest. For a fee ($20,000 is common), prospective adoptive parents can register with the home, specifying the attributes they are seeking in an infant.

A second brokerage practice consists of entrepreneurs, often lawyers, who specialize in what are termed *private adoptions*. These brokerages often advertise for unwed mothers. . . .

Finally, prospective adoptive parents can act as their own brokers and seek to find a baby themselves. Like the agencies, they advertise listing the desirable attributes they possess as parents and hoping to persuade an unwed pregnant woman to supply her baby to them. . . .

Just as the shortage of adoptable infants has tended to turn prospective parents into profane products who must sell themselves to adoption agencies, the resulting commercialization of the adoption market has tended to transform babies into profane commodities. Prospective adoptive parents, especially those willing and able to pay up to $25,000 for an infant, demand an ideal product; historically and currently that perfect baby is envisioned as a healthy, white newborn with blonde hair and blue eyes. Adoptive parents who are willing to accept "less" than this ideal baby consider themselves altruistic. As one frustrated couple reported to Claire Berman, "We never anticipated that we'd run into any difficulty. . . . After all, we aren't looking for a blue-eyed, blond baby." Couples unwilling to adopt must either remain childless or turn to the new reproductive markets [such as surrogate motherhood]. . . .

Surrogate Motherhood and Court Decisions

A surrogate mother is defined by the Ethics Committee of the American Fertility Society as

> a woman who is artificially inseminated with the sperm of a man who is not her husband; she carries the pregnancy and then turns the resulting child over to the man to rear. In almost all instances, the man has chosen to use a surrogate because his wife is infertile. After the birth, the wife will adopt

the child. The primary reason for the use of this technology is to produce a child who is genetically linked to the father.

Although surrogate motherhood is often depicted in the press as the converse of artificial insemination, in fact it differs in several important respects. First, it represents a significantly greater physiological and emotional commitment on the part of the surrogate mother. The surrogate mother not only provides genetic material, her egg, but also gestates and gives birth to the child. Because of these latter contributions, she is paid a substantially larger fee for her services (usually $8,000–$12,000). Further, because under normal circumstances a baby is legally presumed to belong to the woman who gives birth to it, the surrogate mother must sign a contract prior to conception abdicating her possession of the child and agreeing to surrender it upon birth to the man with whose sperm she was impregnated.

Because of the commercial aspects of surrogacy technology and because it involves the intentional conception of a child who will be given up by its natural mother in return for money, this treatment for infertility has raised substantial ethical controversy. Undoubtedly the most vivid exemplar was the "Baby M" case, which involved two sets of parents, William and Elizabeth Stern and Richard and Mary Beth Whitehead, fighting over possession of one baby. Reviewing this case, as presented in the popular press from 1986 to 1988, will help to highlight the consumer policy issues involved.

An article in *Time* notes that the contract in which the Sterns agreed to pay Mary Beth Whitehead to have a child fathered by Mr. Stern raised several issues relating to the sacred/profane exchange dilemma: "Is a womb a rentable space? Should the use of a surrogate mother be a legitimate option for couples who cannot have children? Or is it an odious trade in babies?" The article also introduced several socioeconomic distinctions between the parties to the exchange. In a subsequent article in *People*, Mary Beth raised the issue of exploitation of the poor by the rich: "You cannot contract to sell a baby. If they legalize this contract, they may soon start bringing in poor women from other countries just to be breeders (like me)."

A later article in *Time* elevates the sacred/profane exchange controversy to more abstract, but insightful terms:

> The second half of the 20th century has been full of uneasy trade-offs and Faustian bargains. One after another, life's most intimate and privileged matters—sexual relations, birth, and death—have been delivered to the unsanctified ground of science and commerce. . . . If a society legitimates surrogacy, what has it done? Has it imperiled its most venerable bonds of kinship and the bond between mother and child? Has it opened the way to a dismal baby industry?

Simultaneously, a piece in *Newsweek* makes it clear that a valuable product was at stake in the controversy: a blonde, blue-eyed little girl.

In April 1987, Judge Sorkow rendered his decision, awarding custody of Melissa to the Sterns. "At birth, mother and father have equal rights to the child . . . the biological father pays the surrogate for her willingness to be impregnated and carry his child to term," wrote Sorkow. "At birth the father does not purchase the child. It is his own, biologically, genetically related child. He cannot purchase what is already his." An editorial in *Time* counters,

> Are there any ethical limits on what one person may pay another to do? It is a question that rarely rises in the world of normal commerce, even in the modern service economy (of which the contract drawn between William Stern and Mary Beth Whitehead may stand as the oddest example). . . . The emotions that were being traded have a soul-like sanctity in the sense that they belong to the mysteries of the species and are commonly shared. . . . Whatever Stern and Whitehead thought their pact was about, they were trafficking in goods too elusive to package and too universal for personal property. What you do not own, you cannot sell.

Whitehead's lawyers carried her case to the New Jersey Supreme Court, which handed down its decision in February 1988. The court held that the surrogacy contract violated a legal prohibition against paying money for adoption: "the use of money for this purpose—and we have no doubt whatsoever that the money is being paid to obtain an adoption and not, as the Sterns argue, for the personal services of Mary Beth Whitehead—is illegal and perhaps criminal. . . . There are, in short, values that society deems more important than granting to wealth whatever it can buy, be it labor, love, or life." Despite this ruling, the court awarded custody of Melissa to the Sterns on the grounds that it was in the best interests of the child to reside with her father and his wife. The justices also found no illegality in allowing women to *volunteer* as surrogates, providing the agreement allowed the mothers to change their minds about foregoing parental rights.

The Stern-Whitehead case was important in that it established some legal precedents for consumer policy decisions in a heretofore largely unregulated human market. Over the past decade 2,000 infertile couples have contracted with women to bear them babies for a fee averaging $10,000. The vast majority of these transactions are arranged by surrogate parenting clinics.

Contractual Arrangements

Prospective surrogates are screened to determine if they are physically and psychologically sound and asked several questions to determine other attributes they possess which would make them attractive to a contracting infertile couple. Once accepted by the clinic, a prospective surrogate is interviewed by couples who might desire to purchase her services. It is at this stage that the prospective surrogate most resembles a product-for-sale. One journalist describes the scene at Noel Keane's Dearborn, Michigan, surrogacy center as follows:

> His comfortable two-story offices were full of prospective surrogate mothers, . . . and infertile couples who had come to check out the candidates. The well-groomed couples . . . were each assigned a private office, through which the surrogates were rotated to proffer their fertility. . . . I watched them come and go, the surrogates, young women dressed to please. . . . "Just look at her," said one young man smiling at his pretty young girlfriend and their eight-month-old child, "Her stomach was that flat the day she left the hospital. . . . I'll take care of her when she's pregnant again, but the baby means absolutely nothing. It's like watching someone's car for nine months. We're in it for the money; it's a business—that's the way we look at it."

Once the deal is struck, the contracting couple agrees to pay the surrogate a fee that ranges from $8,000 to $12,000 and to provide for her medical expenses, which usually come to $5,000. The couple also pays a fee to the agency arranging the transaction of from $4,000 to $12,000. There is money to be made in the surrogacy business; Noel Keane's surrogacy agency grossed $600,000 in 1986.

Positive Outcomes

Despite the commercialism described, there is another side to surrogacy. Contrary to the negative publicity and torn emotions engendered by the "Baby M" trials, over 500 children have been born as a result of surrogacy and only a handful have experienced contested custody; the vast majority of transactions have gone smoothly with satisfied parties on both sides of the exchange. Thus, most participants have ended up happy, and 500 children have experienced a life that otherwise would never have occurred.

The reasons for happiness on the part of the infertile couple are obvious. Through surrogacy they have obtained something that otherwise would have been impossible—a child who is in part genetically theirs. And for the majority of surrogate mothers, the experience has been rewarding beyond, and often in spite of, its financial aspects. Amy Overhold summarizes the results from several studies and identifies the primary motivations for surrogates as being altruism, a need to feel good about themselves or make a special contribution to society; guilt over past abortions; personal experiences as adoptive children; and the need to reenact their own childhood abandonment. Others cite the surrogate's desire to create life, to re-experience pregnancy and childbirth, to gain a feeling of self-fulfillment and accomplishment, and to help others attain a family.

If both consumers and producers are satisfied with the exchange, why then does it bother so many others? The most often cited rationale for aversion to the notion of surrogacy is that it commercializes an event—conception and birth—that is widely regarded in Western culture as sacred. The exchange of money for a baby is repugnant to many because it seems to reduce a sacred child to a profane commodity. . . .

By putting a monetary value on the components of human life, the primary ethical reservation to permitting such markets has been that they profane or desacralize all life. Although on the surface, this proposition would appear to be certainly true, on closer examination it may in fact be false. In Titmuss' view, human life, as a sacred entity, must be kept separate from the arena of commerce; to put a price on life inherently profanes it. However, commercial markets in human blood, organs, and reproductive components do not so much put a price on life, as they permit the expenditure of economic resources to *enhance, prolong, or create life.* And, in fact, there are many commercial markets which meet these needs without ethical opposition. For example, few would dispute monetary expenditures on health insurance, medical care, exercise equipment, and nourishing food for oneself or one's family. In fact, the absence of such expenditures might be taken as a sign of moral laxity.

The infertile consumers who enter the reproductive markets . . . have a common sacred goal in mind—they want to become parents to a baby. To foreclose them from achieving this goal and forming that most sanctified of human units—a family—because a fee must be paid to attract a supplier seems a greater blow to communal values than does the money paid. . . .

Although [this] discussion has attempted to put forward these issues dispassionately, . . . it is important to keep in mind the all-too-human desires and tragedies they represent. In reaching judgments as to which exchanges in reproductive markets are acceptable and which are not, one must never lose sight of real people, real parents, and real children whose needs, happiness, and even existence are at stake.

"The best institutions offer emotionally disturbed children a chance at a second childhood. . . . This time they will be protected from harm."

More Residential Communities Should Care for Children

Mary-Lou Weisman

Mary-Lou Weisman is a freelance writer and journalist who has written about social issues for the *New York Times* and the *New Republic*. In the following viewpoint, Weisman, citing experts who testify that some troubled children should not be raised in families, argues that public and private institutions can provide appropriate care for such children. While such a notion opposes most conventional wisdom, the success of many such institutions, Weisman believes, ought to prompt society to reconsider and promote these effective alternatives to adoption.

As you read, consider the following questions:

1. In what ways, according to Weisman, are current residential facilities unlike nineteenth-century orphanages?
2. How well do current family-preservationist policies serve the needs of abused children, in Weisman's view?
3. What evidence does the author present to indicate that public and private institutions can help children become successful adults?

Excerpted from Mary-Lou Weisman, "When Parents Are Not in the Best Interests of the Child," *The Atlantic Monthly*, July 1994. Reprinted by permission of the author.

Orphanages are not what they used to be. They aren't even called orphanages anymore. The residents no longer sleep in metal beds, twenty to a dormitory room. At the Boys Town campus, just outside Omaha, Nebraska, children live eight to a suburban-style home, two to a bedroom. Bureaus have replaced lockers. Uniforms and standardized haircuts are gone. So are the long wooden tables where, in the orphanages of legend, children sat awaiting their portions of cornmeal mush for breakfast, or bread and gravy for dinner. For instance, at the former St. James Orphanage, in Duluth, Minnesota, known since 1971 as Woodland Hills, young people wearing clothes from places like The Gap and Kmart push plastic trays through a cafeteria line, choosing baked chicken or shrimp and rice. The weight-conscious detour to the salad bar.

In 1910 some 110,000 orphans lived in 1,200 orphan asylums throughout the United States. At the end of 1990, according to data from the American Public Welfare Association, there were approximately 406,000 children in out-of-home placements. About three quarters of these children were in adoptive and foster homes. About 16 percent, or 65,000, were emotionally disturbed children in need of therapy, most of whom lived in the group homes and residential treatment centers that are the institutional descendants of the orphanage. (The remainder, less than 10 percent, were cared for by a variety of temporary and emergency services.) What little research is available indicates that most of this smaller subset of "homeless" children have been physically or sexually abused, often by the adults charged with their care. At Boys Town, now a residential treatment center—and no longer just for boys—virtually all the girls and nearly half the boys have been sexually abused. The director, Father Val J. Peter, tells of a teenager who asked him on the day she arrived, "Who do I have to sleep with to get along here?"

Dealing with Disturbed Residents

Child-care workers agree that children in residential treatment today are likely to be far more disturbed than the children who were in need of protective services twenty years ago and who, in turn, were probably more disturbed than the good-hearted orphans with chips on their shoulders who preceded them. These kids have had it with parents—biological, adoptive, or foster— and the feeling is usually mutual. These kids do not trust adults, especially parents. They cannot tolerate the intensity of family life, nor do they behave well enough to attend public school. During a first screening at a residential treatment center a psychiatrist often asks a child, "If you had three wishes, what would they be?" Twenty years ago a typical answer was "I want a basketball," or "I wish my father didn't drink." Today, according to

146

Nan Dale, the executive director of The Children's Village, a residential treatment center for boys in Dobbs Ferry, New York, one is likely to hear "I wish I had a gun so I could blow my father's head off." Child-care professionals call these young people "children of rage." Some of them take antidepressants and drugs to control hyperactivity. In addition to the behavior and attachment disorders common to children who have been abused and moved around a lot, some suffer from having been exposed *in utero* to crack and some from other neurological problems.

What It Costs

Institutional care for children is not cheap. Here is how the 78-bed Mercy Home in Chicago spends its money:

Annual Cost per Child

Staff	$35,000
Room, heat, light, gas	8,000
Clothes, camp, transport	5,000
Food	4,000
Tuition	3,500
Counseling	2,500
Medical, dental	1,500
Total	59,500

Only 7 percent of total is government-funded.

Source: *Newsweek*, December 12, 1994.

Most of the children who live in institutions are between the ages of five and eighteen. According to a 1988 study 64 percent of children in residential treatment centers were adolescents thirteen to seventeen years old. Approximately 31 percent were younger than thirteen, a percentage that has been increasing. According to the same study, the majority, about 70 percent, were male, a factor attributed to the more aggressive nature of the sex. Approximately 25 percent of the children were black, and 8 percent were Hispanic.

A group home may house as few as four children, whereas a residential treatment center may be home to a hundred or more, although in either facility usually no more than eight to twelve are housed together, supervised by house parents or by child-care personnel working eight-hour shifts. At Woodland Hills an old three-story red-brick orphanage building has been renovated so that the first floor can be used for administration, classrooms, and the cafeteria. The second- and third-floor dormitory rooms have been divided into meeting rooms, staff offices, and apartments with bedrooms that sleep two.

Not Meant to Be Long-Term Abodes

Unlike the orphanages from which they are descended, most group homes and residential treatment centers are not meant to be long-term abodes. A typical stay at such a center lasts from several months to two years, after which most children return to their birth, foster, or adoptive families. A significant minority, those who either have no homes to return to or do not wish to go home, move on to less restrictive group homes or to independent living arrangements, also under the aegis of the child-welfare system. . . .

Orphanages as such had virtually disappeared by the late 1970s as a result of a decrease in the number of orphans and a growing conviction that children belong in families. That every child needs parents and a home has become an article of faith and a guiding principle for social-policy makers and a matter of federal law as well. The philosophy of "permanency planning," as set forth in the Adoption Assistance and Child Welfare Act of 1980, considers the goal of the foster-care system to be keeping children in families. The law allows for but discourages "out-of-home placement"—institutionalization in group homes or residential treatment centers—and calls for the return of the children to a family, biological or otherwise, whenever possible and as quickly as possible. But for many practitioners in residential treatment the law has become increasingly irrelevant.

Richard Small is the director of The Walker Home and School, in Needham, Massachusetts, a residential and day treatment center for severely disturbed pre-adolescent boys. Writing recently in a professional journal with Kevin Kennedy and Barbara Bender, Small expressed a concern shared by many of his colleagues.

> For at least the past decade, we in the field have been reporting, usually to each other, a worsening struggle to work with a much more damaged group of children and families, and a scramble to adjust our practice methods to meet both client needs and policy directives that may or may not have anything to do with client needs. . . . Those of us immersed in everyday residential treatment practice see these same guidelines as less and less applicable to the real children and families with whom we work. Many of our child clients and their families suffer from profound disruptions of development that we believe are likely to require long-term, multiple helping services, including (but not limited to) one or more time-limited stays in residential treatment. Despite a policy that seems to see clear boundaries between being "in care" (and therefore sick and vulnerable) and "reunified" (and therefore fixed and safe) our experience tells us that many of our clients are likely to live out their lives somewhere between these poles. . . .

148

Institutional Family Values

In the paradoxical world of "child protective services," an institution may be the first home some children have ever known, providing their first chance to sit down to meals with other people at regular times, blow out birthday candles, and be taken care of by adults who do not hit or even yell. All but one of the staple ingredients of a happy home life are replicated in the best group homes and treatment centers. Intimacy is purposely missing. Love and family bonding may be what these children will need and be capable of having eventually, but for the moment the emotional thermostat must be set at neutral. These children are believed to be too disturbed to handle the intensity of real family life; that is precisely why they have been institutionalized.

The best institutions offer emotionally disturbed children a chance at a second childhood. They are given the opportunity to shed cynicism, develop self-esteem, and grow back into innocence and vulnerability. Candy will become a treat. This time they will be protected from harm. This time they will come to think of adults as kind and dependable. They will learn to play. They will learn to care about others.

Treatment communities teach Judeo-Christian values—the work ethic and the golden rule. Institutions offer vocational training and courses in computer literacy. At The Children's Village the best computer students teach their newfound skills to other children and adults in the surrounding communities, and The Children's Village has its own Boy Scout troop. The kids at Woodland Hills collect and pack supplies for national and international relief efforts. In addition, they split wood and deliver logs to the elderly in the Duluth community. Boys Town children host Special Olympics games.

Structure and a Controlled Environment

A highly controlled environment is required to create a second childhood for severely disturbed children. Safety is the key issue. Keeping these children from harm involves more than keeping them safe from sexual abuse, physical abuse, drugs, and crossfire; they must be kept safe from themselves and their peers. Newly institutionalized children often try to run away. When a young person at Woodland Hills forgets to bring the appropriate book to class, two peers accompany the student back to the dormitory to retrieve it, thereby minimizing the possibility of an escape attempt. At The Children's Village burly guards equipped with walkie-talkies and trained in firm but gentle techniques of physical restraint stand ready to intervene should fights or tantrums develop beyond the regular staff's ability to control them. Children are never left unattended, not even when they sleep. In every one of the twenty-one cottages at The

Children's Village one staff member remains awake throughout the night. The children in these cottages are sometimes suicidal. The bedroom doors in all the cottages open into the corridor, so that youngsters cannot barricade themselves in their rooms. Sexually abused children sometimes become sexual predators. At The Villages in Topeka, Kansas, some young girls will not allow anyone to comb their hair; for girls who have been sexually abused, even grooming can be too threatening.

This antidotal second childhood must be highly structured and predictable as well as safe. Treatment communities impose rules, chores, and schedules, and emphasize neatness, cleanliness, and order. . . . A well-structured day serves the child as a kind of armature within which to build a new, less chaotic, inner self. "How to succeed and how to fail is very clear here," says Daniel Daly, the director of research at Boys Town. "These children are looking for consistency and for an environment they can understand."

Institutional Belief Systems

Often institutions for children, like religions, have their own belief systems. What the faith is may not matter as much as its function as an organizing principle for its adherents. At The Villages the organizing principle is a belief in the therapeutic value inherent in family life. Woodland Hills is committed to a behavioral model called "positive peer culture." Any surrogate who remotely resembles a parent, or any scenario that draws its inspiration from a Norman Rockwell dinner-table tableau, is presumed anathema to this population of disturbed teenagers. Instead the kids confront one another in group therapy, and the staff gambles on its ability to turn the potentially destructive power of the peer group into a positive force. The Walker School, which adheres to a "cognitive behavioral model," has as its article of faith the conviction that every child can learn. As a result Walker places an unusually strong emphasis on academics, although "learning" at Walker can mean anything from solving math problems to practicing sitting still to running in the right direction in baseball. Green Chimneys is well known for using animals to encourage children to love and trust. Through "farm therapy" children learn to be care-givers even if they have not been cared for themselves, thereby helping to interrupt the cycle of abuse.

When it was an orphanage, Father Flanagan's Boys Town put its faith in God and the work ethic. Now that it's a residential treatment center, it also believes devoutly in science and technology. Father Val says, "Boys Town has embarked upon a program of basic research in microbehavioral analysis," the goal of which is to develop practical, replicable techniques for changing the behavior of emotionally disturbed children. These techniques are explained in a 250-page manual that is used to train the "family teachers" who head up each Boys Town "family.". . .

"Family Preservation"

In 1992 legislation called the Family Preservation Act was vetoed by President George Bush. The bill asked for about $2 billion to strengthen families. About half of that amount was earmarked for "family preservation"—programs to preserve troubled families *before* they broke up, so that fewer children would enter the foster-care system in the first place. Families in crisis would be assigned a licensed social worker, who would be available to them around the clock for a period of about three months, for help with problems ranging from substance abuse to landlord-tenant relations. Parents in imminent danger of abusing their children could find relief in a "respite program." Budget legislation for 1993 provided $1 billion for similar purposes, with a substantial portion also to be spent on family preservation. It had the backing of leading child-advocacy groups, including the Child Welfare League of America, the Children's Defense Fund, and The National Association of Homes and Services for Children. The Edna McConnell Clark Foundation has produced media kits claiming that family-preservation programs cost less per family ($3,000 for one family for a year) than family foster care, which it says costs $10,000 per *child*, or institutional care, which costs $40,000 per child.

Directors of some children's institutions are convinced that "family preservation" will take money directly out of institutional pockets. . . .

"It makes about as much sense as closing down emergency rooms and intensive-care units in order to lower hospital costs," says Brenda Nordlinger, the executive director of the National Association of Homes and Services for Children.

"Family preservation? Who can be opposed to that?" says David Coughlin, of Boys Town. "But," he warns, "some kids are going to be in trouble all their lives. These kids are always going to need help. You can't just blow across the top of a family for three months and expect their woes to go away.". . .

De-Institutionalization, Again

Nan Dale, of The Children's Village, thinks that the fervor to reduce the numbers of children in residential treatment is reminiscent of what is now generally considered the disastrous policy of de-institutionalizing adult mental patients in the 1970s. Program directors are very skeptical about whether preventive-intervention programs are really as successful as their advocates claim. Those who believe that family preservation is being over-

151

sold see an ally in John Schuerman, a professor of social work at the University of Chicago. Schuerman has studied preventive-intervention programs and believes that many of the families that were treated and did not split up were not likely to split up in the first place.

Nan Dale is feeling the anti-institutional heat and resenting it. "We're as pro-family a place as you can find. The fact that we serve a child who has been removed from a family does not make us anti-family. We involve parents." Nevertheless, she says, "the lines have been drawn. When the words 'preventive service' got applied to everything up to the doorstep of residential care, some of us had apoplectic fits. We all would have told you that what we did here *was* preventive. We prevent lifetimes in mental hospitals, lifetimes in prisons. All of a sudden some bureaucrat in Washington defines preventive service as preventing placement outside the home, and we become the thing to be prevented.". . .

Going Against the Tide

David Fanshel was until his recent retirement a professor at the Columbia University School of Social Work. A leader in the field of social work, and foster care in particular, Fanshel was the principal investigator in two major longitudinal studies on foster children in homes and institutions. At a time when many experts are questioning the value of residential treatment and promoting family preservation, Fanshel is going against the tide. He foresees a greater need for residential care in the near future. In fact, Fanshel, for decades one of the leading proponents of permanency planning, has modified his views. He now believes that permanent placement with a family is not an appropriate goal for about a quarter of the older, more seriously damaged and criminally inclined children in the system. He would like to see foster care reorganized into a two-tiered system in which permanent placement would remain the goal for the larger group, and the forestalling of criminal behavior through treatment would be the goal for the other group, which he calls "Subsystem B." He sees institutions playing a significant role in treating such dangerous children. . . .

"I wish," The Walker School's Richard Small says, "that there were a place, a group home, where kids could live at those times when they couldn't live at home. We've got a number of youngsters in this society—who knows how many?—who are capable of being connected to people, who wish to be connected, who should be connected, but who can't live full-time with the people they're connected to. When they do, terrible things happen to both sides, the kids and the caretakers. These kids get placed in families repeatedly and they repeatedly fail. What are we going to do with these children? Right now we either put them in an institution or we put them in a family.". . .

Twenty-five years ago 80 percent of the children who "graduated" from The Children's Village went home to some family member, most likely the mother. But starting about five years ago the percentage began to drop. Today only 55 percent go home to family. Nan Dale, citing her own subjective standard of measurement, the "GFF" (gut-feeling factor), estimates that half of that narrow majority are returning to a home situation that is fragile. At Woodland Hills, where most of the kids are released to the care of their families, David Kern says he feels uneasy about the prospects for success almost half the time. He calls sending vulnerable children home the worst part of the job. While he was at The Villages, Don Harris felt uneasy about returning kids to their parents about 80 percent of the time. "The reality is we can help these kids build some bridges to their families, but they probably will never be able to live with them."

Not sending vulnerable children home can also be the worst part of the job. People who work with institutionalized children continually face a quandary to which they have no satisfactory solution: What should they do when, in spite of everyone's best efforts, family seems not to be in the best interests of the child? What the system has to offer is life in a group home followed by independent apartment living, and then nothing.

Life without parents is a difficult sentence to pronounce upon a child, but it's happening more and more often. "Sometimes children have gone beyond the opportunity to go back and capture what needed to be done between the ages of three and eight," says Gene Baker, the chief psychologist at The Children's Village. "Sometimes the thrust of intimacy that comes with family living is more than they can handle. Sometimes the requirement of bonding is more than they have the emotional equipment to give. As long as we keep pushing them back into what is our idealized fantasy of family, they'll keep blowing it out of the water for us."

"*Informal adoption reveals a community adapting and flexibly responding to its own needs.*"

Informal Adoptions Should Be Supported

Charmaine Yoest

Charmaine Yoest is a policy analyst at the Family Research Council, a lobbying organization that applies traditional values to current problems. In the following viewpoint, she contends that extended families in black communities have historically given their children love and supervision within the care of extended families. Although such sacrificial, loving care may not fully satisfy the needs of all children, these informal adoptive arrangements nevertheless provide many children with significant opportunities for a solid foundation for life.

As you read, consider the following questions:

1. In Yoest's view, how does the extended family within the black community typically respond to the needs of black children?
2. Although the author argues that informal adoptions provide a strong measure of care for children, what problems does she list as remaining unsolved?
3. How does Yoest account for the fact that some children of informal adoptions are able to break the cycle of poverty and recurring teenage pregnancies?

Charmaine Yoest, "Points of Light: Informal Adoption in the Black Community," *Children Today*, September/October 1990, published by the U.S. Department of Health and Human Services.

Her young mother had just died at age 31, from asthma, leaving six children between 1 and 12. Her father had left the year before. It was 1965 in Louisiana and the relatives had gathered in the kitchen of Grandmother McKee's house:

> "I can remember, vaguely, they were saying, what are we gonna do with the children? And somebody said, 'Put 'em up for adoption.' But my grandmother said, 'No. I'll raise them.' She didn't want to separate us. So, that's the way it began," remembers Nadine, the fourth child, only 5 years old then.

They called her "MaDear" (ma-dee-a), short for "Mother Dear," and she raised them all on nothing but her own and her daughter's Social Security checks. No welfare. A blind uncle and ten other grandchildren without a mother also needed her care. "She was like the post, the security. You could go there and lay your head down; we may not have had a lot of material things, but that was home. She was always there," says Nadine.

"Taking Care of Our Own"

Many others in the black community share Nadine's memory of being informally adopted by a grandmother. The tradition of "taking care of our own" by taking in needy children is so prevalent in the black community that it is a distinctive part of its culture. In a study published in 1977, Robert Hill, a professor at Morgan State University in Baltimore, Maryland, found that 13% of black children lived in informally adoptive families (compared to only 3% of white children). By an overwhelming majority, those children were being raised by single, elderly women like MaDear. Hill found that almost half of black families headed by women over 65 had informally adopted children.

Grandma Jones (not the real family name) is another woman who, like MaDear, informally adopted her grandchildren. Her daughter gave birth as an unwed 15-year-old to Gale. Subsequently, in two-year intervals, Gale's mother had another daughter and a son. They all lived together in the Jones home even after her mother married.

Though Gale's mother was present, Grandma Jones was always the children's primary caregiver. Gale says of her mother, "It was like she was my sister." Gale distinctly remembers her mother sitting down in the kitchen one day and deliberately deciding that Gale would belong to her grandparents, while the other two children would remain hers. "My mother informally gave me to my grandparents," says Gale.

Eventually, her mother became addicted to heroin and left. "She went off and did her own thing," remembers Gale. Later she returned and, to strike back at the Joneses for trying to get her off heroin, took the children away. She soon returned Gale, but kept the other two with her. However, when the Joneses found out that the two younger children didn't see their mother for days at a time, Grandma Jones went to court and won guardianship of them as well.

The Cycle of Unwed Teenage Pregnancy

Gale's mother was the third generation of women in her family to have become an unwed pregnant teenager. Single parenthood can be the event which effectively extinguishes the light of hope in a young girl's life, introducing her to a dark world of struggle and hardship. In our society today, unwed teenage pregnancy has become an agent of darkness, perpetuating poverty through the generations. For the child of a single parent, the statistical odds of becoming an unwed mother, or fathering a child out-of-wedlock, are staggering. One study found that 80% of the girls who were mothers at 15 were themselves daughters of teenage mothers.

Gale and Nadine are exceptional in having broken out of this vicious cycle. Gale is now studying for her Ph.D. at a northern university and Nadine graduated from college and now works in Washington, D.C. Gale's younger sister, however, did become pregnant out-of-wedlock, carrying the cycle into the fourth generation.

Unwed pregnancy is far from just "a black problem." Regardless of race or class, unwed pregnancy coupled with single parenthood is intrinsically and inescapably difficult in its emotional demands, and usually leads to poverty. According to the National Center for Health Statistics, 65.7% of all children under age 6 in female-headed families lived in poverty in 1986; in female-headed black families the proportion was 71.9%.

The number of white, unwed pregnant teenagers is far greater than the number in the black community, but proportionally the black community is hit harder by unwed pregnancy and its effects. In 1989, 61.2% of all black children were born to unwed mothers. According to Marian Wright Edelman, President of the Children's Defense Fund, a black teenager is twice as likely to become pregnant as a white teenager and five times as likely to become an unwed parent.

Few Choose Formal Adoption

Despite this high level of unwed pregnancy, the black community has a very low percentage of girls choosing formal adoption for their babies. In fact, the percentage is statistically insignificant at less than 1%.

As a result, there is a common perception that the black community is not interested in adoption. Because there is such a low relinquishment rate, it is assumed that unwed black mothers will not consider adoption. And with black children comprising

things she did? You know? Not to receive anything in return. She didn't have any ulterior motives. Nothing from the state, which could have been paying her welfare checks. But that wasn't the case at all. She just took care of us.

For MaDear, her decision about the children's care was automatic—of course they would stay with her. This attitude springs from what Edelman calls "the strong black tradition of self-help." Another writer, James King, talking about this tradition says: "All black families in America have a common sense of 'peoplehood' in the sense that they have had to help each other in the struggle against oppression since arriving in America."

This strong sense of kinship, expressing itself as a network of help, was very much a part of Nadine's young life: "Because my family is so close-knit, they always helped to provide for us," she says. One of her cousins made her clothes, and they all pitched in to make sure the children always had Christmas presents. The aunt that Nadine most admires (and who paved the way as a role model) was able to attend college because the family held dinners to raise money for her tuition.

In the past, close-knit communities have served another purpose—to a large degree the extended family has been the black community's Child Protective Service. A young mother raising a child alone frequently did so in the context of a watchful, protective, extended family. Child abuse or neglect did not go long undetected. One young girl quoted in *All Our Kin*, Carol Stack's study of the black family, said:

> I wasn't living at home at the time, but mamma kept Christine most of the time. One day mamma up and said she was going to take my child and raise her right. She said that I was immature and that I had no business being a mother the way I was acting. All my mamma's people agreed and there was nothing I could do. So mamma took my child.

According to Hill, the lowest levels of child abuse are among informal adoption arrangements. But even in cases when a child is removed from a home by the state, the extended family is still a resource. A study on formal foster care by the National Black Child Development Institute found that relatives were considered for placement assistance in 75% of the cases, and nearly 60% offered some type of assistance. One of the most common reasons for denying placement assistance was lack of financial or housing resources.

Advantages

Informal adoption arrangements offer several major advantages to the children. Because the arrangements are usually made intra-family or within the kinship network, to some degree a sense of belonging and continuity is maintained for the child. Also, informal adoption can provide security and care for a child who might otherwise have to cope with the terrible disruption and impermanency of the foster care system.

Also, the involvement of the young mother's family and the support of the extended family framework in raising the child can somewhat mitigate the stress and isolation a young mother faces as a result of the absence of the father. For instance, Nadine talks with great fondness of the fun of growing up in the midst of so many cousins, all of them raised as brothers and sisters.

Looking at informal adoption reveals a community adapting and flexibly responding to its own needs. Instead of the stereotypical conniving welfare mother, we see great dignity personified. We come away with a picture of hope and possibilities—some, like Nadine and Gale, have indeed made it out of the darkness and into the light with the sacrificial support of loved ones.

Three Disadvantages

The system of informal adoption has been successful in its primary, and most fundamental, objective: providing homes for needy children. But in some other, significant ways, it falls short of the optimal situation for the child. And although in the real world, the optimal cannot always be attained, it must always remain the goal. Hill himself says:

> The informal adoption mechanism appears to perform some vital functions for black families in such areas as income maintenance, day care, services to out-of-wedlock children and unwed mothers, foster care and adoption. But very little is known about the adequacy of these self-help efforts and coping strategies among low-income blacks—a primary target group of most social welfare policies today. And, until one assesses the adequacy of these coping strategies, it is not possible to effectively determine the kinds of additional supportive services and programs that are needed to enhance the quality of life of low-income and minority children in general.

Rather than providing an environment that enables young people to climb out of the intergenerational poverty cycle into self-sufficiency, informal adoption can itself become a factor in perpetuating the cycle of dependency and poverty. This can be seen in three ways:

- lack of a model of an intact, nuclear family;
- perpetuation of unwed pregnancy; and
- lack of legal status and confusing relationships.

The absence of a model of what a family with a mother and a father can be is perhaps the most damaging effect of informal adoption. This is not a problem when the child is brought into an intact home. However, the majority of informal adoptions transfer a child from a single teenage mother to another single grandmother or an aunt.

The child then grows up experiencing the single parenthood

model as normal. And according to Edelman's analysis of the breakdown of the black family, "The failure of first marriages to form among young blacks is the largest single cause of the very high proportion of all young black families that are fatherless." In Sandven and Resnick's study, only 52% of the young girls viewed having two parents as important. Thirty-seven percent said that they would never marry.

The Rise in Out-of-Wedlock Births

Since the 1960s, the rate has risen dramatically for both races, but the numbers are much higher for black women than white women.

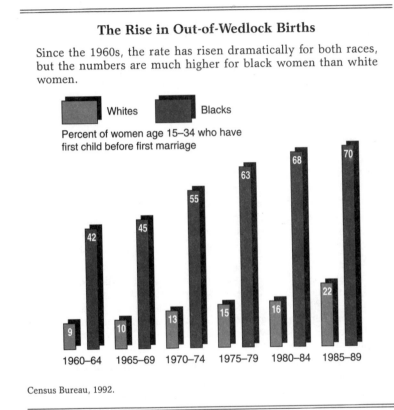

Census Bureau, 1992.

As an adult, Nadine is beginning to see how this lack of modeling has impacted her. She says that she very much missed her mother growing up: "I have always missed not having a momma. I really have. And my grandmother did an excellent job. But I do believe that there's nothing like your own mom."

But she says she never "had an understanding of what a real daddy was." All of her aunts, except for one in Houston, were divorced, so there were no models of a father even in her extended family. She added, "How could you miss something you don't have? For the most part, a dad—he was just an option."

The second negative effect of informal adoption is its contribution to the continuation of the unwed teenage pregnancy cycle. Informal adoption provides a resolution to the pregnancy that may do nothing to address the underlying reasons for the young girl's pregnancy.

Sandven and Resnick found that the young girls whose first babies became "gift" children in an informal arrangement tended to soon "replace" that child by having another. Although Sandven and Resnick report that "the majority had not intended to become pregnant when they did," there are other indications in their study that the girls' intentions were not clear, perhaps even to themselves. For instance, they also note that 67% of the "gift" group, and 56% of the overall group, reported a death of a family member or friend in the past year.

A Path to Adulthood

Motherhood (and fatherhood) becomes a pathway to adulthood. Accordingly, the girls in Sandven and Resnick's study received very few negative reactions to their pregnancies; in fact, their peers tended to react with surprise and excitement and their boyfriends were the ones to respond most positively. In addition, with informal adoption the corollary adult responsibilities may be diluted. The new mother is allowed to remain a child, while her own mother assumes the role of caregiver to the new baby. Significant relational problems can result. According to Hill:

> Several studies have revealed role strain and conflict between grandmothers and mothers concerning the rearing of informally adopted children. Often, the grandmother behaves as the "mother" of the grandchild, and the natural mother as an older sister of her own child. Consequently, the grandmother role may, in fact, be non-existent.

Lastly, informal adoption leaves the child in legal limbo. Should the child's informal parent die, the child is ineligible for Social Security benefits. Nor would the child be eligible for disability benefits to which he would otherwise have been entitled had he been legally adopted. Additionally, if no one present has ultimate legal responsibility for them, informally adopted children are sometimes shuffled from one home to another. This is the dark side of the "revolving door."

In our discussion of informal adoption, we must recognize the deterioration of some of the factors that have made informal adoption possible in the past. During the last 20 years the extended family network in the black community has been seriously weakened. With the decline in the extended family, the resources that have enabled older black women, and others, to take in needy children in the kinship network are diminishing.

The Importance of Role Models

Hearing the details of Nadine's story without knowing her or knowing the outcome, there would be little risk in predicting that she would become an unwed, poorly educated adolescent mother living in poverty. All of the other girls on her block became unwed mothers. But she did not. On getting to know her, one is startled to discover that Nadine comes from an economically deprived background; there are no outwardly visible indications.

Gale's story is likewise a gratifying surprise: A woman who as a very young girl watched her mother shooting up on heroin, grew up to earn a college degree and go on to pursue a doctorate. Her story is a wonderful anomaly.

These are two who were born on the edge of darkness. But light came to them through their grandparents: MaDear McKee and the Joneses. And that light enabled them to see things differently. Nadine explains:

> There is one thing that I know has made me different. I don't want to sound too mystical but the only thing I can say is that I have always, always wanted better for myself! And I don't know where that came from; but I have always, always wanted better for myself. Just because you didn't have, doesn't mean you have to end your life not having.

Gale's outlook is similar. When asked what the difference was between those who were able to make their dreams a reality and those who fell prey to the limitations of their background, she replied, "There's got to be something inside you that says, 'I don't want to live like that.' For some people it's a much clearer vision, they see it as attainable."

If it was a clear vision of a better life which motivated both Nadine and Gale, the path that they both took to get there was the same as well: education.

"It wasn't a big push." said Gale. "When I came home, I was just expected to get A's. My grandfather would have done anything to help me go to college. 'You're smart,' he would say, 'go to school.' All his generation knew was that if you got an education you could be somebody."

Nadine's comments about MaDear echo the same sentiment:

> She never sat us down and preached to us, but we knew she wanted us all . . . it was expected . . . that we would get an education. She wanted me to get an education because she knew she could only do so much for us. She knew that if we got an education, at least we would be more equipped to have what she didn't have, and to have what she couldn't give us. When I finished my college degree, she was so happy she didn't know what to do.

A vision becomes believable when we see it modeled in someone's life. Role models also play a big part in helping young people see something better beckoning. For Nadine, it was her aunt in Houston, the one with the beautiful things and the many bottles of shiny nail polish. Inspired to be like her, Nadine collected and sold soft drink bottles to be able to get her hair done. Her aunt had gone to college, so Nadine did too. To this day, her aunt prods her on, asking about her goals and aspirations.

Human nature is so infinitely variable that there are no simple formulas which guarantee success. Though Gale—despite the obstacles—was able to build a life of accomplishment, her brother did not. And Nadine and one other cousin are the only ones out of the 16 MaDear raised together who finished college. While it is impossible to lay down conditions which ensure that a child will develop to his full potential, experience clearly teaches us that certain fundamental factors enormously improve the odds for positive outcomes.

The sacrificial, loving care, the encouragement, the positive expectations, the discipline, and the taking of responsibility personified by MaDear and Grandmother Jones provide a solid foundation for life, and opportunity to grow, develop and achieve. It is impossible to overemphasize the significance of the security of the consistent individual, personalized attention of an adult in the life of a young child.

Sometimes, children almost seem radiant with their purity and enthusiasm for life. There is a fragile, natural spark of light which begins with a child's dreams, hopes, and imagination and must be nurtured and protected. Just as a candle's wick must be trimmed and the flame protected from a draft, so the light of a child must be shielded from the winds of adversity whose icy blast can extinguish it, leaving only darkness. With nurturing love and care, the light grows and brightens; with neglect and abuse, the light flickers, dims, and finally dies.

But even in the darkness, the dying spark can be reignited into a glowing flame with another point of light. Rekindling the spark in a child's life and nurturing the flame, as MaDear McKee and Grandma Jones did, can illuminate the path to a new and better life, renewing confidence and bringing priceless hope.

After considering whether her identity should be disguised in this article, Nadine returned with her decision:

> "I've always been real open," she said, "and the reason why is in Ecclesiastes. It says the end of a matter is better than the beginning. If anybody reads my story, I would just want it to give children hope. I really do believe God is going to do something with my life.
>
> "Even my name, Nadine, means 'hope.'"

Periodical Bibliography

The following articles have been selected to supplement the diverse views presented in this chapter.

Roberta Achtenberg — *Lesbian and Gay Parenting: A Psychological and Legal Perspective* (1) 1987. Available from the National Center for Lesbian Rights, 1663 Mission, 5th Fl., San Francisco, CA 94103.

Sharyn Anleu — "Surrogacy: For Love but Not for Money?" *Gender & Society*, March 1992. Available from Sage Publications, 2455 Teller Rd., Newbury Park, CA 91320.

Nancy Apfel and Victoria Seitz — "Four Models of Adolescent Mother-Granddaughter Relationships in Black Inner-City Families," *Family Relations*, October 1991.

Chris Bull — "New York Judge Grants Adoption to Lesbian Couple," *Advocate*, March 10, 1992.

Alexander Capron — "Whose Child Is This?" *Hastings Center Report*, November/December 1991.

Victor Groze and James Rosenthal — "Single Parents and Their Adopted Children: A Psychological Analysis," *Families in Society*, February 1991.

Rick Harding — "Florida Adoption Ban Violates Constitution, State Court Determines," *Advocate*, April 23, 1991.

Michele Ingrassia — "The Limits of Tolerance: An Adoption Ignites a Furor over Gay Rights," *Newsweek*, February 14, 1994.

Karima A. Haynes — "Single Black Women Who Adopt," *Ebony*, May 1994.

Deborah Joy — "Going It Alone: The Challenge of Single Parenting," *Ours*, March/April 1994. Available from Adoptive Families of America, 3333 Hwy. 100 No., Minneapolis, MN 55422.

Jack McCallum — "Family Matters," *Sports Illustrated*, April 26, 1993.

Kathleen McDonald — "Love and Surrogacy," *Glamour*, December 1994.

The New York Times   "Lesbian Wins Appeal on Vermont
                          Adoption," June 20, 1993.

Ingrid Ricks   "Fathers and Son," *The Advocate*, February 7,
                         1995.

Cherylon Robinson   "Surrogate Motherhood: Implications for the
                         Mother-Fetus Relationship," *Women and
                         Politics*, Summer/Fall 1993. Available from
                         Haworth Press, 10 Alice St., Binghamton,
                         NY 13904.

Kari Sandven and   "Informal Adoption Among Black Adolescent
Michael Resnick   Mothers," *American Journal of Orthopsychiatry*,
                         April 1990.

Are Some Adoptions More Problematic Than Others?

Chapter Preface

Because the number of adoptable children worldwide has increased dramatically in recent years, adoption professionals actively seek prospective parents, especially for foreign, minority, and special needs children. These attempts to find parents are sometimes accompanied by difficulties and problems that require serious consideration.

How best to care for children with special needs is a concern that illustrates the problem. The term *special needs* is generally used to describe those children for whom it is particularly difficult to find permanent homes. Adoptable children may have special needs, as Judith McKenzie observes, because they are "older children, children of color, children with physical, mental, or emotional problems, or children who are part of a sibling group." When prospective parents begin to consider adoption of such children, they are often asked to fill out an "acceptance scale" indicating the conditions they will consider. This scale not only includes questions about the race, sex, age, and number of children to be considered, but it also seeks to establish the degree to which prospective parents will consider children with problems of mobility, seizure disorders, heart problems, vision and hearing impairments, physical deformities, sickle-cell anemia, hyperactivity, speech impairments, congenital disabilities, and histories of sexual abuse, among other conditions. Parents considering adoption of these children must weigh carefully their resources, communication skills, self-esteem, motivations, and abilities to manage stress.

In the following viewpoints, adoption professionals argue and clarify the fundamental principles and issues associated with adoptions involving foreign, minority, and special needs children.

"The mere acceptance of international adoption overlooks the negative impact on children, birth mothers, adoptive parents, and . . . Third World countries."

Foreign Adoptions Should Be Discouraged

Kenneth J. Herrmann Jr. and Barbara Kasper

Kenneth J. Herrmann Jr. is an associate professor of social work and Barbara Kasper is an assistant professor of social work at State University of New York at Brockport. Writing to social workers, they contend in the following viewpoint that the good of foreign adoptees is not served when such children are removed from one country and placed in another. They argue that in the face of worldwide racism and sexism, children are best served when international adoption agencies work toward developing indigenous local services that will make foreign adoptions unnecessary.

As you read, consider the following questions:

1. In what ways, according to Herrmann and Kasper, are children treated as commodities?
2. In what situation(s) do the authors suggest that adoption might be the best option for a child?
3. What recommendations do Herrmann and Kasper make that will, in their estimate, improve the lives of Third World women and children?

Adapted from Kenneth J. Herrmann Jr. and Barbara Kasper, "International Adoption: The Exploitation of Women and Children," *Affilia*, vol. 7, no. 1 (Spring 1992), pp. 45-58, ©1992 by Sage Publications, Inc. Reprinted by permission of Sage Publications, Inc.

International adoption has become increasingly prevalent in the past 20 years. During the 1980s, for example, more than 40,000 children from Korea alone were adopted by North Americans. Table 1 details the growth of international adoption since 1978.

The literature on adoption generally supports this practice because of the number of children who require care that is not provided in their own countries. The process of adopting children from other countries has been delineated, and guidelines for protecting adopted children and for helping them adjust have been published. This viewpoint contends, however, that the mere acceptance of international adoption overlooks the negative impact on children, birth mothers, adoptive parents, and the Third World countries from which the children are removed.

Worldwide Oppression of Women and Children

The International Year of the Child and the International Year of Women highlighted the unique positions of children and women throughout the world. The historical oppression of both groups has been based on a perception that they are dependent and in need of special protection. This perception has resulted not merely in the exercise of these special protections but in unique forms of victimization and oppression.

Children are commodities. Throughout history, they have been bought, sold, and traded at the whim of adults. Both women and children experience the oppression that results from their financial, emotional, and physical dependence on others. For this reason, their experiences in the realm of international adoption are similar. International adoption operates within a male-dominated system that is based on the laws and expectations of men. If children and women are to benefit, it seems that they must accept what they are given, play by the rules of those in control, and trust that what they experience is in their best interests.

The Third World Baby Market

The psychological, educational, and social effects of adoption on individual children are well known, but the political and social effects on Third World societies from which these children come are not. Adoption is not always a morally justified and praiseworthy event. Many Third World children are legally free, and adoption by adults from developed nations is their only hope for a family or for surviving malnutrition or disease. However, many other children are placed under questionable circumstances:

- From 1976 to 1986, more than 10,000 Sri Lankan children were adopted by foreigners. Parents in that country are given small sums by "adoption agents" to surrender their children. Foreigners stay for a week in a hotel, receive adoption

170

Table 1: Visas Issued to Americans for Adoption: 1978–88

Source Country	1988	1986	1984	1982	1980	1978
Bolivia	21	25	24	9	11	16
Brazil	164	193	117	72	48	15
Chile	252	317	153	113	92	36
Colombia	699	550	595	534	653	599
Ecuador	41	25	12	11	32	42
Paraguay	300	32	8	8	1	0
Peru	142	71	31	35	54	35
Other South American countries	31	22	14	15	16	8
Belize	6	5	5	12	1	2
Costa Rica	73	72	99	108	62	87
El Salvador	88	147	364	199	179	98
Guatemala	209	228	110	98	75	51
Honduras	161	135	148	22	20	24
Nicaragua	8	14	10	4	11	29
Panama	23	25	20	20	11	26
Dominican Republic	54	31	44	45	26	17
Haiti	41	19	13	14	14	7
Jamaica	38	38	16	33	33	27
Other Caribbean countries	7	14	20	11	16	18
Canada	12	13	9	14	64	93
Mexico	123	143	168	98	144	152
China	52	10	6	31	0	0
Hong Kong	49	40	30	18	14	14
India	698	588	468	409	319	149
Japan	69	46	45	30	36	47
South Korea	4,942	6,188	5,157	3,254	2,683	3,045
Lebanon	23	19	15	6	6	8
Pakistan	10	12	14	5	17	3
Philippines	476	634	408	345	253	287
Taiwan	56	90	56	35	0	0
Thailand	75	27	19	19	13	38
Turkey	11	11	8	0	3	2
Other Asian countries	23	14	25	37	90	166
Greece	10	16	8	10	14	25
Poland	51	32	26	12	20	14
Portugal	17	19	16	13	23	12
Other European countries	21	36	29	36	57	90
Oceania	15	21	9	7	2	18

Source: U.S. Department of Justice, U.S. Immigration and Naturalization Service, Statistical Analysis Branch, Washington, DC, based on a recompilation of data.

services, choose a child, and leave as an intact family. Only 2% of the adoptions in 1985 were handled by the government, while 98% were handled by these adoption agents.

- Scouts who work for lawyers in El Salvador are paid $50 for each child they obtain for foreign adopters, mainly North Americans, who pay $10,000 per child. Some babies are kidnapped, and others are coaxed from poor and desperate mothers; all documents are falsified.
- Colombia is another popular source of children. In one instance, children were bought for $600 and sold for $10,000 for adoption. One attorney alone sold 500 Colombian and 100 Peruvian children by this method.
- Military officers in the totalitarian government of Guatemala were accused of exporting 157 babies to the United States for adoption for $5,000 each. Babies in that country have been kidnapped and provided with illegal papers.
- Leonardo Villeda Bermudez, secretary general of the National Council on Social Welfare in Honduras, charged that Honduran children have been adopted by foreigners for the sale of body parts, sexual abuse, and Satanic rites and as couriers in drug trafficking. Many women in Honduras surrender their children for $25–$50, believing they are providing a better life for them. These women are approached by adoption "merchants" at the public hospitals or after giving birth on the sidewalks or in hallways because of lack of bed space.

In some Third World nations, illegal baby merchants have sought to remedy the problem of inadequate prenatal care so healthy babies will be produced for the adoption market abroad. This view of women as "breeders" is clear in the following example:

In Honduras, they have paid teenage girls to get pregnant; the merchants then follow the young women throughout their pregnancy to make sure they eat well and receive some kind of prenatal care. Once a baby is born, and if the baby is healthy, the mother is paid $50.00 for the product. This practice is not very different from what we call "surrogate motherhood" in the U.S.; however, it is substantially cheaper.

India is one country for which it may be argued that adoption is the best option for many children. Because of the worsening problem of poverty, about 16.5 million Indian children, aged 5–14, are in the labor force. Family planning is rarely used, because children add to the family income. The rates of death and disease among children in India are among the highest in the world. Many parents frequently abandon their babies at birth or shortly afterward because they cannot raise them, and the abandoned babies are housed in jails or local orphanages that are ill equipped to provide care. Adoption may be an alternative to death for these babies and to social ostracism or life as one of the millions of street children because they are unwanted.

When examining what may be in the children's best interests, one must consider the social adjustment and identity of internationally placed adoptees. L.G. Balanon, a Filipino critic of international adoption, maintained that the real issue is whether the basic needs of these children can really be met in an environment other than their culture of origin and asked: "What advantage does the Western society offer to deprived children not only during their formative years but for the rest of their lives? What happens to the colored foreign children in a predominately White society when they grow up?" T. Melone questioned if a child can ever become part of a different culture and pointed out that the severing of a child's natural ties is similar to any violent separation from family and surroundings. Therefore, one must examine the difficulty of the adoptees' adjustment in a racist environment and question if the "good" adjustment of these children is accomplished at the cost of their ethnic heritage and identity.

International adoption is often not the best alternative, and children are merely products of an elaborate system that sells them from the Third World to adults in developed nations. Foreign adoptions in Korea, for example, bring in $15–20 million per year of badly needed foreign currency.

Such economic and political forces may allow the global society to avoid its responsibility to ameliorate poverty and to provide family planning services and other necessities. Ironically, although adoption may contribute to the well-being of tens of thousands of children, it may contribute to the continued oppression of tens of millions. It is noteworthy that the very nations from which children are adopted are the ones that the United States exploits economically and militarily.

The Exploitation of Women

International adoption, influenced by traditional patriarchal perspectives, violates the interests of women, as well as of children. Women typically adopt as part of a spousal couple or as individuals, but countries such as Korea do not permit single women to adopt their children. Some adoption agencies or orphanages use the strength of the woman's role in the marriage and *her* willingness to remain at home after the child is placed as criteria for selection. Therefore, they do not consider the mother's income when assessing the adopting couple's finances. This practice may disqualify otherwise eligible couples. [We] contend that international adoption is a political action that frequently reinforces the oppression of women and even sets the stage for women to exploit each other.

Third World women who wish to place children for adoption when no alternative is possible will certainly find placement services, some legal and others illegal or questionable. Although black-market adoption schemes that are occasionally exposed in the United States may be common in another nation, they are illegal everywhere. They violate guidelines established by the United Nations and advanced by several nongovernmental organizations of the United Nations.

Fertility and babies have a market value in a global economy. Whereas a surrogate mother in the United States receives an average of $10,000, in Guatemala, the birth mother may receive as little as $55. Reports from Argentina, Brazil, El Salvador, Guatemala, Honduras, Thailand, and other nations indicate that children are placed for adoption after having been purchased, indentured, or abducted.

Women may be the victims of strong social norms against unwanted pregnancy. If children in Korea cannot be cared for by their biological parents, transferring the babies abroad is usually viewed as the next best alternative in a culture that attaches great importance to maintaining family ancestry. To avoid shame, it is common for the rare adopting mother in Korea to pad her stomach for several months to give the outward impression of pregnancy. This aspect of Korean society is either ignored or glossed over when prospective adoptive parents are oriented.

Unmarried Korean mothers are considered immoral, and unmarried fathers do not have legal responsibilities for their out-of-wedlock children. One home for unwed mothers in Korea reported that initially as many as 90 percent of the birth mothers want to keep their babies. After counseling, however, perhaps 10 percent do so. Many birth mothers experience depression and guilt when they give up their children after delivery.

Women are socialized to expect and embrace the role of motherhood as a primary aspect of their identities. Many women who adopt do so after grappling with the grief and pain of infertility, which, with its accompanying reproductive technology, is fast becoming a profitable business. Much of this technology views women as "living laboratories" and often subjects them to experimental procedures about which they are not informed. In their desperation for a baby, most women do not explore (nor are they typically fully informed of) the conditions under which their adopted child's birth mother surrendered the child.

Issues Concerning Reproductive Technology

A common thread connecting both infertile women and many international birth mothers is their lack of control over fertility. Reproductive technology in developing countries generally focuses exclusively on contraception. Conversely, in industrialized countries, the aim of fertilization, insemination, and surrogacy techniques is to increase pregnancies. Sterilization is often favored in developing countries when controlling the growth of the population is a pressing issue. According to N. Kanno, "The pressure placed on Third World women to use permanent birth control methods raises some of the same ethical issues as those raised by the new reproductive technologies in western countries."

Studies have generally shown Third World women's strong desire for reliable means of contraception and safe ways to terminate unwanted pregnancies. Childbirth kills hundreds of thousands of poor women each year, and the medical complications of improperly performed illegal abortions are reaching epidemic proportions in many areas of the Third World. For example, 20–50 percent of all maternal deaths in Latin America are due to illegal abortions.

In most societies, the control of reproduction is mainly in the hands of male-controlled policymaking bodies. Other factors that influence women's access to contraception and abortion are a culture's predominant religious values and a society's need for cheap labor. Although the birth mothers in developing societies may have little or no access to birth control or abortion, a decision to surrender a child for adoption is often not socially acceptable and further exacerbates the mother's already marginal social status. These women are politically disenfranchised.

Thus the paradoxical situation into which the adoptive mother is placed is particularly graphic from a political perspective. Her efforts to fulfill her needs and those of her child may result in oppressing a woman in another situation or assisting a woman in another nation. That not enough information on the circumstances surrounding the conception, birth, and placement of the baby is ever available may also pose a dilemma for American women who hold prochoice views and who adopt from women who have no choice. . . .

What Needs to Be Done

- Standards, guidelines, and laws should be strengthened and rigorously enforced. The U.S. Department of Justice requires that all documents supporting [international] adoptions meet certain legal standards, and the United Nations has established minimal standards to be observed in such situations. When violations of these guidelines or standards occur, it is rare that penalties or publicity ensues. Both must always occur. Agencies and adoption services should be closed when they violate these standards. The mass media should be alerted, as should relevant advocacy organizations and regulatory bodies.

- Standards regulating international adoption must require the inclusion of information about the birth mothers' circumstances if it is available. Too many adoption agencies in developed nations fear they will lose a source of adoptable children by making such demands on agencies or other sources in Third World nations.

- International adoption agencies must be required to provide prevention and community development services in the nations from which they remove children. The aim of these efforts must be to ameliorate the oppressive climate faced by women and children in these societies. Such services may be established cooperatively with organizations that are already involved in such efforts, including Plan International, Save the Children, and UNICEF.

- Attention must be focused on the children who are left behind. These "unadoptables" are mentally, physically, and emotionally handicapped children and groups of siblings. Because most nations that permit the removal of their children for adoption have woefully inadequate domestic foster care or adoption programs, program development, the sharing of resources, and an international effort to provide for these children are necessary. Such programs may be established contractually between agencies in Third World countries and international adoption agencies in developed nations.

- National organizations and movements that focus on the rights of children and the rights of women should join forces to effect change by, among other things, working for the ratification of the United Nations Convention on the Rights of the Child by all nations and rigorous efforts to advance the goals set during the International Year of Women. The resulting awareness, sensitivity, and resources may result in the recognition of the human rights of all people.

This final recommendation may result in significant change. The United Nations Convention on the Rights of the Child was passed by the United Nations General Assembly in November 1989. The Special Commission on Intercountry Adoption of the Hague Conference on Private International Law is now developing a proposed convention on Intercountry Adoption, which may be submitted to all countries as a regulatory treaty for such adoptions. Ratifying and signatory states to both treaties will be required to strengthen family life, enforce laws against exploitative adoption practices, and adhere to guidelines to protect human rights. These requirements will be monitored by a body established for this purpose. International human rights groups with nongovernmental organization status at the United Nations, including International Social Service, Amnesty International, Defense for Children International, the Anti-Slavery Society, and Radda Baren, will be a vital part of this process, and they have traditionally exercised their responsibilities with a client-centered, progressive activism. The cooperative efforts of such groups within the context of international law may end the rationalizations used to justify this form of exploitation, such as that it is merely an aberration of historically based cultural practices.

Human Rights and Human Dignity

Adoption has been seen as merely a common method of creating a family. However, it must also be seen within the political perspective of human rights and human dignity. In Guatemala and El Salvador, for example, there are about 100,000 war orphans. As C. Aubin questioned:

> Why are the countries from which North Americans adopt frequently in economic/political turmoil? We need to examine the role of our own government, both past and present, in creating or perpetuating devastating economic situations. It is from economic crisis that we can trace the abandonment of many children in our world. Are we adding to a country's economic devastation by removing important resources?

It is important to realize that this country cannot deal with global issues connected to the marketing of children without looking at the market itself. In certain countries, the United States is actually pillaging natural resources as well as their children. As M.K. Benet aptly noted:

> For it is only the developed countries that have in this century been able to care for their own children, and then only for the children of the groups that form part of the capitalist world, not for the children of the satellite groups within developed countries.

The current situation of many ethnic and racial minorities in the United States demonstrates this point. Both developed and developing nations will continue to struggle with this issue until the traditional nations are transformed into an international world government.

Therefore, the questions related to the rights of the woman who adopts, the rights of the birth mother, and the rights of the adopted child must be framed within the national and global implications and realities of sexism and the oppression of children. The political imperative to take these factors into account is clear from ethical, professional, moral, and legal standards of conduct. We social workers must ask the difficult questions about whose best interests international adoption really serves.

2 VIEWPOINT

"The benefits of international adoption far outweigh any negatives."

Foreign Adoptions Should Be Encouraged

Elizabeth Bartholet

Elizabeth Bartholet is professor of law at the Harvard Law School and author of *Family Bonds: Adoption and the Politics of Parenting*. Bartholet writes, lectures, and consults widely on issues involving adoption, reproductive technology, and parenting arrangements. In the following viewpoint, she responds to critics of international adoption and presents both a rationale for such adoptions and recommendations for reforms designed to facilitate and encourage more transnational adoptions.

As you read, consider the following questions:

1. What does Bartholet see as the main objection to international adoptions? How does she answer this objection?
2. How does the author respond to critics who charge that international adoptions work against progressive national programs specifically designed to help children?
3. To facilitate more international adoptions, what reforms and recommendations does Bartholet urge?

Excerpted from "International Adoption" by Elizabeth Bartholet, in the Spring 1993 issue of *The Future of Children*, a publication of the Center for the Future of Children, The David and Lucile Packard Foundation, ©1993. Reprinted courtesy of the publisher.

International adoption is a very important part of the total adoption picture. How various nations of the world shape the rules governing international adoption will define to a great degree adoption's future role as a parenting alternative. This is because the world divides into essentially two camps for adoption purposes, one consisting of countries with low birthrates and small numbers of children in need of homes, and the other consisting of countries with high birthrates and huge numbers of such children. In the United States and other Western, industrialized countries, the number of babies surrendered or abandoned by birthparents has been limited in recent decades by contraception, abortion, and the increased tendency of single parents to keep their children. As a result of these and other factors, very few children are available for adoption in comparison with the large numbers of people who, for infertility and other reasons, are eager to adopt. In the poorer countries of the world, war, political turmoil, and economic circumstances contribute to a situation in which there are very few prospective adopters in comparison with the vast numbers of children in need of homes.

International Adoption as an Alternative

For the infertile people who want to parent, international adoption constitutes the major alternative to infertility treatment and infertility "by-pass" arrangements such as donor insemination and surrogacy. These prospective parents are frustrated and discouraged by the common assertion that "there are no babies available for adoption." There is some truth to this assertion, if the focus is limited to babies born in the United States. But there are many infants and young children in other countries available for adoption and many more in need of homes. . . . For most of the homeless children of the world, international adoption represents the only realistic opportunity for permanent families of their own.

The Controversy

There is, however, great controversy about the benefits and dangers of international adoption. To some, international adoption presents in extreme form some of the problematic issues that are at the heart of all adoption. It can be viewed as the ultimate in the kind of exploitation inherent in every adoption, namely the taking by the rich and powerful of the children born to the poor and powerless. It tends to involve the adoption by the privileged classes in the industrialized nations of the children of the least privileged groups in the poorest nations, the adoption by whites of black- and brown-skinned children from various Third World nations, and the separation of children not

179

only from their birthparents, but from their racial, cultural, and national communities as well.

To others, however, international adoption is a particularly positive form of adoption. Prospective parents reach out to children in need, rather than fight over the limited number of healthy infants available for adoption in this country. The fact that these families are built across lines of racial and cultural difference can be seen as a good thing, both for the parents and children involved and for the larger community. These are families whose members must learn to appreciate one another's differences, in terms of racial and cultural heritage, while at the same time experiencing their common humanity. The evidence indicates that they succeed in doing so.

Recent Trends

The tensions between the different visions of international adoption are evident in recent developments. There has been a vast increase, during the past few decades, in the number of children placed for adoption across national borders. Close to 10,000 children per year have come into the United States from abroad for adoption in recent years. They comprise one-fifth to one-sixth of all nonrelative adoptions in this country and a somewhat larger portion of all infant adoptions. Worldwide, there are an estimated 15,000 to 20,000 international adoptions per year.

This increasing interest in international adoption is colliding with a new hostility to such adoption. The politics are similar to those involved in the debate about transracial adoption in the United States. Children are said to belong with their "roots" and in their communities of origin. Political forces in the "sending countries" have been condemning in increasingly loud voices the practice of giving their countries' children to the imperialist North Americans and other foreigners. South Korea, the country responsible for sending more than half the children who have ever come to this country for adoption, has in the last few years begun phasing out its foreign adoption program in response to such pressures. In combination with other developments, this resulted in a dramatic decrease in the number of international adoptions in 1992. Preliminary data provided by the U.S. Immigration and Naturalization Service indicate that in fiscal year 1992 there were only 6,500 such adoptions. . . .

Real Problems and Mythical Concerns

This viewpoint takes the position that the benefits of international adoption far outweigh any negatives and that international adoption should be encouraged with appropriate protections against abuses. . . .

U.S. International Adoptions 1993

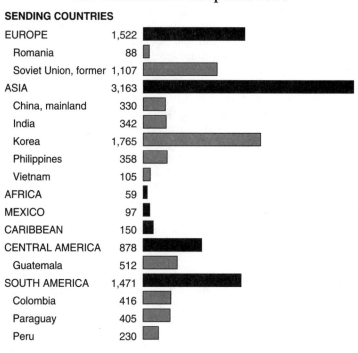

SENDING COUNTRIES

EUROPE	1,522
Romania	88
Soviet Union, former	1,107
ASIA	3,163
China, mainland	330
India	342
Korea	1,765
Philippines	358
Vietnam	105
AFRICA	59
MEXICO	97
CARIBBEAN	150
CENTRAL AMERICA	878
Guatemala	512
SOUTH AMERICA	1,471
Colombia	416
Paraguay	405
Peru	230

Source: U.S. Immigration and Naturalization Service, 1994.

The problems that should be seen as central to the international adoption debate are the misery and deprivation that characterize the lives of huge numbers of the children of the world. Millions of children die regularly of malnutrition and of diseases that should not kill. Millions more live in miserably inadequate institutions or on the streets. Their situations vary: some institutions are worse than others; some "street children" maintain a connection with a family while others are entirely on their own. But there can be no doubt that overwhelming numbers of children in the poor countries of the world are living and dying in conditions which involve extreme degrees of deprivation, neglect, exploitation, and abuse. International adoption should be seen as an opportunity to solve some of these real and desperate problems for some children. It should be structured to maximize this positive potential by facilitating the placement of children in need of nurturing homes with people in a position to provide those homes.

International adoption can, of course, play only a very limited role in addressing the problems that the children of the world face. Solutions lie in reallocating social and economic resources both among countries and within countries, so that more children can be cared for by their birthfamilies. But, given the fact that social reordering on a major scale is not on the immediate horizon, international adoption clearly can serve the interests of at least those children in need of homes for whom adoptive parents can be found.

Some have suggested that international adoption programs might conflict with programs designed to improve the lives of the millions of children now in need or with efforts to accomplish the kind of social reordering that might help the children of the future. For example, some argue that instead of promoting and pursuing adoption, governments and individuals in the well-off, industrialized countries should devote increased resources to more cost-effective programs designed to promote the well-being of children in their native lands. These efforts could include improving foster care arrangements, sponsoring orphanages, and supporting various UNICEF [United Nations Children's Fund] projects.

Such efforts, however, are not inconsistent with supporting foreign adoption. Indeed, the opposite is true. Foreign adoption programs are likely to increase awareness in the United States and other receiving countries of the problems of children in the sending countries. These programs give those who adopt reason to identify, through their children, with the situations of other children not lucky enough to have found homes. Foreign adoption is thus likely to help create a climate more sympathetic to wide-ranging forms of support for children abroad.

Highlighting Social Problems in Sending Countries

Another argument voiced against international adoption is that it might relieve pressure within some sending countries to deal with social problems that need attention. But this argument also collapses upon analysis. Sending children abroad for adoption tends to highlight rather than to hide the fact that there are problems at home. Indeed, it seems likely that a major reason for the hostility exhibited by many sending countries toward foreign adoption relates to their governments' embarrassment at having domestic problems spotlighted by this public confession of their inability to take care of their own children.

Although speculative arguments can always be mounted, it is unlikely that adoption of a relatively small number of the world's homeless children will significantly interfere with the efforts to assist those other children who remain in their native countries. Indeed, the nations of the world are in general agreement that "the best interests of the child" should be the paramount principle governing the placement of children outside their biological families. Given the real problems confronting the world's children, it should be clear that this principle requires laws and policies designed to facilitate the international placement of children in need of homes.

Avoiding New Problems

Care should be taken, of course, to prevent international adoption from creating new problems. Adoption must not be used to break up viable birthfamilies, and those who want to adopt must not be allowed to use their financial advantage to induce impoverished birthparents to surrender their children. There is a need for laws that prohibit baby buying, and for rules governing the process by which a child is removed from one parent to be given to another. The rules should ensure that the birthparents have voluntarily surrendered or abandoned their child, or have had their parental rights terminated for good reason. There is also a need for rules designed to ensure that adoptees receive loving, nurturing adoptive homes, and are protected against any form of exploitation.

But it is patently absurd to talk as if the real dangers for children were the dangers that they might be taken from their birthparents for purposes of abuse and exploitation. Nonetheless, public discourse about international adoption focuses overwhelmingly on its alleged risks. Concern is regularly expressed in the United States and abroad about the dangers that children will be kidnapped or bought from their birthparents for sale to rich North Americans; the media give headline coverage to stories of "kidnapping rings" or "baby trafficking." There are, of course, some documented instances of kidnappings and of improper payments to birthparents. But there is no evidence that these practices are widespread, and it is quite unlikely that they are. Current law makes it extremely risky for adoption intermediaries and would-be adopters to engage in baby buying or kidnapping. Even if some might be willing to engage in such activities if this were the only way or the easiest way to accomplish an adoption, the fact is that it is not. The world is, sadly, all too full of birthparents desperate to find homes for the children they cannot care for, and of children who have already been surrendered or abandoned. When one looks beneath the surface of most media and other stories of "child trafficking," it becomes clear that the term "trafficking" is used very loosely. The stories sometimes involve claims that what is characterized as a "bribe" has been paid to an official, without disclosing the fact that small payments are traditional in the conduct of official business in the country at issue. Often the trafficking stories say simply that the adoptive parents paid a great deal of money to agencies or other adoption intermediaries without indicating whether anything beyond legitimate fees for services were involved. Rarely is there any evidence that birthparents have been paid or that children have been taken from birthparents capable of and interested in raising them. . . .

Seeing International Adoptions as Opportunities

Critics of international adoption often voice concern that children will not receive appropriate care in their new families and countries. Arguments are made that it is unfair to separate children from their racial, ethnic, cultural, and national groups of origin. Loss of the group link and sense of group heritage is said to be a deprivation in itself. And growing up in a foreign land is said to pose risks of discrimination.

Those who voice these concerns again ignore the realities of children's current situations. International adoption represents an extraordinarily positive option for the homeless children of the world, compared to all other realistic options. Most of these children will not be adopted otherwise. They will continue to live in inadequate institutions or on the streets. Foster care is available only to a limited degree and sometimes results in little more than indentured servitude. The homeless children who survive to grow up often will face virulent forms of discrimination in their own country, based on their racial or ethnic status, or simply on the fact that they are illegitimate or orphaned.

The research studies on the outcome of international adoption show that these children and their families function well and compare favorably on various measures of emotional adjustment with other adoptive families, as well as with biological families. This is strikingly positive evidence since most international adoptees have had problematic preadoptive histories which could be expected to cause difficulties in adjustment. The studies show that adoption has, for the most part, been very successful in enabling even those children who have suffered extremely severe forms of deprivation and abuse in their early lives to recover and flourish.

Some of the research hints at the complex issues involved in being part of a biracial, bicultural, binational family. But the studies provide no evidence that the challenge of establishing a satisfactory ethnic and cultural identity causes any harm to the international adoptee. The findings are consistent with those in the transracial adoption studies. Black children who grow up in white families emerge with a strong sense of black identity. At the same time they tend to have a bicultural or multicultural orientation. They apparently enjoy an unusual degree of comfort in both black and white worlds, and are unusually committed to a future life in which they can relate to both those worlds. They are flourishing in all the terms in which psychic health and social adjustment are typically measured. There is no evidence that a multicultural identity is problematic from the perspective of the children involved.

There has been no focus in the studies on determining what special positives might be inherent in international adoption for the children, their adoptive families, or the larger society. But some studies hint at the rich quality of the experience involved in being part of an international adoptive family and the special perspective its members may develop on issues of community.

It seems clear that the debate over international adoption has little to do with genuine concerns over risks to children. Children are being sacrificed to notions of group pride and honor. As B. Tizard has described:

> It is argued that the practice is a new form of colonialism, with wealthy Westerners robbing poor countries of their children, and thus their resources. National pride is involved. However poor the country, they find the implication that they cannot care for their own children to be undignified and unacceptable.

Thus poor countries feel pressure to hold on to what they term "their precious resources," and rich countries feel embarrassed to do anything that looks like colonialist exploitation.

But there is no real conflict between the interests of the sending and those of the receiving nations. International adoption serves a symbolic function for those in power. Sending countries can talk of their homeless children as "precious resources," but it is clear that the last thing these countries actually need is more children to care for. At the same time, the well-off countries of the world have no burning need for these children. Their governments might be willing to permit the entry of adoptees from abroad to enable those struggling with infertility to parent, but international adoption is not seen as serving any strong national interest. So the homeless children end up as "resources" that the receiving countries of the world are quite willing to forgo to improve relations abroad.

New Directions

The starting point should be agreement that children are not to be thought of as "resources," belonging in some fundamental way to their racial or ethnic or national communities of origin. The world should take seriously the sentiments enunciated in international human rights documents that children are entitled to a loving, nurturing environment, and that their best interests should be the guiding principle in the structuring of international adoption.

Receiving countries need to take action to build trust. They must recognize that there are genuine concerns about exploitation, as well as a long history of resentment. Good faith could be demonstrated and children's interests served through offers to develop and fund programs to benefit children's welfare within a sending country, in conjunction with any international adoption programs that are instituted. Mechanisms could be developed to provide sending countries with regular feedback on what has happened to the children sent abroad for adoption. Regular reports could help assure sending countries that their children are receiving good treatment and are thriving in their new adoptive homes.

Sending and receiving countries need to agree on a legal framework for international adoption that would facilitate placement. The model should be one in which each of the key decisions in the adoptive process is made carefully by a responsible agency and then deferred to by all others. All duplicative processes should be eliminated. Several agreements already exist between particular sending and receiving countries which provide examples of how the laws of two nations can be coordinated to facilitate the adoption process. Receiving countries should revise their adoption, immigration, and nationalization laws to remove impediments to international adoption, and to ensure fully protected status to all foreign adoptees.

Implementing a New Legal Framework

For the United States this would mean the following:
- Development of agreements with other nations on a legal framework facilitating international adoption. . . .
- Recognition in such agreements of the principle that children's best interests require that children in need of homes be placed for adoption as expeditiously as possible. Children deserve nurturing homes now and not simply at some distant point in the future. Delay hurts and may do permanent injury.
- Elimination of the immigration law provisions that now restrict the children available for adoption by U.S. citizens to those satisfying the narrow "orphan" definition. [Congress has severely limited the scope of foreign adoption by permitting entry only to foreign adoptees who fit a narrow "orphan" definition. For an adoptee to qualify, both parents must have died or have abandoned the child, or the "sole or surviving" parent must be unable to care for the child.]
- Qualification for entry into the United States of all children that appropriate sending country authorities designate as being available for adoptive placement.
- Revision of U.S. laws to ensure that foreign agency decisions releasing children for adoption and foreign adoption decrees are honored by U.S. agencies and courts. This

would help ensure fully protected adoptive status to children adopted from abroad and would eliminate the necessity for duplicative [federal and state] adoption proceedings.

- Development of simple procedures to ensure that every foreign adoptee receives an English-language birth certificate from a U.S. agency upon submission of a foreign adoption decree.
- Revision of U.S. citizenship laws to make citizenship automatic upon completion of a foreign-born child's adoption by a U.S. citizen, just the way citizenship is now automatic upon birth of a child to U.S. citizens whether they are living here or abroad. . . .

The nations of the world should move beyond political hostilities and symbolic acts to focus on the real needs of children. If they did, they would accept international adoption as a good solution for at least some portion of the world's homeless children and could begin to restructure their laws and policies so as to facilitate rather than impede such adoption.

> "The abominable practice of placing Black children for adoption by white families [is] a practice of genocide unlike any previously inflicted on us."

Transracial Adoptions Should Be Forbidden

Audrey T. Russell

In the following viewpoint, Audrey T. Russell articulates the position of the National Association of Black Social Workers (NABSW), which in April 1972 passed its historic resolution opposing transracial adoptions. Arguing at the 1972 NABSW conference that transracial adoptions are a form of cultural genocide perpetrated by whites, Russell contends that blacks must preserve their culture and personal identities as a distinct people by taking exclusive care of their own children. At its recent 1994 conference, NABSW reaffirmed its 1972 resolution in "Preserving African-American Families" when it declared: "It is the right of a child to be raised in a permanent, loving home which reflects the same ethnic or racial group."

As you read, consider the following questions:

1. What, in Russell's view, are the consequences of transracial adoptions for black children?
2. According to Russell, what motivates whites to seek to adopt black children?
3. How does the author define a "black child"?

From Audrey T. Russell's workshop lecture on transracial adoption, in *Diversity: Cohesion or Chaos—Mobilization for Survival: Proceedings of the Fourth Annual Conference of NABSW*, 1973. Reprinted with permission of the National Association of Black Social Workers, Detroit, Michigan.

It is significant that this, our fourth annual conference, continues to carry forth the concentration on the Black family which we established as our total focus of concern at the first conference in 1969. The overriding emphasis of that conference was for the development of a new social theory based on liberation rather than adjustment and the Black family, defined as *all* Black people, was examined very closely in light of the social forces that impact upon it.

Leverne McCummings, in his foreword to the compilation of papers from that conference, said, "We will see our Black families in a new light, understand by our definitions what their strengths and weaknesses are and practice our work accordingly. We will reject, discard and destroy those forces which seek to force us to do otherwise." Well, Brothers and Sisters, the Black family is in serious trouble now, and we are called upon to reject, discard and destroy some forces which are operating to reject, discard and destroy us.

Trans-Racial Adoptions: Black Genocide

Brothers and Sisters, a terrible scourge is upon us, wreaking devastation to our ranks as Black people. The plague to which I refer is the abominable practice of placing Black children for adoption by white families—a practice of genocide unlike any previously inflicted on us. The power barons have decided against gas chambers anymore (that's much too nasty and obvious and folks get perturbed even 25-plus years later); they now choose more subtle and insidious means for just as lethal a purpose. Black genocide has long been recognized as a real possibility in this country and has long been in motion in the delivery of health services, social services, city planning, political, education planning and economic development. The white power structure already starves our families, pours narcotics into our neighborhoods, stimulates gang warfare and fans the fires of riots. All of which result in scores of more Blacks being killed. Yes, my beloved ones, the potential for Black genocide in this country is a real going thing and we must be eternally alert to its presence, thereby keeping on guard. What is more deadly to a race than killing off its children?

Promoting Black National Identity

Imamu Amiri Baraka has popularized a responsive chant beginning with the question "What time is it?" to which the choral response is "It's nation time!"

Nationtime, Nationhood, Nationbuilding have some very serous implications for us as Black social workers—who are first of all *Black people!!!*

Nation building is the ultimate of our being in this age of revelation of our true reality—that reality being our wholeness, wholesomeness, our historical, social and cultural value as a people; our integrity, strength and beauty. Our minds, our bodies and our spirit—*strong, true and beautiful*. Such a reality has established our need and thrust for unity and the strength that springs therefrom to enable the building of a strong nation.

RESOLUTION

Be it resolved:

that the National Association of Black Social Workers go on record in vehement opposition to the practice of placing Black children with white families;

that such trans-racial placements are contradictory to the essentials for identity building and sustenance;

that such placements are insults to the nation building concept of our very being;

that Black children belong totally in Black familial environments for healthy survival;

that the National Association of Black Social Workers, through its own organization and through all its contacts, will work, educate and prod all agencies, associations and other forces to cease and desist the practice of trans-racial placements of Black children;

that the National Association of Black Social Workers use all its offices, contacts and influences to stimulate the creation of Black-oriented and -directed specialized programs for the recruitment of Black adoptive families;

that the National Association of Black Social Workers use its offices, contacts and influences to stimulate, where necessary, the creation of Black-oriented and -directed specialized programs of alternatives to adoption within the Black community.

Presented to and adopted by the National Conference of the National Association of Black Social Workers, 1972, Nashville, Tennessee.

What does a nation need? Of what is it built? A nation first and foremost needs its resources; without resources there can be no life, no sustenance, no growth. . . . What is our chief resource? Our children!! How then can we pursue the vocation of nation building if we lose the foundation bricks? *Our children!*
Where is there a future for us without our children?
The issues of nation building and identity present the crucial base for our concern about the abominable program of transracial adoption of our children and we must all arise in vigor-

ous, vehement and voracious opposition to this practice and exert all efforts to stop it.

Basic to the concept of nation building is the extermination of a plantation system—the mentality which wants "Chuck" to do it, the inertia which permits him to do it, the lethargy which thrives on his doing it, all of which have supported his dominance and oppressive character. In casting off the plantation shackles we stand tall, self-assured, self-defining and self-determining. If this is to be our stance, then can we continue to let the white man determine the life status of our children? Where then will be our sense of nation or ever evolve the reality of a nation?

"The theory of Black nationalism," writes Walter Palmer, "speaks to the need of unity of Blacks operating as one nation, one family. This is necessary for our survival in a society hell bent on our annihilation." There is no unity when our children are kidnapped and placed in a foreign environment. Lerone Bennett writes in his *Challenge to Blackness*, "We believe in the community of the Black dead and the Black living and the Black unborn." To me, that spells complete uninterrupted unity, steeped in the continuity of heritage which propels us into our heritable future—a continual flow of blackness which impacts on all it touches; and our remaining together to be so touched is a moral, social, and political imperative.

A nation constructs itself, sustains itself and grows on health. Illness is weakening, it saps life, thus destroys. Black children living with white families is as pathological as a case of chronic schizophrenia; therefore it is destructive and must be avoided at all costs.

Problems with Trans-Racial Adoptions

Let us recognize the incongruence of a white family being a family for a Black child. The family is the basic unit of society—that from which flows its history, culture and total civilization. It is the family unit which shapes attitudes, values, self-concepts, and develops one's sense of himself in relation to the world at large. One's whole identity construct is begun and nurtured within his immediate family. Identity grows on three levels—physical, psychological and cultural—the whole mind, body, and spirit spectrum of our very being and development. We normally expect to resemble someone in our family and feel a glow of pride in hearing "you look just like your father—or mother—or great Aunt Minnie." It is important to children and further seals one into the family, his own primary group; his own inner circle of society—he truly belongs. How then can it be sound to place a child in a foreign setting and expect him to develop a healthy sense of identity of himself who is totally different from his relatives? Until quite recently, adoption agencies

191

went to great lengths to match children with adopting couples in an effort to reach as perfect a picture of resemblance as possible. What has happened to the rationale for that policy? It was very soundly rooted in the importance of family resemblance—the physical identity with one's own. So now, are all these theories so completely destroyed that the family resemblance is of no consequence whatsoever?

It shouldn't take much exercise for us to imagine the confusion and conflict stirred up within a Black child placed with a white family. In this society of ours, which is distinctly Black or white, and characterized by white racism which is reflected on every level of existence, is it not cruel to expect a Black child to identify with parents who are representatives of the oppressing arm of this world, while those who look like him are the victims? What then is he? We are all expected to love our parents. Can the Black child really sustain this love toward white parents when he becomes aware of the social system in which he lives? Again, what is he: oppressor or oppressed? What is he—a minority person in his neighborhood, school, church, etc., yes—but who in the hell has ever been a racial minority member of his own family????

How, also, can this white family help a Black child realize, feel and know, on a visceral level, his true heritage? Library shelves of Black literature are not the answer—a good intellectual device for academic learning, yes, but not equal to the Black history he feels as he trudges along beside his mother going about her chores, as he hears his grandparents' tales of long ago, much of which he can relate to his own reality of life.

Lauren Snowden presents another point:

> Another important reality that is not being taken into consideration by adoption agencies is the fact that in our society the developmental needs of Black children are significantly different from those of white children. Black children in Black families are taught, from an early age, highly sophisticated coping techniques to deal with racist practices perpetrated upon them by individuals and institutions. These coping techniques become successfully integrated into ego functions and can be incorporated only through the process of developing a positive identification with a significant Black other and development of a positive self-image as an individual and a Black person.

The Illusion of Integration

There is *NO WAY* a white family can give Black children the survival education they need, or interpret the society to them honestly and objectively. Whites in endorsing the practice of trans-racial adoption of Black children make reference to such nonentities as one world, only one race—the human race. Whites ask if we aren't growing more together and loudly accuse us antagonists of separating the races. They support trans-racial adoption of Black children as a means of bringing the races closer together. Thaddeus Mathis very aptly refers to this as "the empty integrationist philosophy which has existed for so long in this country and which has been repudiated time and time again by the everyday realities of American social and political life as experienced by the masses of Black Americans." Black America's history of pursuit for integration was always founded on our perception of how people *should* relate to one another—on the pronouncements of humanistic values upon which a society *should* be based, without recognition of the American reality which has always been the antithesis of these pronouncements.

A New Neo-Colonialism

Today we are attuned to the reality of the situation and thus recognize that we live in a Black or white world, that there is a Black culture, a Black life style, a Black meaning to all things. We also recognize that when Black and white do get together, Black is submerged by the innate tendency of whites to dominate and control. How then, I ask again, can a white family and community raise a Black child to become a Black adult? At best he can only become a well-fed, well-dressed, well-trained person, but a psychological mongrel—a new spelling of neo-colonialism. Brother Sékou Touré states very tellingly that the environment determines the individual. He says more fully:

> Decolonization must of necessity complete itself by the liberation of the colonized spirit, that is to say, from all the bad consequences (moral, intellectual, and cultural) of the colonial regime. Colonization, to enjoy a certain security, always has a need to create and to maintain a psychological climate favorable to its justification—from whence the negation of cultural, moral and intellectual values of the people. . . . This science of dehumanization of colonized people is so subtle in its methods at times that it progressively succeeds in warping our natural physical carriage and in devaluing our original virtues and qualities, with a view to our assimilation.

Brothers and Sisters, it's one thing to *lose* our resources but it's another and more serious thing to reinforce the enemy with *our* resources—another example of neo-colonialism which, refined further, spells genocide!

Camille Jeffers makes the following salient observation:

> Four hundred years ago the Black experience in this country began on the auction block with children being torn from their mothers' arms. Today, under the mistaken guise of liberalism the attack on the integrity of Black families continues with the separation of Black children from their own people and from their own cultural heritage. The same agencies that have for years on end scrupulously followed the rules of the game in

placing Jew with Jew, Catholic with Catholic, and Protestant with Protestant, now unwittingly or not so unwittingly choose to place Blacks with whites in a society that is acknowledgedly racist to the core. The Black community must claim its heirs and maintain its cultural heritage.

The Complicity of Adoption Agencies and Whites

The adoption of our children by white couples is a cruel, vicious and evil hoax played on young innocents. It is further an insult to Black adults because it says that we do not care for our own. *Adoption* agencies loudly proclaim that Black families will not adopt. We all know the lie of this. Let us be very clear that this vicious activity is sanctioned, Yea, promulgated by the white bastions of professional child welfare work standards and practices—the Child Welfare League of America. Their position was most recently proclaimed at their Eastern Regional Conference in Philadelphia, last month [March 1972]. Therefore, that organization must be a prime target for our concern in dealing with this assault on our ranks. It is well to note here that a resolution from the workshop on trans-racial adoption was presented to the League, calling for the cessation of trans-racial adoptions of Black children.

Trans-racial adoption has been described as a *deviant behavior* by Lauretta Byars, student at the University of Kentucky, who writes, "Parents who participate in trans-racial adoptions are exhibiting a deviant behavior from the mind-set of the American society of which they are a part." She goes on to sketch the historical picture of the white man's justification for our enslavement —that being our lack of human quality, which constituted his mind-set against us as weak, inferior, backward and uncivilized. "Deviancy is defined as a departure from the norm; the norms of the white society prescribe the behavior, to do otherwise is to violate the norms and consequently be labeled deviant."

Now I ask you—do our children need to be raised as the end result of deviant behavior? How can the white man, for whom this is deviance, play a successful charade through all the exigencies of a Black child growing into his own as a Black adult?

Let us take a close look at the whole phenomenon of trans-racial adoption. It was advanced by whites for whites. Have no doubt, it is an expedient for white folk only—the supply of white children has dried up and their human desire for parenthood is being satisfied through this psychological bastardization of our children.

In confrontations with whites about this practice it becomes patently clear that many of the adopting couples operate under the racist assumption they can do a better job in raising Black children than we can, that many are solely motivated by some distorted rescue fantasy, that many view it as a status symbol.

It all becomes much more sickening in relation to those children born of Black-white alliances. Whites have now re-defined these children as either Black-white or interracial children. The most deadly aspect of this amorphous definition is that they are emphasizing the white in these children; thus adopting their whiteness in him, they deny his genesis and he loses any opportunity to gain a healthy projection of his future. This produces a whole crew of folk who are confused about their identity and thus becomes the oppressor—*neo-colonialism.*

Necessary Reaffirmations

Well, let us loudly and clearly and strongly re-affirm our concept of a Black child as a child born of *a* Black parent. For centuries on end, one drop of Black blood made a child Black; this has been *immutable law* for generations. Now that it suits the whim of racist America, such definition can be changed at the drop of an ego from the eternal and infernal arrogance of the white man. I repeat, there is no such thing as a Black-white child or an interracial child. Both terms reflect incompleteness—children are whole beings, not half anything. Thus any child with at least one Black parent is Black!

A most grievous aspect of the trans-racial adoption mania is, regretfully I say, that many Blacks have been co-opted into executing that policy. There is no intent, here, to be harsh with those sisters and brothers, only to recognize and ask them to recognize their victimization by a colonial power which has rendered them incapable of seeing the true nature of the racist society in which we live. Admittedly the subtle is not always easily discernible; it is the poisonous snake without rattles. We have all been victimized by the same proponents of individual and institutionalized racism, well-adorned oppression, subverted humanism and prostituted Judeo-Christian idealism. Many of us have long seen and thoroughly internalized the reality of our existence in white America. It is incumbent upon us to help the others see, feel and internalize this reality and thereby be propelled in the only direction vital to our continued being—*the Black family as Black nation*—and *the Black nation as Black family!!!* . . .

Alternatives to Trans-Racial Adoption

There are several alternatives to trans-racial adoption which negate the need for us Black people to ever entertain it, even as a last resort. It is incumbent upon us to marshall our forces to deal with all adoption agencies and professional associations on plans of our own for development of specialized placement programs for our children. We must design our own program for recruitment of adoptive families. We cannot depend, for the recruitment of Black homes, on that white social work structure which conceived the idea of trans-racial adoption of our children in the first place. We can and must secure access to their financial resources, offices, etc., for our use in developing programs for the proper adoption of our children and for whatever alternatives to adoption are necessary.

It is not enough, Brothers and Sisters, for us to secure commitments from white agencies to stop all trans-racial placements of our children—that we must do, to be sure, but the full circle of service to our children must be the order of the day, hence the need for our programming.

White agencies have demonstrated the limits of their abilities to plan for Black children; they do not even serve Black children as Black children in foster homes. How dare *we* let them continue even another year masterminding the adoption of our children!!

The job is *ours*, Brothers and Sisters—the responsibility is *ours*, Brothers and Sisters. It means WORK—HARD, CONSISTENT, REALITY-FOCUSED WORK—but that's what nation building is all about.

And if I ask you what time it is and you respond, "It's Nation Time," then I say make that more than a slogan.

Make it your way of life and let's get on with nation building by first preserving our seeds!

"Transracially placed children and their families have as high a success rate as all other adoptees and their families."

Transracial Adoptions Should Be Encouraged

Rita J. Simon, Howard Altstein, and Marygold S. Melli

Rita J. Simon is University Professor at the American University's School of Public Affairs in Washington, D.C. With Howard Altstein, former dean of the School of Social Work at the University of Maryland, she has coauthored several books on transracial adoption. In the following viewpoint, Simon and Altstein, along with coauthor Marygold S. Melli, Voss-Bascom Professor of Law at the University of Wisconsin College of Law, contend that recent research clearly indicates that transracial adoptions are as successful as all other adoptions. In addition to summarizing the work of other researchers, they present their own 20-year longitudinal study on transracial adoption and report that it confirms the results of other studies made in the last two decades.

As you read, consider the following questions:

1. In their report on research by Grow and Shapiro, what point do Simon, Altstein, and Melli make about the difficulty in measuring the successfulness of an adoption?
2. According to the authors, what general—and sometimes specific—conclusions can one draw about transracial adoptions?

The case for transracial adoption rests primarily on the results of empirical research. The data show that transracial adoptions clearly satisfy the "best interest of the child" standard. They show that transracial adoptees grow up emotionally and socially adjusted, and aware of and comfortable with their racial identity. They perceive themselves as integral parts of their adopted families, and they expect to retain strong ties to their parents and siblings in the future.

Thus, there is a basic difference in the type and quality of the arguments that are made for and against transracial adoption. The latter are based almost completely on rhetoric and ideology. The National Association of Black Social Workers have never presented scientific data to support their position [against transracial adoption]. They have described vignettes, issued warnings, and made dire predictions. For example, after the findings from the first phase of the Simon-Altstein study were published in 1977—which showed that the transracial adoptees surveyed were aware of their racial identities and adjusted into their adoptive families—the NABSW reacted with a warning: wait until these children become adolescents; then the trouble will start. Other studies and our subsequent work did not support those predictions. The findings in our study, as we show in this review of the literature, were not unique or even unusual. All of the studies—even those carried out by researchers who were initially skeptical—arrived at the same general conclusions.

Research in the Mid-1970s

The work of Lucille Grow and Deborah Shapiro of the Child Welfare League represents one of the earliest studies of transracial adoption. Published in 1974, the major purpose of *Black Children, White Parents* was to assess how successful the adoption by white parents of black children had been. Their respondents consisted of 125 families. . . .

In discussing the specific measures of success they relied on, Grow and Shapiro . . . commented,

> This study of black children adopted by white parents shares the common problem of adoption studies—indeed, of most studies of social programs—that of identifying a valid, operational definition of "success." In an ideal society all adopted children, like their biological peers, would have a happy childhood and develop into well-adjusted, well-functioning adults. In a much-less-than-ideal society, it is evident that many, like their biological peers, will not. Since they do not all become "successful" adults, a series of difficult, usually unanswerable, questions is raised. Is the failure necessarily related to the fact of adoption? Is the rate of failure any different from that observed in the rearing of children by their biological parents? Are the problems of rearing adopted children essentially those

inherent in the child-rearing process and subject to the same risks or are they greater? In the specific type of adoption under scrutiny here, is a black child more "successful" in a white adoptive home than he would have been in a black foster home or a series of them?

In the end, Grow and Shapiro decided on the following measures: (1) the child's responses to the California Test of Personality and the Missouri Children's Behavior Check List Test; (2) three scores based on physical and mental symptoms reported by the parents as present or absent in their child; (3) significant adults' evaluation of the child, that is, mother, father, teachers, and parents' assessment of the child's relations with her or his siblings; and (4) the parents' assessment of the child's attitude toward race.

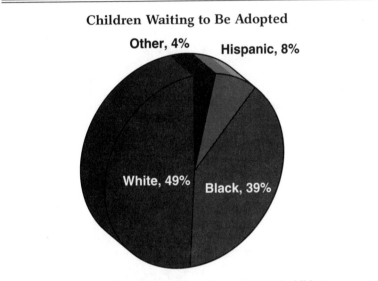

Children Waiting to Be Adopted

Other, 4%   Hispanic, 8%

White, 49%   Black, 39%

Race or ethnic origins of the estimated 17,000 children who are in foster care, waiting to be adopted.

Source: Voluntary Cooperative Information System and American Public Welfare Association, 1991.

On the basis of the children's scores on the California Test of Personality (which purports to measure social and personal adjustment), Grow and Shapiro concluded that the children in their study made about as successful an adjustment in their adoptive homes as other nonwhite children had in prior studies. They claimed that 77 percent of their children had adjusted successfully, and that this percentage was similar to that reported in other studies.

Grow and Shapiro also compared the scores of transracially adopted children with those of adopted white children on the California Test of Personality. A score below the twentieth percentile was defined as reflecting poor adjustment, and a score above the fiftieth percentile was defined as indicating good adjustment. They found that the scores of their transracially adopted children and those of white adopted children matched very closely.

When the parents were questioned about their expectations concerning their adoptive children's adjustment after adolescence and about the children's ties to the home when they became adults, the responses were generally optimistic. One-third of the parents did not anticipate that their adoptive children would experience future difficulties; 18 percent did not believe that any trouble lay ahead.

When the parents were asked why they chose to adopt a non-white child, 54 percent of the parents gave reasons and motivations that were essentially social. Forty-two percent said they wanted to provide a home for a hard-to-place child, and 10 percent characterized transracial adoption as a "Christian act." Forty-nine percent of the mothers and 60 percent of the fathers felt that one benefit of transracial adoption was that they were able to "give a home to a child whom nobody seemed to want." Seventy-one percent of the mothers and 66 percent of the fathers felt that transracial adoption enabled them "to express the deep love for children . . . [they] . . . have always had." Reinforcing the latter statement, and weighed against the idea of transracial adoption as a gesture to right society's wrongs, was the evidence supplied by the parents that "helping to compensate for the inequities in our society" was not perceived to be very much of a benefit of transracial adoption. . . .

Ladner's 1977 Research

In 1977, Joyce Ladner—using the membership lists of the Open Door Society and the Council on Adoptable Children as her sample frames—conducted in-depth interviews with 136 parents in Georgia; Missouri; Washington, D.C.; Maryland; Virginia; Connecticut; and Minnesota. Before reporting her findings, she introduced a personal note.

This research brought with it many self-discoveries. My initial feelings were mixed. I felt some trepidation about studying white people, a new undertaking for me. Intellectual curiosity notwithstanding, I had the gnawing sensation that I shouldn't delve too deeply because the findings might be too controversial. I wondered too if the couples I intended to interview would tell me the truth. Would some lie in order to cover up their mistakes and disappointments with the adoption? How much would they leave unsaid? Would some refuse to be interviewed because of their preconceived notions about my motives? Would they stereotype me as a hostile black sociologist who wanted to "prove" that these adoptions would produce mentally unhealthy children?

Prior to starting the interviews I admit to having been skeptical about whether the adoptions could work out well. Because I was reared in the Deep South, with all of its rigid racial segregation, transracial adoption represented, for me, an inexplicable departure from custom and tradition. I would have thought it just as unorthodox for a black couple to adopt a white child. Racial polarization in America sensitizes everyone to the potential hazards in this kind of "mixing" of the races. On the other hand, I was also unwilling to accept the facile cliches the critics use to describe the motives of the adoptive parents. I wanted to find out for myself what kinds of people were adopting and why they did it. What were their day-to-day experiences? How did the adoption affect their biological children? How were the children coping? It was also important to find out the reactions of their families, friends, and neighbors; their philosophies on race relations and black identity; their experiences with the adoption agencies; and their hopes and expectations for their children's future.

By the end of her study, Ladner was convinced that "there are whites who are capable of rearing emotionally healthy black children." Such parents, Ladner continued, "must be idealistic about the future but also realistic about the society in which they now live."

To deny that racial, ethnic, and social class polarization exists, and to deny that their child is going to be considered a "black child," regardless of how light his or her complexion, how sharp their features, or how straight their hair, means that these parents are unable to deal with reality, as negative as they may perceive that reality to be. On the other hand, it is equally important for parents to recognize that no matter how immersed they become in the black experience, they can never become black. Keeping this in mind, they should avoid the pitfalls of trying to practice an all-black lifestyle, for it too is unrealistic in the long run, since their family includes blacks and whites and should, therefore, be part of the larger black and white society.

Zastrow's 1977 Study

Charles Zastrow's doctoral dissertation, published in 1977, compared the reactions of 41 white couples who had adopted a black child against a matched sample of 41 white couples who had adopted a white child. All of the families lived in Wisconsin. The two groups were matched on the age of the adopted child and on the socioeconomic status of the adoptive parent.

All of the children in the study were preschoolers. The overall findings indicated that the outcomes of the transracial (TRA) placements were as successful as the in-racial (IRA) placements. And Zastrow commented,

> One of the most notable findings is that TRA parents reported considerably fewer problems related to the care of the child have arisen than they anticipated prior to the adoption. . . . Many of the TRA couples mentioned that they became "color-blind" shortly after adopting; i.e., they stopped seeing the child as a black, and came to perceive the child as an individual who is a member of their family.

When the parents were asked to rate their overall satisfaction with the adoptive experience, 99 percent of the TRA parents and 100 percent of the IRA parents checked "extremely satisfying" or "more satisfying than dissatisfying." And on another measure of satisfaction—one in which the parents rated their degree of satisfaction with certain aspects of their adoptive experience—out of a possible maximum of 98 points, the mean score of the TRA parents was 92.1 and of the IRA parents, 92.0.

Research in the 1980s

Using a mail survey in 1981, William Feigelman and Arnold Silverman compared the adjustment of 56 black children adopted by white families against 97 white children adopted by white families. The parents were asked to assess their child's overall adjustment and to indicate the frequency with which their child demonstrated emotional and physical problems. Silverman and Feigelman concluded that the child's age—not the transracial adoption—had the most significant impact on development and adjustment. The older the child, the greater the problems. They found no relationship between adjustment and racial identity.

W.M. Womak and W. Fulton's study of transracial adoptees and nonadopted black preschool children found no significant differences in racial attitudes between the two groups of children.

In 1983, Ruth McRoy and Louis Zurcher reported the findings of their study of 30 black adolescents who had been transracially adopted and 30 black adolescents who had been adopted by black parents. McRoy and Zurcher commented that 60 percent of the TRA parents "seemed to have taken a color-blind attitude to racial differences between the adoptee and family." They described these families as living in predominantly white communities, and their adopted children as attending predominantly white schools. They reported that 20 percent of the transracial parents acknowledged the adoptees' racial identity and the need to provide black role models for them. Those parents enrolled their child into an integrated school, moved to a mixed neighborhood, or became members of a church located in the black community. Their children expressed an interest in contact with other blacks and often discussed racial identity issues with their parents and peers.

Another 20 percent of the transracial families had adopted several black children and acknowledged that their family was no longer white, but interracial. They enrolled their children in integrated schools. Racial discussions and confrontations in the home were common. The children were taught to emphasize their black racial heritage. When the parents were asked to "denote their children's racial background," 83 percent of the inracial adoptive parents (black parents and black children) listed their child's background as black/black, and 17 percent as black/white. Among the white parents who adopted black children, 27 percent reported their child's racial background as black/black, 57 percent as black/white, and the other 16 percent as black/Mexican, Indian, Korean, or Latin American.

In the concluding chapter of their book, *Transracial and Inracial Adoptees*, McRoy and Zurcher wrote,

> The transracial and inracial adoptees in the authors' study were physically healthy and exhibited typical adolescent relationships with their parents, siblings, teachers, and peers. Similarly, regardless of the race of their adoptive parents, they reflected positive feelings of self-regard.

Throughout the book, the authors emphasized that the quality of parenting was more important than whether the black child had been in-racially or transracially adopted: "Most certainly, transracial adoptive parents experience some challenges different from inracial adoptive parents, but in this study, all of the parents successfully met the challenges.". . .

In 1988, Joan Shireman and Penny Johnson described the results of their study involving 26 in-racial (black) and 26 transracial adoptive families in Chicago. They reported very few differences between the two groups of eight-year-old adoptees. Using the Clark and Clark Doll Test (the same measures we used in our first study) to establish racial identity, 73 percent of the transracial adoptees identified themselves as black, compared to 80 percent for the in-racially adopted black children. Interestingly, although three-quarters of the families lived in white neighborhoods, 46 percent of the transracial adoptees named a black among their best friends. The authors concluded that 75 percent of the transracial adoptees and 80 percent of the in-racial adoptees appeared to be doing quite well. They also commented that the transracial adoptees had developed pride in being black and were comfortable in interaction with both black and white races.

In a 1992 unpublished report, Karen Vroegh—a researcher in the Shireman and associates project—concluded,

The majority of the adopted adolescents, whether TRA or IRA (inracially adopted) were doing well. The rate and type of identified problems were similar to those found in the general population. Over 90 percent of the TRA parents thought transracial adoption was a good idea.

In 1988, Richard Barth and Marianne Berry reported that transracial placements were no more likely to disrupt than other types of adoptions. The fact that transracial placements were as stable as other more traditional adoptive arrangements was reinforced by data presented in 1988 at a North American Council on Adoptable Children (NACAC) meeting on adoption disruption. There it was reported that the rate of adoption disruptions averaged about 15 percent. Disruptions, they reported, did not appear to be influenced by the adoptees' race or gender or the fact that they were placed as a sibling group. When examining adoptive parent characteristics, neither religion, race, marital status, length of time married, educational achievement, nor income seemed predictive of adoption disruption. . . .

"Should Race Be a Factor in Adoption?"

To return to a point made earlier, research findings show that transracial adoption is in a child's best interest. Transracial adoptees do not lose their racial identities, they do not appear to be racially unaware of who they are, and they do not display negative or indifferent racial attitudes about themselves. On the contrary, it appears that transracially placed children and their families have as high a success rate as all other adoptees and their families.

When given the opportunity to express their views on transracial adoption, most people—black and white—support it. For example, in January 1991, *CBS This Morning* reported the results of a poll it conducted that asked 975 adults the question "Should race be a factor in adoption?" Seventy percent of white Americans said no, and 71 percent of African Americans said no. These percentages are the same as those reported by Gallup in 1971 when it asked a national sample the same question.

At its seventy-eighth annual national convention in 1987 and again in 1992, the NAACP adopted the following resolution:

WHEREAS, there are a number of black children for adoption; and

WHEREAS, black children are among the most difficult to place in adopted homes; and

WHEREAS, there is a policy, written and unwritten, by many agencies to place black children only with black people;

NOW THEREFORE, BE IT RESOLVED, that the NAACP sponsors and supports efforts for legislation that will encourage policies that place black children for adoption without regard to race.

*"Developing families [for special needs children]
is becoming increasingly difficult and is an
important challenge to be faced."*

Special Needs Adoptions
Should Be Promoted

Judith K. McKenzie

Judith K. McKenzie is executive director of the federal government's National Resource Center for Special Needs Adoption located at Spaulding for Children, Inc., in Southfield, Michigan.
In the following viewpoint, McKenzie reports that although special needs children present a challenge to adoptive parents, with
intensive help and supportive policies most of those who adopt
can become highly skilled and effective parents. She urges a
comprehensive overhaul of adoption services, and lists nine specific proposals for helping special needs children and those who
adopt them.

As you read, consider the following questions:

1. What two definitions of "children with special needs" does
   McKenzie offer? What challenges do these children present to
   adoptive parents, in her view?
2. According to the author, what are the four types of adoptive
   families? What does she say is the dominant feature of
   families that adopt special needs children?
3. What blocks to foster-parent adoption does McKenzie
   mention?

Excerpted from "Adoption of Children with Special Needs" by Judith K. McKenzie, in the
Spring 1993 issue of *The Future of Children*, a publication of the Center for the Future of
Children, The David and Lucile Packard Foundation, ©1993. Reprinted courtesy of the
publisher.

Special needs adoption refers to the adoption of children who are particularly difficult to place in permanent homes. The definition of "children with special needs" includes older children, children of color, children with physical, mental, or emotional problems, and children who are part of a sibling group. However, for those who work in the field of special needs adoption, the term has come to have an additional and broader meaning: a child welfare service which seeks permanent homes for children in foster care who will not ever be able to be reunited with their birthparents. As such, it is the option considered and implemented only after all attempts to reconcile children with their families have failed. These children became labeled as "special needs" not because of a physical or mental disability, although some of the children do have developmental disabilities, but because, through default of parents and bureaucracies, they have become wards of the system. Most of them have experienced some significant trauma in their young lives, including deprivation, physical and sexual abuse, abandonment, loss, and many moves in foster care. As a result, they are prone to emotional, behavioral, and learning problems. Once these children are adopted, they are very challenging to parent. Many of them require highly skilled and specialized educational, psychological, and medical services which are not readily accessible to adoptive parents.

Children in Foster Care

Before children are adopted, those in need of parents are often referred to as "the children who wait." A 1991 report of studies in 20 states documented that children for whom adoption is planned remain in foster care an average of 3.5 to 5.5 years and, in many urban areas, much longer. These long delays are extremely detrimental to children, particularly when their development has already been compromised by early childhood trauma, and longer stays in foster care usually mean more moves for them and a decreased probability of adoption.

Unfortunately, the situation is likely to get worse before it gets better. The American Public Welfare Association (APWA) has estimated that as of June 1992, there were 429,000 children in foster care in the United States, a 53% increase during the past 5 years. Considering that many states estimate that 15% to 20% of the children in foster care ultimately have adoption plans, there may be as many as 85,000 children today who need adoption planning and services. As the numbers of children in care are increasing, many states are reporting growing backlogs of children waiting for adoption. Children of color are overrepresented in these statistics and are known to wait longer than Caucasian children for adoption, if and when they are targeted for this service. All major urban areas are reporting unmanageable numbers of infants and young children coming into out-of-home care as the result of parental addiction, and the vast majority of these are children of color.

Despite the fact that legal pressures have increased for returning children home and/or seeking other permanent solutions for them, such as adoption, states have not been able to keep pace with the growing demand for the services that are needed for these vulnerable youngsters and their families. Child welfare resources, organizational practices, and outcomes have changed very little since the 1970s, even though the needs are changing rapidly. With increased emphasis on reducing lengths of stay and on cost containment in child welfare, we are likely to see new reform attempts in permanency planning. Within the context of broad system reform, special needs adoption must have a more prominent place. Major revisions in child welfare policy and practices and new resources and procedures for doing special needs adoption will be required to keep pace with the increased emphasis on accountability and with the burgeoning need. . . .

Special Needs Adoption Services

Many of the children who will need adoption in the future will have entered care as infants. Although it is believed that the majority of these babies will, with proper support, be able to develop normally, many of them will have been born drug exposed and/or will test positive for the HIV virus. These babies will challenge the system because it is difficult to predict the developmental sequence or long-range effects of prenatal drug exposure on individual children and because, as A. Crocker has predicted, HIV infection will contribute to an increase in developmental disabilities in children. A significant number of these children may live for many years and require the care and nurture of permanent families.

Older children or children who have spent many years in the system will present additional challenges. These youngsters will have experienced emotional trauma, including multiple separations from their families while in foster care. Frequently, they will have experienced deprivation and abusive treatment. A high percentage of them (estimates from workers in the field are as high as 75%) will have been exposed to sexual abuse either at home or while in the foster care system. Current experience of the National Resource Center for Special Needs Adoption indicates that the majority of them will have lived in families where drugs, alcoholism, and violence were prevalent. Many of these youngsters will be members of sibling groups, and the older children who wait will be mostly boys. Of all children waiting, given current demographic trends, a vast majority will be children of color. More than two-thirds of the children will be under 10 years of age by the time they are referred for adoption, a much younger group than has been seen in past years.

Many of these children will be difficult to parent. Their emotional problems—anger, irritability, inability to attach—will continue to be the most challenging problems for families to accept and manage over time.

Four Types of Adoptive Families

Special needs adoption professionals are proud of their work and their association with adoptive parents. The extraordinary progress that parents can make with troubled children has been truly gratifying. Many start out with only a keen commitment to parent children with problems, but with time and experience, they have become highly skilled parents and effective advocates for their children.

Overall, adoptive families of children with special needs are a diverse group of people. They include lower-income and middle-class families, most of whom will have parented other children. Some are childless couples; others single parents. However, the single most dominant feature of the special needs adoptive family is that the vast majority of them have been foster parents first. Some states are reporting that 80% to 90% of their adopters are foster parents. In a 1988 report on minority adoptions by the Inspector General of the U.S. Department of Health and Human Services, it was found that in seven urban area agencies reporting, the average rate of foster parent adoption was 61%, with a range of 40% to 80%. This report also indicated that, in 1984, 14 of 17 states reported a foster parent adoption rate of 50%. Given the current trends, we expect this percentage to increase steadily in the future; and as it does, we predict that many adoptive parents will be from 45 to 60 years of age, and many more will be families of color, primarily African-American families.

Another group of adopters will be extended family members. More and more state agencies are reaching across county and state lines to find relatives willing to care for children whose parents are involved in drugs, alcoholism, sexual abuse, and other dysfunctional behaviors. However, these relatives have no preparation or support to care for their young relatives, who are very likely to need specialized services.

Foster parents and relatives offer children continuity of relationships and a chance at normalization. However, they pose special practice challenges and risks for the child welfare agency. Of particular concern is the practice of placing children in the first available foster care home and leaving them there indefinitely. Many children are not well served by this practice when they are separated from siblings, placed with a family of a different race or culture, and/or placed with families that are unable to meet their long-term needs, possibly because of the advanced age of the foster parents or grandparents. These families are often resistant to agencies intruding in their lives and reluctant to accept preparation for adoption or seek services when needed for fear of losing their children. In relative placements, families are not always informed of their rights to financial support and services through the adoption program, and, in some instances, the children cannot be adequately protected from the conditions that brought them into care in the first place. Foster parent and relative adoption are the most practiced and least well defined and studied areas of special needs adoption.

Why Traditional Agencies Promote Transracial Adoptions

We are seeing more very young babies of African-American and mixed-race heritage adopted by white couples. . . . Given the fact that African-American families throughout the country are waiting to adopt infants and that African-American families adopt at a rate of 4.5 times greater than European-American or Hispanic families, there seems to be a lack of commitment to connect infants with potentially available families and agencies. . . . Many traditional adoption agencies, which are staffed primarily by Caucasian administrators and workers and which place mostly infants for fees, find themselves in the positions where they have accepted custody of a minority child, even though they have no waiting families of the child's race or culture. Because the main funding source for services to the mother and baby is ultimately the paying adoptive parent, the agency places the child with a family that has already been screened and is willing to pay the fee.

Judith K. McKenzie, *The Future of Children*, Spring 1993.

The third type of adopter is the recruited, prepared special needs adoptive family, including single- and two-parent families. Today most of these families differ from foster parents only in that they are definite in wanting to make a long-term commitment to a child at the onset. Most of these families will continue to be lower-income families. Some will have had experience with fostering, perhaps with a different agency than the adoption agency. Many will have had prior experience with children with special needs. Regretfully, most state agencies are reporting a decline in the number of recruited families. Factors that may be influencing this decline are the economy, the aging of our population in general, the predominance of the two-career couple in our society, and the fact that most of the children who are waiting are children of color, while many families of color continue to distrust formalized adoption systems. In addition, agencies have few resources with which to recruit and develop new families, considering current caseload sizes. . . .

The fourth type of family is the infertile couple. Many of these couples are seeking to adopt a normal, healthy infant, but will "settle" for a preschooler or possibly drug-exposed infant. In these cases, it is essential that agencies prepare these couples by providing extensive training, including opportunities to meet with other families who have adopted children with special needs; giving full disclosure of information; including prognostic information; and offering early intervention services. These families may also need future access to adoption assistance for specialized services. . . .

There is a desperate shortage of homes for children with severe disabilities, older minority children, especially boys, and large sibling groups. A national study of adoption exchanges, which are centralized databases listing waiting children and waiting families and containing photolistings of the children, documents the problem that children who wait and the families who wait do not match up. Recruiting and, what is more important, developing families for these children who cannot be adopted by relatives or foster parents is becoming increasingly difficult and is an important challenge to be faced.

Nine Ways to Improve Services

Provide Postadoption Services. Once families adopt, they demand more accessible and more appropriate postadoption services. Many families are discouraged by the way they are treated after the adoption is finalized. Mental health services are often insensitive to adoption issues and to the problems a child brings as a result of having been abused or in foster care. Some families have been subjected to investigations by protective service officials, sometimes initiated by complaints from their child or the school. These families acknowledge difficulties in parenting their children, but when confronted by protective service workers, they are often treated as if they are not "real" parents. Families believe that there is too great a tendency for protective service workers to seek inappropriate and precipitous removal of these children from their now permanent homes. When adoptive families are offered intensive help, they are likely to be more responsive than other families. In an Oregon study of 1,752 families receiving family preservation services, 4.1% of families referred were adoptive families. At intake, the adopted children typically presented as more disturbed than other children in the study and the families were rated as more likely to require out-of-home placement than other families in the study. After being provided intensive services, these families were seen as more stable and no longer in need of placement services.

Offer Financial Assistance. Financial assistance is now and will continue to be critical. All states should provide adoption financial assistance at the same level as is paid a family for fostering a child. In almost all states, the level of financial assistance for adoption is significantly less than that provided for foster care. This serves as a considerable disincentive for foster parents to adopt a child, or children, in their care. Needs tests in determining the amount of assistance are not within the spirit of the law and should be eliminated. Adoption assistance should be made available to all children who are at risk of languishing in foster care, including infants of color and those who have been prenatally drug exposed. . . .

Include Foster Parents and Adoptive Parents in the Process. Foster and adoptive parents can assist professionals in many ways. They are, for example, very credible recruiters of other parents. They can be formally involved in recruiting families for specific children in their churches and communities. They might be involved in preparing recruitment materials such as photolistings for adoption exchanges. Also, foster parents can be taught to help children with preparation of "life books" and to be involved in other meaningful ways to help children make the transition to adoption in their home or to a new family.

Foster parent adoption should be seen as an excellent avenue toward permanency and should receive more emphasis and aggressive promotion. Where foster and adoptive parents have been trained together in programs emphasizing permanency planning, there have been significant increases in the rate of foster parent adoptions. Foster parents who are given therapeutic help in dealing with child problems are also more likely to adopt their children and grow in confidence and competence. Video training programs in permanency and parenting skills can be particularly useful for busy foster and adoptive parents to use at home. Foster parents might be educated to participate more directly in processing their own adoption paperwork and other procedures, thus reducing delays and work on the part of the social worker.

Accelerate the Processes of Family Preservation and Adoption Planning. There must be a strengthened commitment to family preservation on the part of public and private agencies and policymakers. However, when an infant comes into care because a family refuses or is unable to make use of family preservation services or because an infant has been abandoned, immediate preadoptive planning should begin, even as reunification efforts are intensified. Birthparents should be told initially that adoption

211

is a possible consequence of their child's placement, and birth-parents who wish to take part in adoption planning should be offered the opportunity to do so. This should include open adoption and the opportunity to help their child move to a new permanent family. Linking family preservation and adoption efforts will lead to more timely and effective outcomes for children, be they reunification, extended family placement, and/or adoption.

An infant's placement in foster care should offer the chance of permanency within a year. . . .

Eliminate Fees for Adoption of Children with Special Needs. The practice of charging adoptive parents fees to adopt children with special needs, including younger children and infants of color, should be stopped. Public funding is needed to assure equal access to timely adoption placement for these youngsters and quality services to their birthparents. Otherwise, too many of these children will continue to enter the foster care system and remain there for many months and sometimes years before they are placed for adoption. Also, stable funding arrangements are needed to facilitate the networking of more traditional infant adoption agencies and large public agencies who are likely to have children of color waiting for adoption with specialized minority agencies and programs that are likely to have families waiting to adopt.

Improve Data Collection About Children in Care. Who are the "children who wait"? We know more about those who are adopted than we do about those who never reach adoption. State agencies need timely and relevant data about the children in care. Most states need to revise data collection systems and make them usable for management planning. Once the problems are better understood in a state, creative action will be needed by child welfare leaders to improve conditions for all children in foster care. Unfortunately, the children who enter the adoption track may be the least well served children in the system if current trends continue. Thus, adoption must have a higher priority in the states.

Increase and Support More Community-Based, Minority-Operated Agencies. Collaborations between public and private agencies and communities, especially communities of color, are needed to increase the pool of families waiting to adopt and/or foster the increasing numbers of children of color who are coming into the system. More community-based, minority-operated agencies need to be adequately funded and licensed to do adoption work.

Increase Recruitment and Education of Culturally Competent Workers. Specialized recruitment agencies and/or efforts are not enough. Funding should be provided to recruit, educate, and place desperately needed minority social workers. Additionally, workers who understand, and who are representative of, various cultures need to be available to support prospective adoptive families throughout the process leading to the adoption.

Specialized training in the competencies needed by foster care and adoption supervisors and workers should have high priority in states. The Special Needs Adoption Curriculum developed by Spaulding for Children's National Resource Center for Special Needs Adoption has been distributed to all 50 states and is one readily available resource. Whatever training programs are chosen, they should be based in family preservation philosophy and include these competencies: cultural competence knowledge and skills; family and child assessment and preparation skills; crisis intervention skills; decision-making skills; collaborative, consultation skills; resource knowledge and ability to work within communities; and critical record-keeping skills.

Expedite the Goal of Permanency. Juvenile courts must be made more accountable for their inaction on the part of all too many cases. Joint planning between child welfare agencies and juvenile courts is essential in carrying out requirements of Public Law 96-272 and in solving recurring system problems. [In 1980, Public Law 96-272, the Adoption Assistance and Child Welfare Act, was passed. This Act amended Title IV of the Social Security Act, providing for the first time a formal federal role in monitoring the delivery as well as the financing of foster care services. Underlying Public Law 96-272 is the premise that children develop best in their own families and that most families can be preserved. State child welfare agencies are required to make "reasonable efforts" (a term undefined in the original statute) to prevent a child's placement and, if foster care becomes necessary, to make efforts to reunite the family in a timely manner. However, if these efforts fail, they are urged to seek permanency for the child through adoption. High-level citizen advisory boards might be established in some communities to oversee and expedite this process.]

A New Breed of Leaders

A new breed of leaders is needed in child welfare who will carry their mission and commitment to family preservation into their everyday work with birthfamilies, kinship families, foster families, and adoptive families. They will value diversity and work toward developing culturally competent organizations to better serve those families and children who most need them. Many of the new leaders should be persons of color.

"Rearing [traumatized] children requires a set of skills beyond those normally expected of parents."

Special Needs Adoptions Should Be Reevaluated

Katharine Davis Fishman

In the following viewpoint, Katharine Davis Fishman argues that traditional assumptions about adoption do not adequately prepare most adoptive parents for problems they may encounter when adopting "special needs" children. She warns that all involved in arranging for such adoptions need to reexamine their beliefs, attitudes, and resources in view of the physical, emotional, and psychological problems that often surface with hard-to-place candidates for adoption. Fishman is a journalist whose articles have appeared in numerous magazines, including *New York* and *Town & Country*.

As you read, consider the following questions:

1. According to Fishman, how do the realities of special needs adoptions differ from those of more traditional adoptions?
2. In the author's view, what is often the cause of the failure of adoptive families?
3. In Fishman's assessment, what can be done to help ease the problems faced by adoptive parents of special needs children?

Excerpted from "Problem Adoptions" by Katharine Davis Fishman, *The Atlantic Monthly*, September 1992, ©1992 Katharine Davis Fishman. Reprinted with permission.

Every year some sixty thousand children join unrelated adoptive families in the United States. Most of the time adoption is a joyous experience for child and family, but in a significant and growing number of cases it brings turmoil and grief. The story that follows shows a darker side that commands our attention, whether we are potential adoptive parents, policy-makers, or just citizens trying to make sense of the difficulties these families encounter.

Harold, a slender, angelic-looking twelve-year-old with straw-colored hair and blue eyes, has been with the Vogels since he was seven. (Names of this family and some identifying details of their story have been changed.) Eleven months before that Antonia Ferre—Mrs. Vogel—had seen Harold's picture in a "Sunday's Child" feature in *The Boston Globe*. . . .

Adopting Harold

Antonia, now thirty-five, is a pianist; Ted Vogel, five years older, is a computer consultant. When Antonia saw the article (which was upbeat but candid), she and Ted had been married for two years and had lived together for a year before that. They had planned to have one or two biological children and then adopt an older child. . . . Harold, Antonia read, was bright and engaging but had substantial emotional problems. "Still, there was something about the wording of the article and the look of the kid that reached me," she remembers. "I talked to Ted, and he said, 'This is us.'" So, although adopting their first child was a reversal of the Vogels' life plan, they called the Massachusetts Adoption Resource Exchange and soon were invited to a meeting of the sixty families who had expressed interest in Harold. "They were pretty upfront," Antonia says. "They described a lot of the antisocial behavior in his foster home, which ranged from violent tantrums to setting fires in the middle of the night. He got attention by breaking things, and eventually he would bang his head on the wall. Somebody would have to restrain him." Even so, Ted says, "We felt an attraction, a feeling that something larger than us was pulling us into it. The weird thing is that this kid, as much trouble as he is—and he is major trouble—if you could have invented a kid for us, Harold would be it . . . minus all his pathology." Antonia says, "The kid as he was born into the world was just the sort of child we would have designed.". . .

Harold, the Vogels learned, was the youngest of six handsome children born to a mother and father who were addicted to drugs and alcohol; all his brothers and sisters were highly intelligent despite severe emotional problems. The dissolute parents and their neglected kids were already familiar to the local police force and the Department of Social Services when Harold, at nine months, fell down a flight of stairs and dislocated his collarbone, causing the DSS, at last, to remove all the children and place them in different foster homes. By the time the Vogels agreed to adopt Harold, they knew he had been in a foster family for five years and in a residential treatment facility for more than one year, and had been diagnosed as mildly hyperactive. They had yet to discover that he had been physically abused. For fear of subjecting Harold to further rejection, the Protestant Social Service Bureau required the Vogels to commit to adoption before meeting him, which they did after deliberating for several weeks.

During the customary courtship period the Vogels drove up to Harold's treatment center on weekends and hung around the campus with him for progressively longer periods of time, took him to lunch at McDonald's, and then brought him home for day visits and eventually for overnight ones. During the week a social worker talked with Harold, to prepare him for family life. Ted says, "We were dating, falling in love, with all the negatives." Antonia says, "It became more and more difficult to bring him back. I was having a tough time, and sometimes Harold would maneuver us out of the car and lock himself into it so we couldn't leave."

Traditional Models and Assumptions

Neither Harold Vogel, nor his adoptive parents, nor the way they were united, nor the subsequent chain of harrowing events that brought the family to the Douglas A. Thom Clinic, in Boston, where I met them, fits the traditional model of adoption in the United States, in which an infertile couple provides the solution to a crisis pregnancy. That is the model most widely imagined by the general public, and it is arguably the one that still informs most governmental policy. But according to the latest data gathered by the National Committee for Adoption, infants made up less than half the domestic adoptions by unrelated people in 1986. (State by state the figures vary wildly: infants made up more than three quarters of these adoptions in Nebraska, South Carolina, Hawaii, and Utah, but less than a quarter in Maine, New Jersey, Indiana, Virginia, and New Mexico.)

Detailed, authoritative, comprehensive recent data on adoption is hard to come by, because no federal agency regularly collects it. But the figures that are available suggest that, more often than not, current adoptions are more complex than the traditional romanticized picture. More than a quarter of unrelated domestic adoptions involve children with "special needs"—that is, older children, minority children, children with mental, physical, or emotional handicaps, or siblings who should be adopted together. In the adoption world "special needs" means "hard to place." Elizabeth Cole, a senior fellow at the Child Welfare League of America and a widely respected consultant on adoption issues, explains, "A 'special-needs' child is one for whom finding a family is difficult. The margins of that definition have shifted enormously over the past ten years. Fifteen or twenty years ago a three-year-old was difficult to place. Today a youngster below age ten—unless another factor is present—would not be considered special needs." With respect to potential family problems, then, special needs are no more than the tip of the iceberg. And although a 1988 presidential task force estimated that thirty-six thousand children were waiting for adoption (of whom 60 percent were special needs), Cole herself would fix the current figure closer to a hundred thousand.

Broken Attachments Cause Continuing Problems

When infants and young children find themselves abandoned by the parent, they not only suffer separation distress and anxiety but also setbacks in the quality of their next attachments, which will be less trustful. Where continuity of such relationships is interrupted more than once, as happens due to multiple placements in the early years, the children's emotional attachments become increasingly shallow and indiscriminate. They tend to grow up as persons who lack warmth in their contacts with fellow beings. . . .

[When school-age children are] made to wander from one environment to another, they may cease to identify with any set of substitute parents. Resentment toward the adults who have disappointed them in the past makes them adopt the attitude of not caring for anybody; or of making the new parent the scapegoat for the shortcomings of the former one.

Joseph Goldstein, Albert J. Solnit, and Anna Freud, *Beyond the Best Interests of the Child*, 1973.

Figures on the number of adoptions that end in disruption (the child is returned to the adoption agency before the adoption is made final) or dissolution (the child is returned after the adoption is final) vary widely: in their book *Adoption and Disruption: Rates, Risks, and Responses*, Richard P. Barth and Marianne Berry, of the School of Social Welfare at the University of California at Berkeley, report that "somewhere between 4 and 40% of 'permanent' older child adoptions do not last." Barth and Berry also observe that "unofficial disruptions—in which the child's departure from home is not reported to the adoption agency—may be more common than formal disruptions, but they are not reflected in the statistics." It is even more troubling, however, that the stories like Harold's are those of families who soldiered on: their cases would therefore be recorded among an agency's successes.

One more figure is worth pondering: in 1986, according to the Department of Health and Human Services, more than a million children suffered from abuse or neglect, half of these from outright physical, sexual, or emotional abuse, and the other half from neglect of their basic needs. These were cases in which a state or local child-protection agency either substantiated maltreatment or had reasonable cause to believe the child had been maltreated. "Because of the increased detection of maltreatment by professionals," according to the National Committee for Adoption, "the number of children in substitute care may grow substantially in the near future. This will present an even greater challenge for public agencies, and could result in increases in the number of children in care waiting for adoptive homes."

In truth, adoption—whatever the age or circumstances of the child—is not a simple solution to any problem: it always carries its own complications. Senator Orrin Hatch, introducing a bill to offer a tax deduction for expenses incurred in adopting a child, said that legislators "must make sure our laws treat families formed through adoption the same as families formed biologically." We would serve adoptive families (and they would serve themselves) better, however, by recognizing that they are not the same as families formed biologically. When adoptive families come to grief, it is often from a disparity in expectations: either the parents expected something the child can't deliver, or the child delivers something the parents didn't expect. Much of the blame for this should be shifted to agencies, who ought to know better. . . .

Particularly when agencies may be reluctant to predict (and, to be fair, they are never entirely able to) how a given child will adjust to his adoptive family, prospective parents need to think carefully about what they can put up with. . . .

A New Point of View

One would have difficulty finding a clinician more knowledgeable about extreme situations than the Vogel family's therapist, Hugh M. Leichtman, the administrative director of Wediko Children's Services, a Boston-based mental-health agency serving seriously disturbed children, their families, and their schools. Wediko's operations include a residential treatment milieu (a community in which daily life is structured to be therapeutic), in the form of a summer program and winter boarding school in Windsor, New Hampshire; and a clinical consulting service that provides follow-up therapy to Wediko clients through the Boston public schools' special-education program. Wediko is affiliated with the Douglas A. Thom Clinic. Leichtman, forty-eight, an intense man with sharp eyes, boyish features, and receding silver hair, has been co-directing Wediko for twenty-two years. By the time families reach him, they are pretty much at the end of their rope.

Leichtman estimates that nearly 40 percent of his milieu clients are adopted or foster children. "Back in the late seventies we began to have a run of adopted children from Connecticut," he remembers.

> Somehow the Connecticut Open Door Society [a parents' support group] found out about Wediko, and these kids started to trickle north to us. What struck me about them as a group was how high-functioning the parents were and how extraordinarily disturbed the children were, and how the way we perceived the children varied remarkably from the clinical report—how the home therapist saw the children.

> Almost always the therapist's formulation was made in terms of the standard theory of the day—that these children's symptoms represented family conflict. They were playing out the struggle of the parents and allowed these family systems to stay together. One formulation was that because a child is adopted, the parent isn't giving the child enough, is communicating somehow that the child is second-class.

> Many of these families had biological children who were doing very well. But these adopted kids seemed to be blowing out left and right, causing havoc to the family, so much so that the other kids would start to become symptomatic. As we worked with the parents to get the adopted children's histories, we saw the way these terribly traumatic stories played out. We still didn't have an appreciation of how attention-deficit disorder or other constitutional factors could magnify the effects. But we began to understand the stress these children could bring to their families. It's important to see the direction of the effect: it's not the parents producing it.

> In the past ten years we have treated probably four hundred complex adoption cases, so we have a pretty sizable sample. You can point to your successes and your failures. We believe the only way you're going to save these kids is by preserving the adoptive families, and these families require extraordinary services: expert diagnosis, extensive treatment for the kids, and respite care. . . .

Harold's Therapy

Harold Vogel's behavior had been violent. Harold's residential school had trained the Vogels in the holding techniques used on disturbed children when they have long tantrums. "Even though I had seen other kids being held," Antonia says, "I wasn't prepared for the fury of that first tantrum. It was like two hours of fighting with a wild animal. There was this little seven-year-old, who must have weighed all of fifty pounds, and I just could not get him under control. I'd put my hands out and he'd try to butt me with his head. All the training went out the window. Finally it got to the point where he was sobbing, and his body would soften and get limp, and at this point you could snuggle up. He wasn't seven; he was two."

Over the next two years Harold's tantrums became so frequent that Antonia couldn't play the piano: her wrists were constantly damaged, and they never got to heal before the next episode. Harold was taken to a series of play therapists, whose offices he wrecked, with no positive effects. The therapists—who often said, "Harold, you must be very angry"—told the Vogels to develop Harold's self-esteem by giving him experiences that made him feel successful. "We followed their advice and things got worse and worse," Ted says. Antonia adds, "All this makes sense up to a point, but with his intelligence and the profoundness of his problems, he can keep avoiding the whole point of therapy. He'll just keep his secrets to himself and hang on to his disturbed behavior and wreck his own life—and yours while he's at it."

A Measure of Hope

Finally the Vogels' social worker heard a lecture of Leichtman's and sent the family to the Thom Clinic. "We sat down and Harold went right to the toys," Ted says. "He's a veteran. Hugh said, 'Harold, I need you to come over here,' and Harold continued to fool around. Hugh bounded over to Harold and grabbed his face and said, 'Harold, do I have to hold you and look in your eyes while we have this conversation?' and we looked at each other and said, 'This guy's got it.'"

Over several years Leichtman, through techniques ranging from gentle questioning to re-enactment to imagery induction—"I told him to use his eyelids as a movie screen where he could project the interior of his foster home, and he vividly described the layout and where the abuse occurred"—has elicited precise descriptions of physical abuse and hints of sexual abuse. "The question here is how do we put the feelings that come from these early traumatic events in the appropriate place?" Leichtman says. "How do we get these kids to tie the rage to its original source, instead of having it displaced like a shadow in the grass? With Harold we have three families. We're not even going to try to get to the biological mother. If we can just tie some of the anger to the foster family he was with for five years, instead of having it always fall on the Vogels . . ."

Since signing on with Leichtman, the Vogels have had periods of tranquillity lasting several months. Harold has been to Wediko twice, but only the second visit, a three-month stay in the winter program, helped. Other therapists' efforts were completely inef-fective; Leichtman's successes are of limited duration. A year ago Harold "broke the attachment" by riding off on his bicycle on a highway in a snowstorm with cars whizzing around him. Another time he needed two weeks in a mental hospital. When Harold makes progress, some credit goes to Prozac, the anti-depressant, which enables him to benefit from therapy. His own cognitive development has also helped his understanding. At twelve, Harold is moving away from tantrums and violence and is into stealing and firesetting; the prognosis is uncertain. Still, the Vogels feel that Leichtman is the first therapist to grasp the problem, and that he has saved their family. "Kids like Harold are very difficult for even the most skilled of parents to manage and control," Leichtman says. "These people have admittance to St. Peter's gates already, and Harold will test them further.". . . "Most parents don't understand about the length of this [testing], and they also don't understand that every time the child goes through a new developmental era, the testing usually has to re-cycle. Why? Because the trauma is still with the child. The child reformulates identity and coping capacities with each new devel-opmental era. You have this undigested part of your life—you were traumatized. The scarring, the disconnection that comes with trauma, gets recycled as the child moves through the vari-ous life passages.". . .

Adoption: One Intervention Among Many

Although a child's temperament and constitution affect the way trauma will be played out, Leichtman says, many parents who adopt traumatized children are essentially turning their homes into a therapeutic milieu. Rearing these children requires a set of skills beyond those normally expected of parents, and parents should not expect their affection to be returned in the normal way. The children's multiple problems require a compli-cated, long-term treatment plan; Harold, for example, has re-ceived medication, many years of individual outpatient psy-chotherapy, family-systems therapy, and residential treatment. The parents risk emotional and financial disaster: marriages sometimes break up, and in addition to paying for services not funded by insurance or the government, parents lose consider-able work time. Children whose parents are at work may need supervision to a fairly advanced age, and destructive children will incur expenses that are probably relatively minor but are surely demoralizing.

"There's still a lot of denial about the effects of early trauma, and consequently a lot of blaming the adoptive parents," says Lauren Frey, the post-adoptive-services coordinator at Project Impact, a special needs adoption agency in Boston. "We typically try to look at adoption as an exit service for kids. You get adopted, and 'See you later.' We don't want to pay for the ordeals after this, because we believe adoption is going to cure you. We need more of a view that adoption is one intervention in the life of a child, the first of many that will have to take place.". . .

Some Kids Are Too Damaged to Adopt

The most enlightened state adoptive-services policies at the moment are those of New Jersey. "I used to believe that every child is adoptable," says Rose Zeltser, the acting regional administrator for adoption field operations, who supervises the state's adoption program.

> I still think every child deserves the opportunity for adoption and should be assessed for whether they can live in a family. But some kids we've tried in families cannot deal with the intimacy and the divided loyalty, because they've been too damaged by their early experience. It's not fair to the adoptive family or the child to continue the process if the child cannot live in a family setting.
>
> Institutional care is not an answer for these kids either. They've got to go out in society. You have to teach them how to get control over the rage they feel, express it, get it out, so they don't need to turn it on every adult they come in contact with. For the past several years we've been developing group homes for children prior to placement, because they're so detached that they do not have the capacity to stay in families. These are little kids between the ages of five and twelve. They get intensive milieu therapy before we place them for adoption.
>
> Traditional therapists did not know how to deal with some of the adoption issues. They tended either to blame the child or blame the family. The whole theory of separation and attachment has to be understood, so when you see the behavior the child is exhibiting, you can help the parent back off from it and start asking, "Is this me or is this the birth mother?" So we realized if we were going to avoid disruption, we had to offer families support. . . .
>
> Today when we're placing a high-risk child, the family has to agree to get involved with the counseling service right away. We're saying that whenever any family adds a child you have a readjustment of the family dynamics, and the kids we are adding have a history. The occurrence of problems is normal. We tell the adoptive parents that we don't know about all the things that probably happened to the child: kids trying to survive in foster care learn to cover up. This child may come into your home and, once he trusts you, share a lot of information with you that may scare you. You need to know you have somebody to talk to. Then the family knows who to call when they see a problem, instead of waiting for a crisis.

The state also sends therapists out to adoptive homes for intensive crisis counseling. . . .

Speak Honestly About Adoption

Clearly too few people speak honestly about adoption in the United States, and wishful thinking in the adoption world has caused parents and children considerable grief. Perhaps adoption agencies and others who wish to promote the institution fear that parents who hear too many negatives will not adopt, and in some cases that will certainly be true. But several families I interviewed who had taken on very difficult children went on to adopt again (and the second child proved to have a sturdier temperament). "People who adopt special-needs children really are taking on a lifelong task that will require many more types of services than infant adoptions do," David Brodzinsky says. "Yet you'll hear time and time again that despite the complexity it's often a very rewarding experience. If they measure progress not in leaps and bounds but in small steps, they get tremendous satisfaction." [Brodzinsky, an associate professor of clinical and developmental psychology at Rutgers, has studied samples of adopted children in comparison with their non-adopted peers, has specialized in treating adopted children and their families in his private practice, and has written widely about adoption issues.] Some parents—generally those who seem to feel a calling—will not be deterred by a strong dose of truth, and the children will benefit from the more perceptive handling they'll receive. Other adults will go home childless, and that may be better for everybody.

Innumerable improvements in child-welfare, mental-health, and education policy should flow from an honest approach to adoption. For example, parents who take on special needs children should not have to fight schools, mental-health institutions, and social-welfare agencies for credibility, and government policy should seek to make their arduous job easier. Children who languish or shuttle back and forth in foster care develop layer upon layer of serious problems. Thus agencies and judges should be more efficient in deciding whether children's birth families are competent to rear them, and if they decide in favor of the birth family, services to shore that family up should be readily forthcoming, so that the child doesn't bounce right back into foster care. Furthermore, new techniques of psychotherapy for traumatized children need to be studied and appraised, to determine which ones work.

Infant adoption, which carries complexities of its own, should not be touted as the ideal solution to unwanted pregnancies (birth mothers grieve for their relinquished babies). Once children who cannot be reared by their biological parents are born, however, they will not go away, and the state will pay either for post-adoptive services now or for shelters and prisons later. As Goldstein, Solnit, and Freud wrote back in 1973, "Each time the cycle of grossly inadequate parent-child relationships is broken, society stands to gain a person capable of becoming an adequate parent for children of the future."

To assume that legions of saintly folks are waiting to adopt the growing number of difficult children who will need substitute care seems foolhardy. Moreover, some children turn out to be simply too badly damaged to adapt successfully to family life. No one would now suggest that old-style orphanages are conducive to restoring children's mental health, but a logical alternative might be small group homes in which a few children live with a couple of trained child-care workers who don't pretend to be Mommy and Daddy; thus the child needn't struggle with an intense relationship that may lead to intolerable loyalty conflicts. Another version of this arrangement is what Leichtman calls a friendship family: ten or twelve kids live in a permanent relationship with Mary and John, their adult friends. These alternatives need more thorough research. Not all children thrive in traditional nuclear families, and an honest view of adoption difficulties dictates that we now explore other options.

Periodical Bibliography

The following articles have been selected to supplement the diverse views presented in this chapter.

Elizabeth Bartholet	"Where Do Black Children Belong? The Politics of Race Matching in Adoption," *University of Pennsylvania Law Review*, May 1991.
Susan Brooks	"Rethinking Adoption: A Federal Solution to the Problem of Permanency Planning for Children with Special Needs," *New York University Law Review*, October 1991.
Molly Davis	"Transracial Adoption," *Crisis*, November/December 1992. Available from PO Box 1006, Notre Dame, IN 46556.
Thorwald Esbeusen	"Children Need Homes, Not Ethnic Politics," *Crisis*, November/December 1992.
Kim Forde-Mazrui	"Black Identity and Child Placement: The Best Interests of Black and Biracial Children," *Michigan Law Review*, February 1994.
Peter Hayes	"Are Transracial Adoptions Bad for Black Children?" *CQ Researcher*, November 26, 1993. Available from 1414 22nd St. NW, Washington, DC 20037.
Peter Hayes	"Transracial Adoption: Politics and Ideology," *Child Welfare*, May/June 1993.
Valerie Hermann	"Transracial Adoption: 'Child-saving' or 'Child-snatching'?" *National Black Law Journal*, Spring 1992.
Malcolm Hill and John Triseliotis	"Subsidized Adoption Across the Atlantic," *Child Welfare*, May/June 1991.
Carl Kallgren and Pamela Caudill	"Current Transracial Adoption Practices: Racial Dissonance or Racial Awareness?" *Psychological Reports*, April 1993.
Julie Lythcott-Haims	"Where Do Mixed Babies Belong? Racial Classification in America and Its Implications for Transracial Adoption," *Harvard Civil Rights–Civil Liberties Law Review*, Summer 1992.
Leora Neal and Al Stumph	"Transracial Adoption: If It Happens, How White Parents and the Black Community

Can Work Together," *Adoptalk*, Winter 1993. Available from the North American Council on Adoptable Children, 970 Raymond Ave., Suite 106, St. Paul, MN 55114-1149.

Bruce Porter — "I Met My Daughter at the Wuhan Foundling Hospital," *The New York Times Magazine*, April 11, 1993.

Mike Powers — "Finding Homes for Children with Special Needs," *Human Ecology Forum*, Winter 1994.

Joan Ramos — "The Tough Ethical Issues of International Adoption," *Ours*, January/February 1994. Available from Adoptive Families of America, 3333 Hwy. 100 No., Minneapolis, MN 55422.

Rita Simon and Alice Thompson — "Should White Families Be Allowed to Adopt African American Children?" *Health*, July/August 1993.

Jill Smolowe — "Babies for Export," *Time*, August 22, 1994.

Irene Thomas — "Yours, Mine, and Whose," *Hispanic*, December 1993. Available from 111 Massachusetts Ave. NW, Suite 200, Washington, DC 20001.

David Wheeler — "Black Children, White Parents: The Difficult Issue of Transracial Adoption," *The Chronicle of Higher Education*, September 15, 1993.

Monica Wightman — "Criteria for Placement Decisions with Cocaine-Exposed Infants," *Child Welfare*, November/December 1991.

Lena Williams — "Transracial Adoption: The Truth Comes in Shades of Gray," *The New York Times*, March 23, 1995.

Jean Young, Kelly Corcran-Rumppe, and Victor Groze — "Integrating Special-Needs Adoption with Residential Treatment," *Child Welfare*, November/December 1992.

Should Adoption Policies Be Changed?

Adoption

Chapter Preface

One of the most interesting places to obtain current information and concerns about adoption is on the Internet, especially in the newsgroup "alt.adoption." Notices, inquiries, and responses posted by participants in this newsgroup show how vitally important numerous adoption issues are to many people. On any given day, adoptees in search of birth parents post requests for help, couples seek information on how to adopt children, and birth parents share stories about their experiences. Often the discussion is heated, and the issues debated are significant. Whenever the national media cover a high-profile adoption story (like that of Baby Richard in late 1994), the newsgroup is flooded with messages as concerned people file their observations and post their viewpoints. All this activity indicates not only that many problems about adoption remain unsolved, but also that by thoughtful dialogue people continue to seek better answers to hard questions.

The viewpoints presented in this chapter provide basic background information and arguments helpful in understanding unresolved adoption issues. They provide a foundation for those who wish to enter current discussions on adoption policy, practice, and reform.

"Secrecy and anonymity [are] undesirable within the adoption system."

An Open Adoption Policy Is Best

Annette Baran and Reuben Pannor

Annette Baran and Reuben Pannor are clinical social workers in Los Angeles, California. With Arthur D. Sorosky, they are the authors of *The Adoption Triangle*, first published in 1978. Examining the complex relationships among birth parents, adoptees, and adoptive parents, that pioneering study advocated that laws be changed to permit adult adoptees access to their original birth records. In the following viewpoint, based on their observations over forty years of practice as psychotherapists and researchers, Baran and Pannor warn of the negative effects of and misconceptions about closed adoption and present a positive perspective of open adoption.

As you read, consider the following questions:

1. According to Baran and Pannor, how do closed adoption policies negatively affect birth parents, adoptees, and adoptive families?
2. What, in the authors' view, are the advantages of open adoption policies?
3. What responsibilities do the authors mention for each of the three parties in open adoptions?

Excerpted from "Perspectives on Open Adoption" by Annette Baran and Reuben Pannor, in the Spring 1993 issue of *The Future of Children*, a publication of the Center for the Future of Children, The David and Lucile Packard Foundation, ©1993. Reprinted courtesy of the publisher.

Statutory requirements that adoption be confidential and that the original birth certificate and adoption records be sealed [were first created in the early twentieth century]. The early laws, beginning with the Minnesota Act of 1917, were designed to shield adoption procedures from public scrutiny, so as to provide privacy for both the birthparents and the adoptive parents, and to remove the stigma of illegitimacy from the child. The intent of these original statutes was not to create anonymity between birthparents and adoptive parents or to keep secret from adopted children any information about their past. During the ensuing 30-year period, ideas about who should be protected and from whom changed. By the early 1950s virtually every state had amended its adoption statutes to create complete anonymity for the birthparents. Even in private adoptions where the law permitted the birthmother to choose the adoptive family, rarely did she meet the adoptive parents face to face or maintain any contact with her birthchild. In effect, both public and private systems for adoption were tightly closed. . . .

Our decades of experience in counseling individuals affected by adoption suggest that requiring anonymity between birthparents and adoptive parents and sealing all information about the birthparents from the adopted child has damaging effects on all three parties. These damaging effects are discussed below.

Effects of the Closed System

Relinquishment of a newborn child may be profoundly damaging to birthparents and cause lifelong pain and suffering. Even when relinquishment is a carefully considered and chosen option, birthmothers—and often birthfathers—may suffer from a heightened sense of worthlessness after giving away a child. They may feel guilty about their actions. These birthparents may believe that their offspring will not understand the reasons for relinquishment and that these offspring will blame and hate their birthparents for rejecting and abandoning them. The birthparents may want their children to know that they continue to care about them and, in turn, may wish to learn about the kind of people their children have become. No matter how many children they may have subsequently, birthparents may still desire knowledge and contact with the one they gave up.

In traditional closed adoptions, such knowledge and contact is not possible. Birthparents do not know who adopted their child, where he or she lives, or even whether the child is alive or dead. Even in so-called open placements where all parties know the identity of all other parties, birthparents often have no ongoing contact with the child. In these instances, birthparents may feel powerless. They have no knowledge of what is happening to their child and no opportunity to let the adoptive family

What Adoptive Parents Think of Open Records

Responses of 120 adoptive parents to a survey concerning access to records:

	Yes	No
Vital medical information should be available for adoptees and birthparents seeking the information.	100%	0%
All states should have a state reunion registry allowing information to pass if both adoptee and birthparents register.	97%	3%
A national registry should be established.	93%	7%
Adult adoptees should be able to receive any information that doesn't identify the birthparents.	92%	8%
Adoption agencies should have the legal right to help adoptees conduct searches.	83%	17%
Birthparents as well as adoptees should be allowed to conduct a search.	80%	20%
New laws concerning open records should be retroactive so that children adopted before the law goes into effect can access records.	75%	25%
The legal age for an adoptee to receive birth information should be at age 18.	74%	26%
Adult adoptees should be able to petition the state to conduct a search.	73%	27%
Prior to reaching 18, adoptees should be able to conduct a search with the consent of their adoptive parents.	68%	32%
Once adoptees become adults, they should be able to receive a certified copy of their original birth certificate unless the birthparents have filed a written objection.	68%	32%
Birthparents who request anonymity should have their wishes granted.	68%	32%
Once adoptees become adults, they should be able to receive a certified copy of their original birth certificate even though birthparents have filed a written objection.	33%	67%

Ours magazine, May/June 1993.

know of significant events in their own lives.

Adopted children also frequently suffer from the secrecy imposed in closed adoptions, particularly during adolescence when they often experience greater identity conflicts than members of the non-adopted population. The process of developing an individual identity is more complicated for adoptees because they live with the knowledge that an essential part of their personal history remains on the other side of the adoption barrier. In closed adoptions, any desire on the part of an adopted child to learn more about the birthparents is blocked, often leading to fantasies and distortions. Easily escalated, these may develop into more serious problems. In our studies, we described these adoption-related identity conflicts as resulting in "identity lacunae [gaps]," which can lead to feelings of shame, embarrassment, and low self-esteem. In addition, adoptees may experience a deep fear of loss and separation. Many adopted children feel that they were given away because there was something wrong with them from the beginning.

We observed that, in late adolescence, negative feelings and questions about being adopted increased. In young adulthood, plans for marriage may create an urgent desire for specific background information, particularly about family history. For adopted adult women, pregnancy and the birth of a child may raise fears of possible unknown hereditary problems. Becoming a parent may also trigger intense feelings in the adoptee toward his or her own birthmother. These feelings may include not only empathy for her difficult emotional situation, but also anger and disbelief that she could have given up her own child. The feelings frequently create a need in adoptees to search for birthparents and the hope for a reunion to bring together the broken connections from the past. Such a search, if undertaken, often is prolonged, painful, and fruitless.

Finally, closed adoption can also have negative psychological and emotional effects on the adoptive parents. With no knowledge of or contact with the birthparents, adoptive parents may find it difficult to think and talk about birthparents as real people. They may be unable to answer truthfully their adoptive children's inevitable questions about why they were given up, what their birthparents were like, and what happened to these parents in later life. The ghosts of the birthparents, inherent in the closed system, are ever present, and may lead to the fear that these parents will reclaim the child and that the child will love these parents more than the adoptive parents.

The Movement Toward Open Adoption

Having observed and documented these psychological and emotional effects during the 1970s, we became convinced that secrecy and anonymity were undesirable within the adoption system and recommended reform through opening of sealed records for adult adoptees. We also sought ways of possibly preventing some of the psychological problems we had observed. This led us, in 1975, to advocate open adoption placement of infants and children, an idea regarded by many as new and radical. In fact, open adoption had existed throughout history. Closed adoption was begun in this country, in this century, and soon became the standard of adoption practice. While originally we recommended open adoption only as an option to be carefully chosen in special cases, in 1984 we recommended that open adoption become standard practice.

In the discussion that follows, we present our definition of open adoption, address some of the major objections to it, indicate the potential benefits of open adoptive placements, and finally propose what we consider to be appropriate long-term responsibilities of birthparents, adoptive parents, and adoptees.

Open Adoption: A Definition

An open adoption is one in which the birthparent(s) at least meet the adoptive parents and may even participate in selecting them. In contrast to closed adoption, open adoption includes the exchange of identifying information and the making of agreements regarding future contact and communication. The frequency and extent of this contact and communication will vary and may need to be renegotiated at different times in the lives of the individuals involved, depending upon their needs and desires and the quality of the relationship that evolves. At present, after the adoption is finalized, the adoptive family is recognized as having the final authority to determine the nature and extent of ongoing contact.

Misconceptions About Open Adoption

As open adoption became more common in the 1970s and 1980s, several popular misconceptions were challenged. They deserve further scrutiny.

• *Couples will not adopt children unless they can be guaranteed anonymity and secrecy.* Such guarantees, we now know, were never ironclad. The adoptees' reform movement spawned a nationwide network of search groups that often successfully located birthparents and nullified guarantees of secrecy and anonymity given by adoption agencies to these parents. Furthermore, experience in adoption during the past decade, when fewer newborns were available, has clearly demonstrated that couples, eager to parent children, are willing to adopt under a variety of circumstances. Although once only healthy babies were considered adoptable, now children with disabilities, from mixed racial backgrounds, and in sibling groups are being welcomed by families. It was our belief that couples would accept open placement if adoption agencies made it standard practice. At present open adoption is accepted by many adoptive parents, and this practice appears to be increasing, particularly in independent adoptions.

• *Birthmothers want and need anonymity to move forward in their lives and put the experience of pregnancy and relinquishment behind them.* This misconception was fostered by maternity homes and adoption agencies. It was sustained, in part, because some adoption social workers found it difficult to deal with the continuing pathos and misery of the birthmothers in the post-relinquishment period. Our studies of birthmothers in the 1970s indicated that, when they contacted agencies regarding their relinquished children, they often were made to feel emotionally unstable and at fault for carrying this experience with them. Apparently few caseworkers took the time or made an effort to question birthmothers about their inner feelings, although many birthmothers were eager to be interviewed and to have their feelings heard. These observations were contrary to the belief that birthmothers had emotionally resolved giving up a child, recovered from the trauma, and wished to remain hidden. These birthmothers had not been advised or counseled about the possibility that they might have lifelong anxiety and distress. Even those birthmothers who had not revealed their past to husband and children indicated that, if it were possible to protect themselves, they would want to know and meet their offspring. Not to know whether their children were alive or dead was a continuing source of sadness for some.

• *Adoptees will be confused by contact with their birthparents and may become emotionally disturbed as a result of being aware of and dealing with two mothers during their developmental years.* Our experience has led us to conclude that closed adoptions did not protect adoptees from emotional disturbances. On the contrary, it is our belief, based on years of work with adoptees of all ages, that some of them are particularly vulnerable because of feelings of loss and abandonment, exacerbated by the secrecy and anonymity of closed adoptions. However, because open adoption placement is still comparatively new, we cannot state conclusively what effects it has on adoptees. Long-term studies on the adjustment of adoptees to open adoption are few in number and vary in quality. At present it must be stated that the results are inconclusive, and it is evident that much additional research on this important aspect of open adoption remains to be done. Marianne Berry states, however, that "professionals generally agree that the child is least confused about loyalties to either parent when the open relationship between the adoptive and biological parents is clear and positive."

The Benefits of Open Adoptive Placements

There are several important benefits to open adoptive placements. First, the birthparents assume more responsibility for the decision to relinquish, and as full participants in the placement and entrusting of the child to a known family, they are better able to cope with feelings of loss, mourning, and grief. If contact with their birthchild is permitted, they are able to further ameliorate these feelings.

Next, adoptees' feelings of rejection by the birthparents also can be greatly diminished. A realistic understanding of the problems that led to adoptive placement permits acceptance of the situation. The continuing link with the birthparent dispels the notion that the children were abandoned and forgotten. In open adoption the need for search and reunion is eliminated. Important background information—including genetic and medical histories—is readily available.

Finally, for adoptive parents, knowing the birthparents of their children can prevent the fears and fantasies that might otherwise have a negative effect on their relationships with their adopted children. Knowing the birthparents will enable adoptive parents to provide their children with background information based on first-hand knowledge and direct contacts.

Responsibilities of Birthparents

Relinquishment should not end the role of a birthparent. Birthmothers are responsible not only for providing careful and continuous nurturing before birth, but also for supplying ongoing emotional support to the adoptee following relinquishment. We know, from years of experience in counseling and psychotherapy of adoptees, that feelings of initial rejection and abandonment may cause emotional and psychological problems. Being told by an adoptive parent that one was given up out of love may be a poor palliative for children who feel that anyone who loved them would not have deserted them. Birthparents have a responsibility to let the children they relinquished know that they continue to care about them and are concerned about their well-being.

Birthparents can show this support for a child in many ways. A card, gift, letter, telephone call, or photograph each year on the child's birthday can demonstrate that the child's special day is important to the birthparent. Remembrances of this kind indicate that the child is not ignored, forgotten, or unloved.

Birthparents may feel that continued contact with their child and the adoptive family is painful and brings back difficult memories; however, birthparents need to understand how important they are to the well-being of their child. Other responsibilities and obligations include providing ongoing medical and social information and being available to both child and adoptive parents as needed.

Responsibilities of Adoptive Parents

Adoptive parents share in this obligation to help in the adjustment of the adoptee. Acknowledging that adoption is different from having a child born into the family is an important step toward being successful parents. Adoptive parents must accept the dual identity in their adopted child's life and recognize the continuing importance of the birthparents' contribution to their child's self-concept. Adoptive parents must realize that, no matter how compelling and understandable the facts surrounding the adoption are, the adoptive child may still feel rejected and unworthy. Adoptive parents must work in partnership with birthparents to provide the child with a healthy identity and self-image. To achieve this goal, the birthparents and adoptive parents must each respect the other's role in the child's life and feel comfortable with and trusting of one another. Prospective parents should not adopt unless they feel able to deal with all of the complexities inherent in this kind of parenting. Finally, adoptive parents have a continuing responsibility to share vital information about the child, such as descriptions of serious medical problems and news about a death in the family, with birthparents. Adoptive parents also should help maintain contact between the adopted child and siblings and other significant relatives.

Rights and Responsibilities of Adoptees

In some ways, adoptees are the victims in the adoption triangle. Others made decisions for and about them. They had no role in being conceived, born, relinquished, and placed for adoption. However, as they move out of their childhood into maturity, they should assert certain rights and assume certain responsibilities. Adoptees who are growing up with knowledge of two sets of parents should be encouraged to gain knowledge about adoption and to explore ways of understanding their dual identity and its impact on them. Adoption is one aspect of their being which needs to be woven into the fabric of their lives.

The Best Approach

In conclusion, our decades of experience lead us to believe that open adoption is the best approach. It minimizes emotional and psychological harm, and it allows all parties to meet their continuing responsibilities to each other.

There is, however, more to be done. More research on the effects of open adoption is needed. Also, we must be vigilant to potential abuses. Scanning want-ad columns in newspapers across the country or the Yellow Pages of phone books in any of the major cities reveals the extent to which adoption has become a business and the degree to which open adoption can be used to expand that business. Under the heading Adoption Services appear such statements as "You can choose your child's parents." The possibility of open adoption is frequently used to encourage relinquishment, particularly with young teenagers who are led to believe that they will have all the benefits of knowing their babies with none of the risks or responsibilities. Deceit of this kind unfairly encourages relinquishment and offers promises that often are not kept after the adoption occurs.

Thus, the central question today is not whether adoption shall be open or closed. Adoptive placements of older children are generally recognized as being open, and most infant adoptions now begin as open. Independent adoptions are predominantly open, and many agencies offer open adoption as an option. Rather, the challenge, in our view, is to ensure that open adoption continues to evolve in the best way possible. Every effort must be made to prevent abuse. The respective roles of birthparents, adoptive parents, and extended family in promoting the success of open adoption deserve careful consideration. However, in the final analysis, it is the adoptee whose well-being is central. Carefully designed, long-term studies are needed to investigate the impact of open adoption on adoptees more thoroughly and to generate recommendations for change and improvement.

"Open adoption can harm the very people it purports to help."

A Sealed Adoption Policy Is Best

A. Dean Byrd

A. Dean Byrd is the director of evaluation and training at Latter Day Saints Social Services in Salt Lake City, Utah. In the following viewpoint, Byrd argues that for all concerned—birth parents, adoptees, and adoptive parents—the claims made by open-adoption advocates are unsubstantiated. Indeed, he maintains, open adoption can harm all members of the adoption triangle.

As you read, consider the following questions:

1. According to Byrd, what difficulties may birth parents and adoptive parents encounter in an open adoption?
2. How does the author refute the arguments of those who believe that open adoptions promote the psychological and moral development of adoptees?
3. How, in Byrd's estimate, does open adoption resemble the care of children by foster parents?

A. Dean Byrd, "The Case for Confidential Adoption," *Public Welfare*, Fall 1988. Copyright ©1988 A. Dean Byrd. Reprinted by permission.

To its advocates, open adoption seems to be a panacea: a wonderful, modern approach that strips away secrecy, insecurity, and doubt and allows members of the adoption triangle to deal with one another's needs frankly and honestly. For these advocates, the readily apparent rightness of their cause has already assured its eventual universal acceptance. To quote one forum [the 1988 National Convention to Attend Exclusively to Open Adoption], "Open adoption is no longer an experiment. It has come of age. Given its growth, general acceptance, and potential, open adoption may well represent the future for adoption practice."

I have a problem with all this, however. This alleged acceptance of open adoption seems to me unsupported by anything other than the sparsest anecdotal data—data with virtually no sound theoretical rationale or scientific research to back it up. Indeed, I believe that open adoption can harm the very people it purports to help, especially in the case of adopted children. In this viewpoint I will focus on some of my concerns, in the hope that increased awareness will slow the movement toward open adoption.

Defining the Terms

Before going any further, I should pin down exactly what it is I am talking about. This may seem unnecessary, but terms like "openness" and questions like "Can open adoption be confidential?" are amorphous enough that an exact definition of terms will probably be useful. Social work educators Reuben Pannor and Annette Baran define open adoption as "a process in which the birth parents and the adoptive parents meet and exchange identifying information. The birth parents relinquish legal and basic childrearing rights to the adoptive parents. Both sets of parents retain the right to continuing contact and access to knowledge on behalf of the child."

With this definition in mind, I will discuss the psychological implications of open infant adoption, particularly in regard to the adopted child. After briefly examining the potential psychological impact on birth parents—with an emphasis on birth mothers—and on adoptive parents, I will explore the probable psychological impact on adopted children, based on empirical research from the field of developmental psychology.

How Open Adoption May Affect Birth Parents

It seems apparent that open adoption practice primarily "benefits" the birth parents. Proponents suggest that the postplacement grieving process of the birth mother is made easier in open adoption because firsthand knowledge of the child's well-being is readily available. I think another outcome is equally

239

plausible: that the increased knowledge and contact available through open adoption may encourage birth parents to avoid experiencing the loss, to postpone or prolong the separation and grieving process. Ongoing contact may serve as a continuous reminder of the loss, or as a stimulus for the fantasy that relinquishing a child is not really a loss at all.

The Openness in Adoption Continuum

Traditional, confidential adoption ("closed adoption")   Experimental adoption ("open adoption")

A	B	C	D	E	F	G

A = Complete anonymity between birth and adoptive parents.

B = Knowledge of social and demographic circumstances but no knowledge of identities.

C = Birth parent involvement in selecting the types of acceptable adoptive parents.

D = Exchange of letters and photographs, sometimes using first names only, mediated by the adoption agency.

E = One-time meeting, sometimes on a first-name basis only, without identities known.

F = Knowledge of identities but no contact between birth and adoptive parents.

G = Ongoing contact between adoptive and birth parents.

A–C
Known to work well.

F–G
Risks and benefits to birth parents, adoptive parents, and adoptees unknown.

Source: National Committee for Adoption, *Adoption Factbook*, 1989.

As [A.C. Kraft and others have] noted, "In open adoption . . . the issues revolve around the fact that it is expected that contact will exist, that letters will be exchanged, etc. To this extent, the adoption cannot be really experienced as a loss. It is a bittersweet event in which something is given in exchange for hoped-for relief." [These researchers] conclude: "Mourning for the loss is circumvented because adoption is not viewed as a loss, in spite of the fact that in reality the child has been given up. . . . In a confidential adoption, the loss experienced can be mourned by the birth mother." In other words, open adoption for the birth mother may well take on the characteristics of foster care, an ongoing arrangement around which she may build her life emotionally to the detriment of her own personal progress.

An interesting complement to the information regarding emotional development is associated with cognitive or intellectual development. According to extensive data compiled by Swiss researcher Jean Piaget, adolescents are just beginning to function at the formal level of intellectual development. Many people do not fully develop characteristics such as an ability to relate future consequences to present decisions or to deal with abstract concepts until as late as age 25. These poorly established formal operational stage activities, coupled with the emotional crisis associated with pregnancy, may make it impossible for adolescent birth mothers to make informed decisions about open adoption. In essence, the birth mother is confronted with a situation that is emotionally, cognitively, and practically beyond her coping capabilities.

Adoption decisions are extremely difficult to make. But once the decision to place is reached, dealing with the loss must be an important focus of the counseling process. If this loss is not treated appropriately, the birth mother may not only have psychological problems regarding the resolution of her pregnancy, but also be hindered in her movement to the next developmental stage. The prominent theories of adolescent development suggest that open adoption poses a serious threat to the psychological health of the birth mother. Research questions need to be seriously addressed prior to considering open adoption as an acceptable practice.

I have deliberately avoided discussing the effects of open adoption on birth fathers because they are often uninvolved in adoption decisions. I believe, however, that the factors that pose potential problems for birth mothers would pose similar problems for birth fathers under similar circumstances.

Possible Effects on Adoptive Parents

The area that seems to have the greatest psychological impact on adoptive parents in an open adoption is bonding. Once the adoptive parents fulfill the child's psychological need for parents, the bonding process begins. The adoptive mother, in particular, becomes the nurturing caretaker who must remain readily available throughout the child's developmental years. A child's failure to bond properly can lead to an inability to develop and maintain social relationships, as well as possible psychopathology.

Open adoption has great potential for interfering with the bonding process. Adoptive parents are continually reminded that the child is not really theirs. Do they dare bond with a

241

child who is not really theirs? As [A.C. Kraft and others] conclude: "Whether the contact included meetings, videotapes, letters, pictures, gifts, or progress reports, the adoptive parent's sense of security may be threatened. . . . Contact with the child's parents is viewed as an impediment to the needed bonding process." Contact with the birth parents, as it serves to remind the adoptive parents that they are not the biological parents, may not only reemphasize biological infertility, but lead to feelings of psychological infertility as well. They are not allowed to really psychologically parent the child. Open adoptions certainly do not promote the bonding process between the adoptive parents and the child.

Proponents of open adoption suggest that the need for current medical and genetic information is a valuable reason for adoptive parents to support open adoption. I concur that such a need exists, but it hardly seems to me that open adoption represents the only way these data can be made available.

Open Adoption and the Adopted Child

I feel the welfare of the adopted child must be primary. Proponents of open adoption state that, in a confidential adoption, the child will suffer from an incomplete identity and not be able to develop properly. One would assume from such statements that confidential adoptions would inevitably lead to pathology for the child. Available research does not support this contention, however. In 1985, a study by K.S. Marquis and R.A. Detweiler found that "adopted persons were significantly more confident and viewed others more positively than their nonadoptive peers." Another study concluded that adolescent adoptees were as healthy as those who were not adopted. Finally, the largest and most credible study to date [P.M. Brenich and E. Brenich, 1982] on clinic patients found that adoptees were not overrepresented among populations under psychiatric care. To put it simply, there is little evidence to indicate that confidential adoption leads to child pathology.

There are elements of open adoption, however, that I feel clearly hinder a child's development. And while there is little comparative research examining this area, much of the work done in the field of developmental psychology is applicable. Confidential adoptions provide opportunities for adoptive parents to nurture children as their own and in turn allow those children to internalize a single set of parental values. Open adoption allows the involvement of birth parents who may offer a differing set of values.

It seems apparent that the involvement of the birth parents will influence adoptive parents' relationship with their child. The effect this influence will have on the child depends on the

242

nature of the birth parents' involvement and on the cognitive development of the child. Piaget has theorized that children in the early stages of cognitive development process information only through emotional and sensory motor activities. In other words, their development at this stage is largely shaped by what they feel, see, and touch. A sense of being different can come only from the perception that they are being treated differently by their caretakers. Ambivalence or reservations at this stage on the part of the adoptive parents would likely be felt and could lead to serious future problems for the child.

Unconditional acceptance, emotional constancy, and nurturing are vital if the child is to develop processes of attachment, separation, and individuation, as well as a sense of identity. Adoptive parents should be encouraged to maximize their attraction to the child without reservation. Any sense of permanent indebtedness to the caseworker, agency, or birth parents should be discouraged. Open adoption advocates either require or encourage levels of contact. This contact can seriously interfere with child-parent relationships. Adoptive parents need to be supported in a comfortable pattern of relating to the child with as little interference as possible. Anxiety or guilt about contact can disrupt their relationship with the adopted child.

Adjusting to Adoption

How successfully children adjust to adoption is a function of their cognitive development. One study has noted the difficulties when a child is presented with adoptive information prior to the resolution of the Oedipus complex, which usually occurs between ages 3 and 6. Children at this age are unable to understand and process adoption information; and data suggest that this information may have traumatic effects, including anxiety, confusion, and regression. Preschool children are simply not equipped psychologically to deal with information regarding open adoption. The developmental sequence is negatively influenced from its outset. This may be particularly noted during adolescence, which is often characterized by anxiety and confusion under the best of circumstances. When adolescents go through a turbulent period, conflicts are reflected in their relationships with their parents. Sex role conflicts may become more pronounced. In open adoption, adolescent adoptees are likely to vacillate between sets of parents—moving helplessly through a cycle of unresolved conflicts.

I found no research on how adoption affects moral development. According to theorist Lawrence Kohlberg, value systems and a sense of right and wrong follow a developmental sequence similar to Piaget's theory of cognitive development. The moral development of children emerges from parent-child relationships. When a child is presented with differing value systems, the consequences may include a rejection of both. Difficulties in moral development are directly linked to psychopathology. Sociologist C.V. Brittain concluded that, while peer influence dominated during adolescence regarding such matters as friends, fashion, and fads, the parental value system dominated moral and social issues. In an open adoption, the child may reject one or both parental systems. Depression has been related to loss: the rejection of both value systems is comparable in some ways to the loss of both sets of parents.

Examples of Problems with Open Adoption

It appears that open adoption of newborn children greatly resembles foster care. The adoptive parent is prevented from becoming a complete psychological parent, with the child paying the ultimate price. Developmental issues are difficult to resolve, complicating transitions from stage to stage. Moral development, in the context of open adoption, offers the greatest source of potential psychopathology.

Testimonials are often offered as proof of the advantages of open adoption. Perhaps sketches from some less successful open adoptions will stimulate thought, reasoning, and research. In a case in Canada, an open adoption became unusually open. The birth mother moved in with the adoptive family. Shortly thereafter, the adoptive mother moved out. The adoptive parents' marriage ended in divorce, while the birth mother remained with the adoptive father and child. In another case, a child gained a third father. Besides the adoptive father and the birth father, the birth mother remarried. When the birth father marries again, the child will have a third mother. In another instance, two children were placed in an open adoption. The birth mother of the first child made frequent contacts; the birth mother of the second child, few contacts. The second child suffered from rejection and other psychological problems.

With one child for whom I provided care, the birth mother contacts increased around the beginning of adolescence. Value system conflicts resulted in the adolescent going from one parent to the other. Conflicts were not resolved. The child ended up anxious, depressed, and uncertain about herself. In a traumatic session, she blurted out, "I want to be like my adoptive mother, but my birth mother says I'm like her. I don't know what to do or who I am. My whole life is messed up. It's not my fault. It can't be fixed. My birth mother talks about lawsuits when things go wrong. Isn't there someone that I can sue?" I wonder if caseworkers and agencies can be sued for what appears to be emotional child abuse.

Child development literature raises some serious questions

about the wisdom of open adoption. The potential for negative impact throughout the developmental process appears great. For children, relating to one set of parents is difficult enough. Expecting them to do more than that appears to exact an emotional and psychological toll. Pannor compares open adoption to a custody agreement. I would not rate it so highly.

"For the most part, adoptive families are strong, and their teenagers are quite well-adjusted."

Myths About Adoption Should Be Dispelled

Peter L. Benson and Anu Sharma

Peter L. Benson is president of Search Institute, a national non-profit organization dedicated to practical research benefiting children and youth. Anu Sharma is a research scientist for the institute. In the following viewpoint, Benson and Sharma attack what they characterize as myths and stereotypes about problems with adoption that are promoted by the media. Summarizing findings of a study funded by the National Institute of Mental Health, they argue that these findings dispute much conventional wisdom about adoption; in fact, they assert, adoptive teens do as well as or better than their nonadopted peers.

As you read, consider the following questions:

1. According to Benson and Sharma, what indicators suggest that, on the whole, adoptive teenagers are doing well?
2. As reported by the Search Institute's study, how do adopted teenagers generally work out identity problems?
3. In the authors' view, what comfort and challenges does this study present to those who wish to help adopted teenagers?

Peter L. Benson and Anu Sharma, "The Truth About Adopted Teenagers," *Adoptive Families*, July/August 1994. Reprinted with permission of *Adoptive Families*, © 1994 Adoptive Families of America, 3333 Hwy. 100 North, Minneapolis, MN 55422.

If you see adoption in the news and prime-time television, you likely see it fraught with conflict, danger, and drama. If the story focuses on adopted teenagers, the image can be even more worrisome.

But the largest study ever conducted of adopted teenagers and their families puts many of those fears to rest. Like any population of youth, there are adopted teenagers who have problems. But, for the most part, adoptive families are strong, and their teenagers are quite well-adjusted.

Conducted by Search Institute, a Minneapolis-based research organization, the study was supported by a major grant from the National Institute of Mental Health. It examined in detail the dynamics of family life for more than 700 families who have teenagers who were adopted as infants. [The sample included 1,262 adoptive parents, 881 adopted youth, and 78 non-adopted siblings who were born to the adoptive parents.] The families adopted their children through agencies in four states (Colorado, Illinois, Minnesota, and Wisconsin), but now live throughout the United States.

Because of its breadth and scope, the study begins to answer many key questions about adoption that arise during the teenage years—a time in life filled with more changes than any other time besides infancy.

How Well Are Adopted Teens Doing?

One of the major worries and debates about adopted teenagers involves whether they have trouble growing up healthy and successful because of factors related to their adoption. In the past, researchers have noted that adopted teenagers are disproportionally represented in counseling and treatment, and earlier Search Institute research on public school students found that they are slightly more involved in a variety of at-risk behaviors than non-adopted teens.

This new study found that, on the average, adopted teens seem to be doing well. Half of adopted youth say they are as happy as their peers, and 38 percent say they are happier. The study examines numerous measures of well-being, and it finds many indicators of strength and support for adopted teenagers:

- They benefit from lots of support from family, friends, and others.
- They are involved in many positive, structured youth activities, such as sports, music, congregational youth programs, and community organizations.
- They see themselves as being as strong as their peers in personal identity and self-esteem.
- They show high levels of caring values and behaviors, such as volunteering.

247

There are, however, areas of concern. One involves school. Adopted teens are less likely than their non-adopted siblings (those born to the adoptive parents) to report doing above average in school (50 percent vs. 74 percent), and just 20 percent of adopted youth say they get mostly A's, compared to 45 percent of non-adopted siblings. At the same time, however, they are as likely as their siblings to report liking school and trying as hard as they can.

What Happens During Adolescence?

All teenagers deal with identity issues during adolescence. They experiment with clothes, hair styles, music, and dozens of other choices as they ask: Who am I? What am I becoming? How am I different from others? How am I the same as—and connected to—others? Issues of race, ethnicity, and heritage burst to the forefront as teens seek to sort out the pieces. It's little wonder, then, that questions about adoption are raised during these years.

Our study confirms that these issues become more complex during adolescence, but adoption does not seem to make the search for identity more difficult. Adopted teenagers have as clear a sense of purpose, belonging, and self-esteem as their non-adopted siblings. For example, 79 percent of adopted teens say they have "a good sense of who I am," compared to 77 percent of non-adopted siblings. Similarly, 86 percent of adopted teens say, "All in all, I am glad I am me."

For these teens, adoption is not a major identity problem. Seven questions asked about general feelings about adoption. On average, 69 percent of adopted teens have a positive perspective on adoption based on these questions. More specifically, 73 percent say they feel good that they were adopted, and 84 percent say they are glad their parents adopted them. Only 10 percent believe their parents would love them more if they were born to their adoptive parents, and only 7 percent say being adopted makes them angry.

As we would expect, older youth (ages 16–18) think about adoption issues more than younger youth (ages 12–15). Only 25 percent of adopted teens said they often thought about adoption when they were in grades three to five. For grades six to eight, the percentage rises to 35 percent. Among ninth- to twelfth-grade youth, 41 percent say they often think about adoption.

In addition to the age differences, we also see differences between boys and girls, with girls tending to think more about adoption issues. For example, while 76 percent of adopted boys say "being adopted has always been easy for me," only 63 percent of adopted girls agree with the statement. Similarly, 54 percent of girls in grades nine to twelve say they think often about adoption, compared to only 25 percent of boys.

Adopted girls are particularly interested in getting more information about adoption. Seventy-two percent of girls wish their parents would tell them more about their adoption, compared to 17 percent of boys. Similarly, girls are more interested in learning more about and meeting their birthparents.

Adoptive Family Life

Among adopted teens . . .

83% say their parents often tell them they love them.

80% agree that each family member has at least some say in major family decisions.

75% say they get along with their parents.

74% say they really get along well in their families.

72% agree that their families have "all the qualities I've always wanted in a family."

Adoptive Families, July/August 1994.

These differences make sense developmentally. When confronted with a problem or crisis, girls are much more likely to internalize the issue, to think and reflect. Boys are more likely to "act out" physically. Thus adopted boys are more likely than adopted girls to exhibit risky behaviors such as aggression or substance abuse.

How Strong Is the Parent-Teen Bond?

The importance of attachment—the mutual bond between parent and child—is well-known in adoption. Adoptive parents take special care when a child comes home to build a strong relationship, and many experts point to a lack of attachment as a potential problem for children who are adopted at older ages.

For some parents, however, all the work of attachment that took place during childhood may appear to come unraveled during adolescence. Suddenly the teenager wants distance—to be left alone. The question becomes, does adoption make the attachment weaker so that it breaks at the first sign of conflict? Or is this apparent distance just part of growing up as teenagers search for their own identity and independence?

On the whole, our data show no consistent problems with attachment among adopted teenagers. In fact, they like spending time with their parents (79 percent like to spend time with their mothers, and 78 percent like to spend time with their fathers), and they typically say there are a lot of things they admire about their parents.

In comparing adopted teens with their non-adopted siblings, we find few major differences in levels of attachment. In fact, adopted youth are about as likely as non-adopted youth to say they have similar values, personalities, and interests as their mother and father. The only major area where they see differences involves physical appearance. In all, just 24 percent of adopted teens say they look like their adoptive mother, and 26 percent say they look like their adoptive father.

At the same time, we do find some interesting differences between perceptions of closeness to mothers and fathers. On average, adopted teens are less likely than their non-adopted siblings to report that they "feel close to their mother" (69 percent vs. 79 percent) and to their father (63 percent vs. 73 percent). While these differences are slight, they suggest that something may be occurring that creates emotional distance for adopted youth.

How Much Do Families Talk About Adoption?

Most adopted teens can't remember a time when they didn't know they were adopted. About 68 percent say they first learned they were adopted before age 3, or they can't remember when they learned. Another 27 percent knew by the time they were 7. Nowhere in our study do we see evidence that typical adoptive families intentionally hide information about adoption.

At the same time, there's little evidence that adoption is a regular topic of conversation in adoptive families. Almost two-thirds of adopted youth say they have had no meaningful conversations with their father about adoption in the past year. Forty percent say the same about these conversations with their mother.

One reason adoption may not be a major issue in most families is that it is not used as a weapon against teenagers. Only 2 percent of adopted youth say their parents try to explain away problem behaviors by saying that the problem is because of adoption. And only 5 percent say their parents often do things that remind them that they were adopted. In general, young people feel that their parents know and accept their differences (63 percent for mothers; 61 percent for fathers), yet their parents don't insist on pointing out those differences.

When teens do talk about adoption, both girls and boys are most likely to talk to their mothers, not their fathers. Two-thirds (65 percent) of teens say they are comfortable talking with their mother about adoption. Yet only 47 percent are comfortable

250

talking with their father about it. However, many adopted teens, particularly girls, want to talk more with their parents about the subject. In all, 52 percent of girls wish their parents would tell them more about their adoption, compared to 38 percent of boys.

Part of the difference between boys and girls may come from parents' encouragement. Overall, only 29 percent of adopted teens say their mothers encourage them to talk about adoption, and only 19 percent say their fathers do. However, girls are more likely to say that both parents encourage them to talk about adoption. While 35 percent of girls say their mothers encourage them to talk about adoption, only 20 percent of boys say their mothers do. Similarly, 22 percent of girls say their fathers encourage talk about adoption, compared to 13 percent of boys.

How Does Transracial Adoption Affect Teenagers?

Few issues divide the adoption community more than transracial adoption. While this study cannot answer many of the questions in this debate, it does give insights into the dynamics of transracial adoption, since 29 percent of the youth in the study were transracially adopted (primarily Korean children in Caucasian families).

The study includes indicators that young people who were adopted transracially have quite positive racial identities. Only 20 percent say they wish they were a different race. And 79 percent say their parents want them to be proud of their ethnic background.

Responses from parents show similar patterns. Parents rarely view transracial adoption as a problem. In fact, only 3 percent believe transracial adoption has had a negative impact on their child. And just 1 percent of parents say transracial adoption has a negative impact on their family.

Most transracially adopted teens seem to have assimilated into a multicultural perspective and lifestyle. In this study, 78 percent of teens say they get along equally well with people of their own racial background and with people of other ethnic backgrounds. Only 8 percent feel more comfortable with people of their own ethnic background than with people of other backgrounds.

This comfort level is reflected in the friendship patterns among transracially adopted youth. For a majority of these youth (63 percent), none of their closest friends is the same race as they are. An additional 19 percent have just one of their five closest friends of the same race.

These findings suggest that transracially adopted youth may be isolated from peers with their same ethnic heritage. Only 37 percent report that one or more of their five best friends is of the same race. This apparent isolation may be explained, in part, by the fact that a vast majority of families in the study live in non-urban communities.

Comfort and Challenge

One of the dangers of national studies is that they can gloss over individual needs and issues as they look at "average" and "typical" teenagers. On every item in the survey, there is some variability. While most adopted teens may be a certain way, that doesn't mean your own teenager is the same. Nor does it mean that he or she is a problem just because he or she doesn't fit into the national averages.

Rather, the study raises questions and issues that can both comfort and challenge adoptive families. Parents can find comfort in the fact that—despite sensationalized media images—most adopted teens seem to be doing rather well in their adoptive families. For most, adoption is a positive experience.

The national study also offers a challenge to families to recognize the many different developmental issues that arise during the teenage years and how adoption may play a role. By understanding the issues and discovering appropriate ways to address them, adoptive families can enrich their relationships and the experience of adoption for everyone involved.

*"Adoptees should have access to their birth
records, if they so desire, when they reach the
age of eighteen."*

Adoptees Searching
for Birth Parents
Should Be Helped

Arthur D. Sorosky, Annette Baran, and Reuben Pannor

Arthur Sorosky is a child psychiatrist in Encino, California.
Annette Baran and Reuben Pannor are clinical social workers in
private practice in Los Angeles and coauthors of *Lethal Secrets:
Shocking Consequences and Unsolved Problems of Artificial
Insemination.* In the following viewpoint, excerpted from the
1989 update of their 1978 book *The Adoption Triangle*, Sorosky,
Baran, and Pannor urge that the courts and adoption professionals develop creative and open access to information to assure
sound mental health and psychological growth for all involved in
the adoption process.

As you read, consider the following questions:

1. In the view of Sorosky, Baran, and Pannor, what
   contradictions in the current adoption process must be
   resolved?
2. According to the authors, how do adoptive parents tend to
   feel about birth mothers?
3. What changes do the authors recommend to make searches
   by adoptees and reunions between birth parents and
   adoptees possible?

The controversy over the sealed records in adoptions initially focused our attention on the adult adoptee and his/her right to identifying information about his/her birth parents. We now recognize that the issues are more profound and pervasive. Taking a child from one set of parents and placing him/her with another set, who pretend that the child is born to them, disrupts a basic natural process. The need to be connected with one's biological and historical past is an integral part of one's identity formation. The sealed record in adoptions blocks this process. The search and ultimate reunion between adoptees and their birth parents provide the means for bringing together the broken connections from the past.

Questioning the Entire Adoption System

Opening the sealed records is merely the tip of the iceberg, under which lies a vast mosaic of contradictions that questions the entire institution of adoption as it has been practiced:

• Unmarried pregnant women are told that they have freedom of choice; yet they are made to feel that the best answer for every child born out of wedlock is adoption.

• Birth parents are assured that relinquishment of their child will be a resolution to their problem and the experience will be forgotten; yet their continued pain and mourning, to which no one listens, tell them otherwise.

• Adoptive parents have to promise to be honest and tell the child about his/her adoption and birth parents; yet adoptive parents are told only the positive facts because they aren't trusted to know the whole truth.

• Agencies accept the fact that adopting is different from giving birth to a child; yet they try to match babies to families as if it is the same.

• Adoptive families are counseled that adoptees need a positive identification with their origins; yet parents are rarely helped to work through their own feelings about infertility and their negative attitudes toward the birth parents.

• Families are encouraged to bring their children back to adoption agencies for information; yet the agencies assure parents they will divulge nothing to the children.

• When adopted adults, seeking background information, return to agencies, it is viewed as evidence of family failure and/or personal pathology. No one assumes they have a right to know. They are made to feel sick and abnormal for asking.

We believe it is time to re-evaluate our current and past adoption policies. The premise that has governed the philosophy and practice in the field of adoption has been that the relinquishment of a child by his/her birth parents permanently severs all ties. Although the present standards of anonymity were developed as a safeguard to all the parties involved in adoption, they may in fact have been the cause of insoluble problems.

Adoption is a lifelong process for the birth parents, especially for the birth mother; for the adoptive parents; and for the adoptee. Although the birth parents relinquish all of their rights and responsibilities to the child and have no physical contact, their feelings of loss, pain, and mourning do not disappear. Our study indicated that birth parents continue to care about the children they relinquished and wish to know "how they turned out." They are worried that the children do not understand the reasons for relinquishment and adoption. In general, birth parents are grateful to the adoptive parents and have no desire to disrupt the adoptive family relationship. Available for reunion, the majority of birth parents would not initiate it themselves.

Appreciating the Concerns of Adoptive Parents

When we began our study [of the adoption system, open and sealed adoptions, and adoptee–birth parent reunions], most adoptive parents we approached felt that if their children came in contact with publicity of our research, they would be "infected," turned away from them, or hurt by finding out awful truths. These adoptive parents feared losing the adopted child to a birth parent. This was a resurgence of the old preadoption childless feeling of failure, deprivation, separation, and loss. As our study progressed, we were pleased to find that adoptive parents we interviewed came to feel less threatened and realized that the adoptee's quest for genealogical information or an encounter with a birth parent was a personal need which could not be fully comprehended by a nonadopted person. Even though the adoptive parents' anxiety diminished, there remained a great deal of protectiveness toward the adoptee and concern over the possible negative effects of a reunion.

Tearing Down Walls

Before I built a wall I'd ask to know
What I was walling in or walling out,
And to whom I was like to give offense.
Something there is
    that doesn't love a wall,
That wants it down.

From "Mending Wall" by Robert Frost.

In general, the adoptive parents' attitudes toward the birth mother are both protective and restrictive. They are concerned about reopening the trauma of pregnancy, birth, and relinquishment of the child. They also feel that, unlike the adoptee, the birth mother was a party to the original decision regarding adoption and does not really have the same right to initiate a reunion as does the adoptee. This dichotomy remains a current source of controversy. Some adoptive parents insisted that they would not have adopted had they felt their children would one day leave them to search for their "real parents." They refused to be considered as "caretakers" or "baby sitters" for others. This is now heard less and less. Most know deep within themselves that they adopted because they wanted the chance to parent, not because they were promised a lifetime of secrecy.

Understanding the Needs of Adoptees

Our research data and case histories of adoptees corroborated our initial impression that adoptees are more vulnerable than nonadoptees to identity conflicts in late adolescence and young adulthood. Many of these adoptees seem preoccupied with existential concerns and have feelings of isolation and alienation resulting from the breaks in the continuity of life through the generations that their adoption represents. For some, the existing block to the past may create a feeling that there is a block to the future as well. The adoptee's identity formation must be viewed within the context of the life cycle, in which birth and death are linked unconsciously. This is evident in the frequency with which marriage, the birth of a child, or the death of an adoptive parent triggers an even greater sense of interest in the birth parents.

It would appear that very few adoptees are provided with enough background information to incorporate into their developing ego and sense of identity. The adoptive parents are reluctant to impart known information, especially any of a negative nature, that might hurt the child. The adoptees in turn are often reluctant to ask genealogical questions because they sense their parents' insecurities in these areas. Information given to adoptive couples at the time of adoption is scanty and usually describes immature, confused, adolescent unwed mothers and fathers.

We believe that all adoptees have a desire to know about their origins. However, those adoptees who are basically curious and questioning individuals appear, from our study, to be more likely to initiate a search and reunion. This is not necessarily related to the quality of the adoptive family relationship, although some adoptees' searches are based upon neurotic needs or poor nurturing.

What stand out most in our study of reunion cases are the positive benefits the majority of the adoptees gained. Most were enriched by a new, meaningful relationship with their birth relatives. More important was the effect upon the adoptee who was able to resolve the conflicts of his/her dual identity.

Regardless of what kind of relationship, positive or negative, existed between the adoptee and adoptive parents prior to the reunion, the effect of the experience was in some way enhancing to that relationship. The feelings of the adoptees toward their adoptive parents became more concretely positive and assumed a new meaning, even when the reunion resulted in an ongoing relationship between the adoptee and the birth parents. The realization emerged for the adoptees that their adoptive parents were their only true "psychological parents" and that the lifelong relationship with them was of far greater importance than a new connection with the birth parents.

The Nature of Reunion Experiences

Many adoptees talked about their reunion experiences with both awe and personal satisfaction. This knowledge brought us to the realization that it was often the fear of searching or the fear of hurting the adoptive parents that prevented an adoptee from acting upon his/her desire to find out more about his/her background. Solving the unknown mysteries made it possible for the adoptee to be better able to accept the real value of the adoptive family relationship.

For the majority of the birth parents, the experience provided an opportunity to resolve old guilt feelings and to erase years of wondering about the fate of their relinquished child. For the adoptive parents the reunion threatened to be the actualization of their lifelong fear that their child would someday be lost to the birth parents; the fact that this did not occur provided them with a sense of relief and final reassurance that they were the true parents.

Facilitating Change

It is our conviction that adult adoptees should have access to their birth records, if they so desire, when they reach the age of eighteen. For those adoptees who are determined to find their birth parents, the information available in the original birth records may not be sufficient. In order to avoid situations where adoptees spend agonizing years and large sums of money tracking down trivial clues, we would support methods to facilitate the search. Regional or national registries where adoptees and birth parents could indicate their interest in reunion, for example, have been suggested. In addition, agencies could provide identifying information and reunion services upon request.

In order for registries to be efficient, they could operate in conjunction with a board composed of mental health professionals, which would meet with representatives from each sector of the adoption triangle: adoptees, adoptive parents, and birth parents. The board would be available to offer assistance and counseling to all persons involved in or affected by an adoption reunion who requested such counseling. Whenever a request for reunion was made by either an adult adoptee or a birth parent, attempts would be made to contact the person sought. The board could also be helpful when one party desired a reunion and the other did not.

The role of the birth parents, after the adoption proceedings have been legally completed, must be reconsidered. Birth parents have always had a more direct involvement with adoptive parents in private adoptions than in agency-arranged adoptions. There are positive aspects to the direct-involvement policy that should be studied more carefully by adoption agencies. Allowing the birth and adoptive parents to meet one another at the time of the adoption enables each to have a clear, concrete picture of the other thereby avoiding the almost certain fantasies and distorted images that would otherwise emerge later.

We feel that adoptive parents should be provided with continuing reports of the birth parents' welfare by the original adoption agency. The adoptive parents can use the information to answer their child's inevitable questions and thus minimize the chance that the adoptee will resort to excessive fantasizing in an attempt to fill in identity lacunae [gaps]. Information also should be available to the birth parents about their child's progress and development.

Professionals in the mental health field need to realize that past adoption practices have led to numerous psychological problems for adoptees, birth parents, and adoptive parents. Future adoption practices should stress the continuing needs of individuals placed for adoption in the past, as well as those of their birth parents and adoptive parents. Creative and open approaches to meet the challenges of the future need to be developed.

Recommendations

We recommend that adoption laws and practices be changed to permit the following:

1. The opening of original birth records to adult adoptees and the providing of background and identifying information to them on request.
2. The establishment of appropriate boards that would be available to intercede, on a voluntary basis, on behalf of those adult adoptees and birth parents who wish to effect a reunion.
3. Continuing commitments by adoption agencies to all members of the adoption triangle for as long as necessary, including the provision of viable, current information to any of these parties. This will involve the re-establishment and

continuation of contact by the agency with the adoptive family and birth parents.

4. The setting up of counseling services which recognize that adoption is a lifelong process for all involved.
5. Consideration on the part of the authorities of new adoption alternatives to provide stable homes and families for children who would not be relinquished otherwise.

In Great Britain, Finland, and Israel, adult adoptees may obtain their original birth certificates. There is no evidence in those countries that this policy leads to fewer adoptions, an epidemic of reunions, or unhappy adoptive families. The number of adoptions in the United States is greater than the total for the rest of the world. The American institution of adoption is also more highly structured and secret than in most other countries. Rigidity and secrecy have created the dilemmas now faced by American adoptees, and only new attitudes and practices can end them. Above all, it is essential for us to realize that openness and honesty must replace the secrecy and anonymity that has prevailed in adoption practice. We hope that the controversy over sealed records, which has brought these issues to the fore, will enable us to develop sounder practices to meet both past and future needs of millions of people whose lives are touched by adoption.

"Holding adoption agencies to a reasonable standard of investigation enhances the effectiveness of the adoption process overall."

The Courts Should Do More to Protect Adoptive Families

Harvard Law Review

The *Harvard Law Review* analyzes current legal practices and often makes recommendations in its unsigned "Notes" section. In a "Note" excerpted in the following viewpoint, the journal describes and critiques certain legal devices that allegedly protect the rights of adopting parents—disclosure statutes, annulment proceedings, and wrongful adoption suits. Concluding that these devices do not adequately protect adoptive parents from misrepresentation and negligence, the journal proposes the creation of a new wrongful adoption tort that integrates these three devices into one unified proceeding.

As you read, consider the following questions:

1. According to the *Harvard Law Review*, how does the culture of concealment affect the success of the adoption process?
2. What problems does the author see in the current use of wrongful adoption suits?
3. How is the author's proposal for a unified wrongful adoption tort projected to improve the rights of adoptive parents?

Adoption offers children who are orphaned, abandoned, neglected, abused, or simply unwanted a chance to live in a stable, loving environment. Families who adopt believe that adoption provides them with an opportunity to play a meaningful role in the lives of needy children. Ideally, adoption enriches the lives of both the adopted child and the adopting family.

Unfortunately, adoption does not always live up to this ideal, in part because parents seldom receive vital background information about the child they bring into their family. For example, parents may not know that their adopted child has languished in an abusive home or suffers from hidden health problems. As a result, prospective parents cannot anticipate, much less evaluate, the emotional and financial responsibility they assume by inviting a child into their family. Even when an adopted child develops physical or psychological problems that could have been reasonably discovered and disclosed by the adoption agency, the parents still have little legal recourse. By forcing adopting parents to make decisions without requiring agencies to disclose the complete medical and life histories of prospective adoptees, the current law fails to safeguard adequately the rights of adopting parents.

The Current Legal System

The legal system has not been entirely unsympathetic to the plight of adopting parents. Most states have enacted disclosure statutes that require agencies to reveal an adoptee's relevant history to prospective adopting parents. Unfortunately, these statutes suffer from many defects and do not furnish parents with the type of information necessary for them to make an informed decision. In many states, the law also offers adopting parents the possibility of annulling the adoption decree. However, courts have been understandably averse to granting this severe remedy. Finally, a few states have forged a new legal remedy called the tort of "wrongful adoption." This cause of action grants relief to adopting parents if they can show *misrepresentation* by the adoption agency.

Each of these three legal devices—disclosure statutes, annulment proceedings, and wrongful adoption suits—suffers from defects. Furthermore, because these three mechanisms were not explicitly designed to work together, their combined impact has often been contrary to the fundamental goal of securing the equal rights of all the parties to an adoption, especially the rights of adopting parents.

To achieve the goal of equal and fair protection for adopting parents, this viewpoint advocates the theoretical unification of the policies underlying disclosure statutes, annulment proceedings, and the tort of wrongful adoption, and the creation of a single legal proceeding based on the notion of fault. This viewpoint proposes the creation of a new "wrongful adoption tort" that places an affirmative duty on adoption agencies to investigate and to disclose with reasonable care all relevant information about the adoptee. If an adoption agency violates this duty, the adopting family should be awarded monetary damages and, possibly, an annulment of the adoption decree. In particular, this viewpoint argues that courts should no longer conceptualize annulment as a separate and independent legal procedure, but rather as one possible remedy for the newly constructed wrongful adoption tort. . . .

Adoption and the Culture of Concealment

The goal of the adoption system is to provide every child with a "family-like living situation" that is permanent and safe. Adoption provides greater benefits than long-term foster care and therefore is the preferred form of placement. Although much attention has been paid to what Harold D. Grotevant and Ruth G. McRoy call the "demographic and social-psychological factors associated with [the] parents' decisions to adopt," little attention has been paid to the factors associated with successful adoptions. Recently, some of the basic assumptions upon which modern adoptions are based have been questioned.

One assumption of modern adoption practice is that adoption is a "rebirth." This fiction assumes that the adopted child never had a birth family; adopted children leave behind all traces of their past and are fully "reborn" into a new family. Consistent with this assumption, social workers try to eradicate all traces of the birth family. For example, adoption agencies actively discourage communication between a birth mother and the adopting family, and states seal all records identifying an adoptee's birth parents and issue new birth certificates listing the names of the adopting parents. These measures are intended to facilitate adoptions and to finalize them, both psychologically and socially.

The assumption of rebirth, however, does not comport with the realities of adoption. A growing number of adoptions, particularly those that involve older children, end with the termination of the parent-child relationship. In fact, it has been estimated that as many as one in every ten adoptions is terminated. The failure rate increases with the age at which the child is adopted, and one of the factors influencing the success of the adoption is the amount of information provided to the adopting family by the adoption agency.

Research shows that full disclosure of an adopted child's history offers psychological and practical benefits to the child and to her family. But often this history is not disclosed. A recent study by Richard P. Barth and Marianne Berry indicates the magnitude of the problem. Of the families surveyed, roughly one-third of those that had adopted physically abused children were not informed of the abuse at the time of the adoption; more than one-half of the families that had adopted sexually abused children were not told of the abuse before they finalized the adoptions. When agencies do not provide families with this type of information, any behavioral or psychological problems the children might have often come as a surprise to the families. In fact, many of these families often report that agencies provided them with misleading information about the child.

Problems with Current Disclosure Statutes

Consistent with the modern studies that favor greater openness in adoptions, many states have enacted disclosure statutes that require adoption agencies to disclose to the prospective parents, either initially or upon request, any material information known about the child. These statutes protect the rights of adopting parents by acting as a prophylactic to prevent adoptions that are most likely to end in the termination of the relationship. Given accurate, complete information about the prospective adoptee, the parents can make an informed judgment about whether they are emotionally and financially capable of adopting a particular child.

Unfortunately, these statutes suffer from a myriad of defects, too numerous and varied to enumerate here. However, two major defects warrant specific attention. First, most disclosure statutes fail to articulate a specific standard of duty that adoption agencies must meet in disclosing information. Often plagued with ambiguity, these statutes allow great agency discretion by mandating disclosure of material facts only "if available," "where practicable," or "to the extent [the facts] are available." Second, and more important, disclosure statutes impose no penalty on adoption agencies that do not disclose information as the law demands. Disclosure statutes therefore create a toothless duty that offers little relief to adopting parents.

The Inadequacies of Annulment Proceedings

The second way in which the legal system helps to protect the rights of adopting parents is the annulment of the adoption decree. The legal act of annulment revokes the original adoption decree and relieves the adopting parents from all legal obligations and duties to the adopted child. Although this procedure can theoretically be invoked by either the birth parents or the adopting parents, most annulment requests come from birth parents who seek to reclaim parental rights over their child.

Courts in all jurisdictions will grant an annulment if it is in the best interest of the child. However, if annulment is not in the child's best interest, states disagree on the standard that must be met before they nonetheless grant an annulment. In approximately half the states, statutes regulate the annulment process. In the jurisdictions without any explicit statutes, some courts have held that they have no authority to grant annulments. Other courts have held that they retain the equitable power to set aside their own decrees.

In states with annulment statutes, the legal standards for granting annulment vary significantly. Some statutes treat annulment like any other civil decree and leave vast discretion in the hands of judges. Without specific standards, very few annulments of adoption decrees actually occur. This is because courts realize that an annulment means abandonment for at least the second time in the adopted child's life. Understandably, judges who are sympathetic to the plight of the unwanted child often refuse to grant this extreme remedy. Thus, annulment statutes that give the judiciary great discretion do not protect the rights of adopting parents sufficiently.

Problems with Explicit Annulment Statutes

Other more explicit annulment statutes authorize annulment within a limited time period only if the adoption decree is itself procedurally defective. Examples of such defects include lack of notice to the birth parents and lack of personal jurisdiction over the birth parents. These statutes were enacted largely to safeguard the rights of birth parents and not the rights of adopting parents. Generally, these laws give birth parents a window of opportunity to regain custody of their child and to attack the adoption after the formal adoption decree is granted. Usually, these statutes also attempt to protect the interests of the child by limiting the time in which an adoption decree is susceptible to collateral attack. Because these statutes only contemplate harm to birth parents and to children, these laws often do not help adopting parents void the adoption decree through procedural means.

Still other types of annulment statutes delineate specific, substantive grounds upon which parents can contest the adoption decree. Unfortunately, these statutes resist categorization because many of these laws contain idiosyncratic requirements that do not easily lend themselves to doctrinal classification. Nevertheless, two types of statutes merit specific discussion because they affect adopting parents most directly. First, several states allow the annulment of an adoption decree if the adopting parents can prove fraud by the adoption agency. Second, California allows annulment whenever an adopted child manifests a medical condition that existed but was unknown to the adopting parents at the time of adoption.

The statutes that recognize fraud as grounds for annulment suffer from two acute problems. First, adopting parents have only a limited period in which to petition the court for an annulment. Because fraudulent concealment of a child's health or past often cannot be discovered in such a short period of time, these statutes offer little protection for many adopting parents who are defrauded. Second, a duty not to commit fraud inadequately protects adopting parents who may still become victims of adoption agencies that act with gross negligence.

California's annulment statute is unique because it provides a much lower standard for annulment than the statutes that permit annulment upon a showing of fraud. A fair reading of the law suggests that even if the adoption agency acted reasonably in relaying information about the adoptee to the adopting parents, California courts must nonetheless grant the annulment if the child suffered from a medical condition that the parents were unaware of at the time of adoption.

In a recent case, *In re Adoption of Kay C.*, a family adopted a six-year-old girl and expected that she would have only some minor emotional difficulties adjusting to her new home. The family had informed the adoption agency that they were not prepared to adopt a child with severe emotional problems. The two doctors who had examined Kay C. for the adoption agency disagreed about her mental health. One physician recommended that she not be removed from her foster home; the other believed that she was ready for adoption. Soon after adoption, however, Kay C. began to behave disruptively and was diagnosed with a borderline personality disorder. After upholding the constitutionality of the annulment statute under state law, the California Court of Appeal annulled the adoption because Kay C.'s disorder existed prior to the adoption and because her parents had no prior knowledge of her condition.

California's annulment rule, which imposes a form of strict liability on adoption agencies, places too heavy a burden on adoption agencies and relieves prospective parents of the responsibility to think carefully through the risks inherent in adoption. Moreover, under a strict liability standard, the adopting family returns the child as if she were a dangerous or defective product. The strict liability standard, with its connotations of economic analysis and utilitarian calculus, commodifies children in a way that fails to respect their dignity as persons.

Problems with the Current Wrongful Adoption Tort

Misrepresentation. The third legal structure that aims to protect adopting parents is the newly forged tort of "wrongful adoption." However, the vast majority of states do not recognize this tort. Only Ohio, California, and Wisconsin have enforced a tort of "wrongful adoption" against adoption agencies that intentionally misrepresent a child's medical condition or negligently misrepresent the condition.

"Wrongful adoption" was virtually unheard of before the 1986 Ohio Supreme Court decision in *Burr v. Board of County Commissioners.* Russell and Betty Burr sued a county welfare department for intentional misrepresentation in the adoption of their son Patrick. A county caseworker had told the Burrs that Patrick was born to an eighteen-year-old unwed mother whose parents had treated the child cruelly. Soon after the adoption, the child developed a variety of mental and physical complications, including hallucinations, and was eventually diagnosed with Huntington's disease.

The Burrs obtained a court order to unseal the adoption records of their child and discovered that Patrick's birth mother was, in fact, a thirty-one-year-old psychiatric patient diagnosed with a "mild mental deficiency, [and as] . . . idiopathic, with psychotic reactions." Although the identity of the father was unknown, the agency assumed that he was another patient at the same mental hospital. The Burrs also discovered that before Patrick's adoption, the county had evidence that the child was at risk of developing medical problems, including Huntington's disease.

The Ohio Supreme Court based the action of wrongful adoption on the common law tort of fraud. Because the agency had intentionally misrepresented the child's background to the parents, the court ruled in the parents' favor. However, the court limited the scope of the tort of wrongful adoption to agencies found guilty of intentional, affirmative misrepresentation.

The Cases of Michael J. and Erin

Two years after *Burr*, the California Court of Appeal granted relief for wrongful adoption in *Michael J. v. Los Angeles County Department of Adoption.* The state adoption agency advertised Michael J. on television in order to recruit prospective parents. The adoption agency considered Michael hard to place because he had a "large port wine stain on his head, face, chest, and back." The caseworker did not tell the prospective parents that the agency's examining doctor had refused to "make a definite statement" on Michael's condition. Eleven years after his adoption, Michael began to suffer from epileptic seizures and was diagnosed with Sturge-Weber syndrome, a rare congenital, degenerative nerve disorder. The court held that the agency's *intentional concealment* of the doctor's refusal to make a prognosis gave rise to a valid claim. In so doing, the court established a standard of "good faith[,] full disclosure of material facts concerning existing or past conditions of the child's health." However, in holding that agencies "should not be liable for mere negligence in providing information," the court limited causes of action to intentional concealment and misrepresentation.

The State of Wisconsin has also recognized a limited claim for negligent misrepresentation by an adoption agency. In *Meracle v. Children's Service Society*, the Supreme Court of Wisconsin refrained from imposing on adoption agencies an affirmative duty to disclose information, but held that if an agency voluntarily provided information, it could not do so negligently. In *Meracle*, a caseworker had assured the adoptive parents that Erin, a twenty-three-month-old girl, had no higher chance of developing Huntington's disease than did the general population, even though Erin's grandmother had died from the disease. Four years after the adoption, Erin was diagnosed with Huntington's disease. The adopting couple then discovered that the caseworker had negligently misrepresented Erin's chances of developing the disorder. The court held the agency liable for presenting the information negligently.

Negligence: The Duty to Investigate. The *Meracle* court established that when an agency discloses information, it has a duty to use reasonable care. But to date, no court has found a duty to investigate reasonably the adoptee's medical and social history. On the contrary, one state court has expressly rejected a wrongful adoption cause of action based on such a claim. In *Foster ex rel. Foster v. Bass*, the Mississippi Supreme Court held that an agency had no duty to order a test for a rare disease, even though it was standard practice for the agency to report such test results. The agency normally copied each child's hospital medical records onto a standardized form, which included a space for the results of a PKU test [given to locate a possible genetic, but treatable, disorder]. The adopting family's doctor thought that the blank space for the PKU results meant that the hospital had already tested the child for the disease but was simply waiting for the results. In fact, the child had never been tested and subsequently suffered from severe brain damage. The court held that the adoption agency was liable neither for the hospital's failure to order the test nor for leaving a blank space on the standardized form.

Misrepresentation Threat Creates a Perverse Incentive

In sum, all three cases that have recognized the tort of wrongful adoption have grounded it in the tort doctrine of misrepresentation. Both the *Burr* and the *Michael J.* courts found liability in cases of *intentional* misrepresentation caused either by an affirmative statement that misled the adopting parents or by a deliberate failure to state material information. By contrast, the *Meracle* court found liability in cases of *negligent* misrepresentation. No case, however, has imposed a duty to investigate the adoptee's past.

In these three states, the creation of this limited new tort has created a perverse incentive structure: the less agencies know about the adoptees, the less likely agencies will be found guilty of any wrongdoing. If the tort of wrongful adoption in its present form gains acceptance in other states, the combined effect of a common law duty not to misrepresent and a statutory duty to disclose will result in adoption agencies that simply strive to know as *little* as possible about the children they place. Without an additional duty to take reasonable measures to investigate the adoptee's past, the growth of the tort of wrongful adoption, as presently conceived, will hurt—and not help—the cause of adopting parents.

A New Wrongful Adoption Tort: A Unified Proposal

To protect adequately the interests of adopting parents, courts should combine the legal structures that are already in place and create a single legal procedure. This new wrongful adoption tort would impose a duty on adoption agencies to investigate the social and medical histories of adoptees. It would also create a duty to disclose the information thus uncovered. Moreover, the new wrongful adoption tort would require adoption agencies to satisfy these duties—to discover and to disclose—under a standard of negligence. Finally, this proposal would consolidate the legal procedure of annulment into the remedial component of the wrongful adoption tort. In other words, annulment would no longer be a separate legal procedure that revokes adoption decrees based upon highly eclectic and discretionary standards.

Independent of any requirement to reveal known material information, adoption agencies should bear a responsibility to research reasonably all material information about a child's past. As with all negligence standards, the amount of diligence that constitutes reasonable care cannot be defined by bright-line rules. For example, an agency reasonably might not know the history of an abandoned child who was not previously in the social welfare system. On the other hand, an agency should be expected to know the social and medical history of a child who has been a ward of the state for years. Some factors that courts could use to determine whether information is reasonably knowable include the availability of the birth parents for questioning, the existence of a record of previous state intervention, and the availability of reliable medical tests for certain conditions, such as the PKU.

Furthermore, independent of existing disclosure statutes, courts should impose upon adoption agencies an affirmative duty to disclose all material information with reasonable care. This duty differs from the one established in *Meracle*, because that court explicitly rejected any duty to disclose information to adopting parents. The *Meracle* court required only that if the agency chose to reveal information about the adoptee, the agency could not do so negligently. By contrast, the duty to disclose proposed by this viewpoint would require agencies to disclose with reasonable care *all material information* about the adoptee. . . .

If an adoption agency commits the wrongful adoption tort proposed here, courts should have the discretion to award money damages and even to grant an annulment. Monetary damages would compensate a family for the unexpected financial burdens incurred in caring for a physically disabled or emotionally disturbed child. Courts should calculate these damage awards in the same manner as they do in other tort awards. The decision to grant annulments should be made through a two-part analysis. First, as in the status quo, courts should always abrogate the adoption decree whenever annulment clearly would be in the best interests of the child. However, in situations that involve a child's placement in a home with substance abusers or physical or sexual abusers, annulment should not be used. Instead, the usual procedures for terminating a parental relationship, with its accompanying moral opprobrium, should be used. Second, if the child's best interests would not be clearly served by an annulment, the court must balance the competing interests of the child, the birth parents, the adopting parents, and society. The alternative to this judicial discretion—a bright-line test—is inappropriate because each case involves complex factors and relationships that cannot be reduced to a simple rule. . . .

Fostering Confidence in the Adoption Process

This viewpoint has proposed the creation of a wrongful adoption tort that unifies the three existing legal devices of disclosure statutes, annulment proceedings, and wrongful adoption suits. Not only would this new tort correct deficiencies in the existing legal devices, but it would more accurately balance the interests of the adopted child, the adopting family, and the public at large through the twin duties of investigation and disclosure.

Holding adoption agencies to a reasonable standard of investigation enhances the effectiveness of the adoption process overall. The greater the confidence that prospective parents have in adoption agencies, the more likely they will be to adopt. However, a relationship of trust will arise only when prospective families are confident that adoption agencies will make good faith efforts to investigate and disclose all material facts. By fostering such confidence, the proposed wrongful adoption tort would create a climate in which more adoptions can take place.

"*Adoption professionals and agencies alike now know that postlegal adoption services are essential to making adoptions succeed.*"

Adoption Agencies Must Provide More Post-Adoption Services

Kenneth W. Watson

Kenneth W. Watson is assistant director of the Chicago (Illinois) Child Care Society. In the following viewpoint, Watson traces changes in views of adoption and in the nature of the adoption process itself over the past few decades. He observes that, contrary to earlier beliefs, "adoption is really a complex and usually painful process that presents an ongoing challenge to all of those involved." In light of the changing nature and improved understanding of adoption, Watson recommends that adoption agencies take the lead in providing better post-adoption support and services for adoptees, adoptive parents, and birth parents.

As you read, consider the following questions:

1. How does the author describe the changes in thinking that have occurred among adoption professionals in the past few decades?
2. How, according to Watson, have adoption agencies generally responded to the need for postlegal services?
3. In Watson's view, what three concepts must be accepted in order to validate postlegal adoption services?

Excerpted from Kenneth W. Watson, "Providing Services After Adoption," *Public Welfare*, Winter 1992. Copyright ©1992 American Public Welfare Association. Reprinted with permission.

Just how much we change over time—that we ever believed and did certain things that are a documented part of our history—is often hard for us to realize. No less is true of our attitudes and beliefs about adoption.

Agencies change, too. Most adoption agencies now view post-legal adoption services as essential if adoptions are to succeed. Agencies have learned that adoption is not just a legal act that transfers parental rights, but an event that profoundly affects all of the participants for the rest of their lives. They have come to realize this truth as a result of the painful experience of denying it. Professionals who have been involved in adoptions over the past few decades can attest to that fact.

I have worked in adoption for more than 37 years, and in the agency where I am now employed for more than 25 years. . . .

"A Perfect Solution"

In the past, we honestly believed we had finished our work when an adoption was legally consummated. Further agency involvement, we thought, would interfere with an adoptive family's effective integration. We believed adoption was a perfect solution to three of society's most vexing problems: homeless children, infertile couples, and unintended pregnancies outside of marriage. Now we know that adoption is really a complex and usually painful process that presents an ongoing challenge to all of those involved.

The "perfect solution" was but one of a series of myths that shaped past adoption services and that continue to influence the way many people view adoption today. Some other myths were that

- infertile couples had a right to experience parenting and that adoption agencies existed to accommodate them;
- birth parents who surrendered their children were then free to "go on with their lives"; and
- participants in an adoption should not know each other—in fact, should know as little about each other as possible.

Two forces propelled agencies to examine and discard these myths. One was the focus on "special-needs" adoption placements, and the other was pressure from those who had participated in earlier adoptions and who were returning to agencies in search of information or further services.

A New Focus on Special-Needs Adoptions

Most adoption agencies initially came into being to meet the needs of infertile couples who wished to become parents and who could afford the expenses entailed. The children "served" through such adoptions were the kind of children to whom these parents could envision giving birth. They were healthy,

271

white infants. Many other children were growing up in foster care because they were too old, too ill, too different, or too problematic for couples seeking healthy infants in adoption. Other families, however, were interested in adopting these special-needs children. As agencies expanded their adoption programs to meet the needs of a broader range of children, families responded. Many such families received subsidies—adoption assistance—because it was clear when placing the children that meeting their special needs was going to cost more money.

How Times Have Changed

In going through some files recently, I came across an old policy statement about providing service to participants in an adoption once the decree had been issued. The policy stated that when families who had adopted children from the agency subsequently called because they were experiencing difficulties, we were to remind them that adoptive parents had the same rights and responsibilities as any parents and to refer them to other community resources for assessment and help. If surrendering birth parents called to inquire about the whereabouts or well-being of their children, we were to tell them that by surrendering their children they had left the planning in the hands of the agency and to assure them that their children were being well cared for. I shared the memo with current staff, and we smiled and shook our heads at how adoption workers could possibly have been so wrong. When I checked the memorandum more closely, I discovered I had written it.

Kenneth W. Watson, *Public Welfare*, Winter 1992.

Even though these children by definition had special needs and were probably going to present special developmental problems, agencies initially built in no other services for the adopting families. Once the adoption was consummated, agencies regarded these families—as they did all adoptive families—as families whose children had been born into them. If such families returned for help, they were referred to other community agencies or mental health settings. Many of these resources were unaware of adoption issues or of their impact on families. Therapists in such settings often viewed the special-needs adoptive family as pathological for adopting such a child and sometimes even counseled the parents to return the "damaged" child.

As the placement of special-needs children increased, so did the rate of such returns, of "adoption disruptions." A disruption occurs when the agency removes a child from an adoptive family and makes another plan, even though the intent at placement had been for the child to grow up in that adoptive family. Concern about disruptions spawned research to discern what factors contributed to the success of special-needs adoptions. Four studies on disruptions, published in the eighties, relying on different samples and using somewhat different definitions of special needs, suggested various ways in which the disruption rate might be lowered. Although the studies did not agree about specific causes of disruption, remarkably they concurred that one of the surest factors in preventing disruption was the provision of continuing services beyond the point of legal consummation.

Requests for Search Information

At the same time, adults who had been adopted as infants were returning to agencies to raise questions about their adoptions. Many wanted background information about their birth families or help in locating the birth parents whom they had lost through adoption. Some adoptive parents helped their children in searching because they believed it was the best way to help their children resolve the issues of loss and identity. Birth parents, too, were returning to agencies, asking where their children were and how they had fared.

Agencies did not challenge the research findings—their own experience validated them—nor could they deny the pressure of returning members of the adoption triangle—adopted persons, birth parents, and adoptive parents. For example, at 24, "Arnold" wrote a letter from prison to the agency from which he had been adopted as a toddler. As an adolescent he had become estranged from his adoptive parents. Now he was asking for information about his birth parents and asking if he had a sister. He thought he vaguely remembered that he did and wondered if she might have been adopted by a different family. In response, the agency sent background history, a description of his birth family, and confirmation that he indeed had a sister who was placed in another adoptive family. The letter also assured him that the information could be verified both from the agency records and by workers who remembered Arnold and his birth family. By return mail came a letter from him that began, "Does someone really remember me?" When he was released from prison, Arnold hitchhiked across the country. He wanted to visit the agency to reaffirm his origins and to begin a search for his sister.

Initially, agencies thought that the only adoptees who searched were those, like Arnold, whose adoption experience had not been positive. But many persons who had experienced "good adoptions" also came back to agencies. It was harder for them to initiate a search. Most experienced a sense of disloyalty to their adoptive parents as a result of their interest in their birth families. "Robert," as a 3-day-old infant, was adopted into a stable family that met his developmental needs throughout his childhood. At 18, he graduated in the top 10 percent of his high school class and was voted by his classmates as "Most Likely to Succeed." He made plans to go away to the college of his choice. He also began a search for his birth parents. He said that his adoption was great, but that in spite of how good his family was, he had never had a good birthday. Each year at that time, he wondered if his birth mother was "celebrating" his birthday or if she even remembered him. He became moody and unpleasant with his adoptive parents then, but could never tell them why. Each year they tried to compensate for the previous year's bad birthday by celebrating in some new and better way. That never worked. After 18 years he decided he wanted to find the missing pieces in his life and returned to the agency. He needed to know if his birth mother remembered him. He needed to ask her the question that all adopted persons want to ask their birth mothers: "Why did you give me up?"

Birth Parents Search, Too

Birth parents, too, were returning to agencies with their questions and concerns. A few years ago, as I walked through the waiting room of the agency where I work, a woman caught my attention. She smiled and asked if I remembered her. She looked familiar, but I could not place her until she said her name was "Lorraine" and that the last time I saw her was 21 years before. Then I remembered her clearly. I had seen her as a 15-year-old who had come with her mother to the agency in the early stages of her pregnancy. . . .

As Lorraine and I now sat in the office 21 years later, I told her that I clearly remembered her and our earlier contact. She asked if I recalled what I had said to her when she signed the paper [to relinquish her newborn daughter for adoption]. I said I was certain that I repeated what I usually said to surrendering mothers then: "Now you can go on with your life." She nodded agreement and said, "Let me tell you something, Mr. Watson. My life stopped the day I signed that paper. Not one day has gone by that I have not thought of my daughter, and not one week has passed that I have not cried for her."

I asked about her life since that time. She had finished high school, worked steadily as a secretary and now as an office manager, and still lived at home with her mother. Her father had died a few years after the baby's birth. The baby had not been mentioned after she went back home, and as far as Lorraine knew, her father died unaware of the child's existence. "So," I said, "for 21 years the only person you have had to talk with about the baby has been your mother." "Wrong," she said. "Not once since I signed the surrender have my mother or I ever mentioned the baby. That's why I am back here today. I need to talk about my daughter. She is 21 this month and I want to find her."

Agency Responses

Experiences with special-needs adoptive families and those of people like Arnold and Lorraine have caused agencies to think about the kinds of postlegal adoption services clients need. Such services fall into four categories:

- continuation of agency service, beyond consummation, to a family with whom that agency has placed a child;
- agency intervention with adoptive families when those families are experiencing difficulties and request help;
- agency-initiated services offered to adoptive families on a planned basis in response to developmental needs; and
- service to members of the adoption triangle who are seeking information about, or contact with, others who were a part of that adoption.

Continuing service beyond consummation. Continuing service helps families more fully integrate new members or to locate the community support they will need. For example, a family adopted an 8-year-old child who totally rejected their affection and attempts to parent. She acted self-sufficient beyond her age and ignored the parents' efforts to treat her as the little girl she was. The parents used agency help to understand that her behavior related to the poor parenting she had received during her first three years. Because her basic needs had not been met by adults then, she had not learned to trust that adults could meet them now. The parents also needed ongoing support to allow their daughter to act like a 2-year-old so she could learn from the parents' concern how to trust and love. They also needed agency advocacy to help maintain the child in a public school. Any delay in the consummation of the adoption would have added to the child's sense of insecurity and the parents' concerns that they were inadequate. A limited period of extended service beyond consummation met the needs of both child and family.

Agency intervention at the request of families. Postlegal adoption services may be provided to families who adopt and subsequently experience difficulties. Such families have expected to be able to handle the tasks of parenting their adopted child on their own but have run into crises with which they need help. For instance, a family adopted sisters ages 8 and 5 and had no immediate problems. They recontacted the adoption agency when the younger child was 7 because she had begun wetting the bed and having nightmares. The agency reviewed the girls' prior history and noted that the older girl had been sexually abused when she was 7, which was what brought the children into placement. A few meetings with the adoptive parents

275

helped them recognize that the younger girl's behavior might have been connected to memories of her earlier family and fears related to possible abuse or replacement. Openly discussing with the adoptive family the children's history and supporting the parents as they reassured both girls about their current security eliminated the nighttime disturbances.

Planned services in response to developmental needs. Some communities offer services to adoptive families in response not to crises but to anticipated developmental needs. Included are agency support groups, adoptive parent education classes at certain critical developmental levels, and planned respite care. In some communities, for instance, the public agency holds an annual weekend retreat for families with special-needs adolescent children. The families attend, eat, and sleep as family units. There are separate meetings and program activities for the parents and for their children and activities for the whole family together. The retreat provides support, respite, and opportunities for direct therapeutic interventions.

Information and search assistance. Earlier I told about agency involvement with participants in past adoptions who are seeking information about, or contact with, others who were part of those adoptions. As the number of requests for such information and searches has increased, most agencies have responded by developing services; but the extent and structure of services vary. Some agencies are uncomfortable and defensive about these requests and share minimal information. Some ally themselves more actively with the searchers. They may refer the searchers to support groups or to individuals who conduct searches, they may engage directly in the search process, or they may offer to be intermediaries if the missing parties are located. Some agencies have spread the responsibility for responding to information and search requests throughout the regular adoption caseloads, whereas other agencies have identified particular workers or established special units to handle such cases.

Agencies, then, have begun to offer postlegal adoption services in all four service areas. They have done so with understandable reluctance. Most have felt taxed to their limits trying to place children waiting for adoption and have felt they do not have the conceptual, technical, and fiscal capacity to extend services to those whose adoptions had been completed. Of special concern was that agencies would have to offer such services for the lifetime of the triangle members.

Conceptualizing Postlegal Adoption Services

To develop postlegal adoption services, one must recognize and examine how those involved in adoptions view the adoptive family as being different from other types of families and identify how adoption complicates normal development. Three concepts are fundamental to accepting the validity of postlegal adoption services.

First, adopted children, adoptive families, and service providers must accept that although adoptive families are like other families in most respects, fundamental differences affect them at every developmental stage. Foremost among these differences is that adopted children always belong to two families: their family of origin, which gives them their genes, ancestors, birth, and often some early shared history; and their family of nurture, which provides their everyday care and meets their ongoing developmental needs. All the principals in an adoption must reconcile this dichotomy.

A second important concept is that placement in adoption, no matter how early, how benign, or how successful, means that the child always experiences a painful loss of the birth family. Older children bring memories of this family and the pain of the loss with them. Infants placed from the hospital come to grips with this loss when they are able to understand that they do, indeed, have another family.

Complicating the resolution of this primal loss is a third basic concept. Such a loss is a serious blow to the adopted person's self-esteem. Adoptees speak of adoption as being "given up" or "given away." Regardless of the facts of the placement or how well nurtured and cared for the children are in their adoptive families, they view adoption as a rejection or abandonment by their birth families and seek the cause within themselves.

Agencies must find ways to help adoptive families with these concerns and to help other community resources recognize and counsel families about adoption problems. Since adoption has impact at every developmental level, concerns and problems may occur at any point in the adoptive family's life. Because families seek help when they need it, mental health and school personnel should be familiar with adoption and the ways it affects children and their families.

More importantly, however, agencies must reexamine their own adoption beliefs and programs. Service provided after the legal consummation of the adoption must be developed to meet real needs and must become an integrated part of the adoption process. Agencies must decide which postlegal adoption services are most important; how they can best be provided; and who should take responsibility for developing, coordinating, and funding these services. Agencies must also integrate what they are learning about postlegal adoption services into the way adoption service is viewed and delivered at other points in the adoption process. . . .

Since the adequate provision of a wide range of postlegal adoption services will depend upon developing a network of community resources, the public agency must engage the other service providers in this process to decide who is responsible for what services. This means helping other providers understand the importance of service to this client group and setting its own boundaries with respect to direct service. Because drawing boundaries early in the process is difficult, the agency should be careful not to set policy too rigidly too early. Flexible guidelines that are frequently reviewed are much preferred. If such a loose structure is to be effective, however, a knowledgeable person must be in charge—someone at a sufficiently high administrative level to assure impact on agency practice who can both respond to the evolving program with appropriate changes in the guidelines and accept responsibility for some inevitable confusion. . . .

So, over the years adoption has changed. We have learned more about how the members of the adoption triangle are affected. As a result, our attitudes and beliefs about adoption have changed. Adoption professionals and agencies alike now know that postlegal adoption services are essential to making adoptions succeed. Consequently, agencies are confronted with the need to change. The challenge they face is to develop programs that recognize and effectively meet the lifelong needs of the members of the adoption triangle—adopted children, adoptive families, and birth families. The principal player in providing these programs and services must be the public child welfare agency.

"Our laws and . . . practice continue to place young children in continued jeopardy and ultimately cause long-term, often permanent damage."

Unnecessary Barriers to Special Needs Adoption Must Be Eliminated

Lynn G. Gabbard

Lynn G. Gabbard and her husband have adopted seven special needs children over a twenty-year period. Gabbard is also an adoption caseworker for a private child-placement agency, in which she is responsible for the placement of special needs children. The following viewpoint is taken from her testimony in a 1993 hearing before the U.S. Senate Subcommittee on Children, Family, Drugs, and Alcoholism. Gabbard urges the subcommittee to introduce legislation that will remove unnecessary barriers to adoption—especially, she asks, when such legal and bureaucratic impediments contribute to long-term or even permanent psychological, mental, and physical damage to children.

As you read, consider the following questions:

1. What evidence does Gabbard present that children are victimized by the social, legal, and bureaucratic systems?
2. How, in Gabbard's view, will the establishment of national standards for child care promote the welfare of children?
3. According to the author, what resources must be made available to adoptive families of special needs children?

Lynn G. Gabbard, prepared statement on barriers to adoption presented before the U.S. Senate Subcommittee on Children, Family, Drugs, and Alcoholism, Committee on Labor and Human Resources, 15 July 1993.

During the past 18½ years, my husband and I have adopted seven children, now ranging in age from 2 years to 19 years, all of whom were placed from situations somewhat conducive to the development of special needs. We are active participants in, and past co-presidents of, a statewide adoptive parent support and advocacy group and serve on many local, state, and federally focused committees and boards addressing various child advocacy and adoption-related issues. Additionally, I have been employed since 1985 as an adoption caseworker for a private child-placing agency in Connecticut, where I have primary responsibility for the adoptive placement of special needs children and the provision of appropriate preplacement and postplacement services. It is from this somewhat multi-faceted perspective that I approach the issues of special needs adoption and attempt to relate my own personal experiences as they apply to the more global problems at hand.

Barriers to Adoption

When I reflect on the barriers to adoption that we personally have faced with respect to the adoptions of our children, I think primarily of the societal, legislative, and bureaucratic factors that magnify and exacerbate the physical and emotional injuries to children that actually result in their "special needs." Our oldest son, now 17 years old, was born to a 13-year-old mother, who, despite her extremely young age, evident emotional instability, and clearly verbalized ambivalence toward parenting this child, was encouraged to take her baby home from the hospital and assume the many responsibilities of parenthood. A birth defect that necessitated a full body cast made the care of her baby an even more difficult task for this young mother. The extreme neglect and physical abuse that followed, while not to be condoned, could almost be explained when viewed from the perspective of the [immensity] of the daily parenting task demanded of a 13-year-old child. The neglectful and abusive treatment of our son was to continue for nearly 2 years, interspersed with brief hospitalizations and foster placements, until the decision was made to terminate parental rights and allow both of these children, mother and child, to move on toward safer and more productive lives.

Still another precipitating factor in the development of children's "special needs" is the problem of substance abuse. Another of our children, a daughter now 11½ years old, was born both heroin- and methadone-addicted, a victim of Fetal Alcohol Syndrome, a 2½-pound infant born 2 months prematurely at the bottom of a staircase where her mother was thrown following a domestic dispute. This child, medically and intellectually fragile since birth, endured the disruption of 17 foster placements dur-

280

ing the first 3 years of her life and severe physical and sexual abuse while in the care of a mother struggling with substance abuse, family problems, and her own intellectual and emotional limitations in addition to her child's; all of these factors add severe and permanent emotional injuries to the burden of handicapping conditions with which our daughter must struggle daily. Extremely frustrated with the lack of a permanency plan for our daughter after several years, my husband and I ultimately met with her birth mother and [coordinated] our efforts, thereby allowing a mother who sincerely cared for her child, but was unable to provide day-to-day care, to be part of the decision-making for her child's future. She continues to maintain sporadic contact with her daughter and, insofar as the law protects our right to legally parent our child, this is a comfortable arrangement for us and an appropriate one for our daughter.

Our youngest child's permanency has been successfully impeded for several years by an incarcerated parent whose parental rights are protected despite a sentence of 75 years' imprisonment for an extremely violent crime. This man who has lost the right to vote has not lost the right to further damage his child.

The Inadequacy of the Current System

I realize that many people have come before this committee with many other examples of the victimization of children by laws and systems whose sole intent is to protect them from such victimization. I recognize that none of this is new to you as legislators and that much hard work and close scrutiny has been focused upon righting the wrongs, closing the gaps, correcting the inequities in our child welfare systems, and in instituting, supporting and funding the services needed to protect children and families. Yet despite all that has been accomplished, despite all of the accessible, sound medical and academic research emphasizing the extreme importance of nurturance, safety and quality care on healthy development, our laws and certainly our practice continue to place young children in continued jeopardy and ultimately cause long-term, often permanent damage to their physical, intellectual and emotional development. Children and families continue to endure living conditions so impoverished that minimal health and living standards cannot possibly be maintained. Intervention services are often short-term, inadequately funded, and/or administered and frequently perceived by families to be intrusive, judgmental, and disrespectful of family dynamics and cultural values. Children continue to reside with substance-abusing parents for excessively open-ended periods of time while their physical and emotional safety is at serious risk. And our clearly acknowledged problem of teen pregnancy in this country has been progressively exacerbated by the extreme problems associated with children parenting children. My children would have been better served by a system that recognized a birthparent's inadequacy to provide care on a day-to-day basis while at the same time respecting her need to maintain her status as the biological parent.

Our son—and countless others like him—is plagued by a devastating inability to trust that pervades every aspect of his life. Despite his many successes, his self-esteem and confidence in his own worth and abilities are severely impeded. Impairments in such areas as cause-and-effect thinking make it virtually impossible for him to generalize from one situation to another, to learn from his mistakes, to grow and develop in meaningful ways. His relationships and interactions with others are adversely impacted by his anger and mistrust and he struggles in so many aspects of day-to-day life that come so easily to others.

Our daughter's emotional injuries appear to be even more profound. While the physical effects of the drugs and alcohol and her prematurity are difficult, they are correctable on some level, and she has undergone frequent surgical and medical procedures over the years. The neurological, intellectual and emotional deficits are far more extreme and far-reaching. Intellectual retardation is a daily struggle. Seventeen foster placements and numerous other disruptions appear to have permanently impaired her ability to form intimate, meaningful attachments to other people; at best, her relationships with others are exceedingly superficial and she is virtually unable to relate to others in anything other than a self-focused, self-absorbed way, lacking the normal give-and-take reciprocity of even an immature human relationship.

A Call for a National Standard

Increasing societal problems—and our handling of them—have had profound effects upon adoption in this country. My own children and the growing population of children for whom we seek adoptive placement are dramatically—and permanently— affected by the significant traumas of their young lives. These traumas are becoming more far-reaching and more extreme. We must attempt to facilitate legislation and services that minimize such traumas, an extremely difficult charge given the added responsibility of protecting simultaneously the rights of the adults involved. A national call for standards of child care in each state may be a mechanism by which we can encompass and address such issues as how long substance-abusing parents can be allowed to place their children's immediate safety and their future development at risk while they struggle to solve difficult, sometimes insurmountable problems. Should we continue to allow drug-addicted mothers to leave the hospital with their drug-addicted infants? Standards may also be implemented to address minimum age requirements for "independent parenting," that is, to establish an age at which a person may be expected or allowed to parent without intervention or services; I believe that my son's life—and perhaps even his mother's life—would have been positively affected had this system been in place at the time of his birth. Perhaps individual states need to be encouraged to provide a process by which parents can permanently relinquish day-to-day care of their child to nurturing caretakers while maintaining the opportunity to continue to receive information about their child's well-being. While this is clearly not appropriate in all cases, I know that in Connecticut, families are consistently told that open adoption agreements are not legal and there is no process in place to address flexibility and individuality of planning for children whose birth families feel the need to have some ongoing contact or access to information. Clearly, I do not presume to be qualified to set, or even to recommend, what these national standards or guidelines for quality child care would be, but I feel confident that there are numbers of competent people in each state that are well able to address these issues.

Permanent Problems

Many problems are inherent in the day-to-day parenting of children suffering the often permanent effects of emotional and/or physical injury. As I described in telling about my own children, these children often carry with them to their new families a deep-seated rage and profound inability to trust that permeates every aspect of their lives and therefore every aspect of their families' lives. Our children's emotional instabilities have made their lives at home, at school and in the community extremely difficult ones. It was a painful learning experience for us as parents to come to terms with the reality that there are some aspects of their personality development and their very beings that no amount of our love, nurturance and family stability can overcome. Since it is so profoundly difficult for our son to trust, he has been virtually unable to receive and therefore benefit from the positive feelings of others; family occasions are extremely difficult for him, as is communication and expression of affection, and it is extremely painful, as a parent, to watch a child remain on the periphery of a family that wants so desperately to welcome him inside. We have had to learn, with the invaluable help of other adoptive and foster families, not only to accept the inconsistent and minimal attempts at connection that are so small yet so extremely difficult for him to make, but to validate them for him and to explain and sometimes justify them for our other children. Each day we watch him struggle to conform, or more accurately, to appear to conform, to the world's expectations of how a person needs to act and react; we watch him struggle to maintain his anger, to hide his mistrust of others, to build relationships that are comfortable for him that don't threaten and overwhelm his impaired capacity for understanding human interaction and reciprocity. We watch our daughter's struggle with her limited understanding of her own intellectual, physical and emotional deficits. Even more profoundly than her brother, her ability to connect to people in a meaningful way has been devastatingly impaired and her superficiality and complete disregard for the feelings and needs of others meet with understandable rejection from adults and peers alike. Her need to control is closely linked to her instinct to survive and results in extreme forms of manipulative and controlling behaviors that make her extremely difficult to manage at home and at school.

The Rights of Children

My mother was 15 years old when I was born. . . . When I was about 4 years old, [I was] abandoned by my mother. . . . Although my mother was unable to recover from her addictions, she was unwilling to relinquish her rights as a parent. . . .

Before my childhood was complete, I lived in a total of nine different foster, adoptive and group homes. I don't think this would have happened if the courts had terminated parental rights of my parents within one or two years after I was removed. It is a miracle, Senators, that I am able to speak before this distinguished body as a functioning adult. The system that was supposed to protect me when my parents could not, did not.

This does not have to keep happening to innocent children. . . . The rights of parents should not come before the rights of children who have no control over their destinies.

Shane Salter, testimony before the U.S. Senate Subcommittee on Children, Family, Drugs, and Alcoholism, July 15, 1993.

Behavioral issues are with both children on a regular basis and it has been consistently difficult for us and for other families to find resources and services that appropriately address the complexities of our children's trauma, loss, anger and grief. Understandably, conventional therapy often approaches children's difficulties from the vantage point of positive or negative family dynamics, yet in adoptive families of special needs children, the children themselves often have a significantly negative effect on family interactions. Many more therapists are needed who are familiar with the complex issues particular to our children's special needs. Also, adoptive and foster families are consistently viewed as part of the problem, not part of the solution, when behavioral or mental health issues arise, as it continues to be society's expectation that the love and nurturance of a stable family can overcome all obstacles and repair all of the damages of the past, no matter how devastating they may have been. Schools and other institutions, though well intentioned, continue to set standards of conformity that for my children—and for many emotionally injured children—are virtually unattainable, causing further rejection for children who expect nothing else; families then find themselves in the position of advocating, not only for their children, but, in essence, for their own right to be parents and responsible decision-makers.

Loving Without "Fixing"

To summarize, adoptive families need to be encouraged to take risks, to love and to nurture children without assuming the responsibility of "fixing" them. If indeed we believe that children grow better in families, we need to nurture and respect those families, understanding that they are not perfect and do not need to be, that they cannot repair the injuries and damages that their children have sustained. We need to encourage school systems and other institutions to develop mentally healthy environments, capable of accepting children who may never be capable of conformity. We need therapists who understand the dynamics of adoption; pediatricians, dentists and other practitioners who will accept an adoption subsidy for medical care; coaches, teachers and community members who understand that our children's actions and reactions may be inappropriate at times. We need to help adoptive families to continue to emotionally and legally parent children who can no longer live within the family system or who require residential treatment.

In the meantime, we are and will continue to be families. Like all families, we are strong in some areas and weak in others; we love our children and we do the very best that we can.

Periodical Bibliography

The following articles have been selected to supplement the diverse views presented in this chapter.

Annette Baran and Reuben Pannor	"It's Time for Sweeping Change," *American Adoption Congress Newsletter*, Summer 1990. Available from 1000 Connecticut Ave. NW, Suite 9, Washington, DC 20036.
Richard Barth	"Adoption Research: Building Blocks for the Next Decade," *Child Welfare*, September/October 1994.
Elizabeth Bartholet	"Family Matters," *Vogue*, November 1993.
Robert Clifford and Pamela Menaker	"'Wrongful Adoption' Gains Acceptance," *The National Law Journal*, September 28, 1992.
Renee Cordes	"Parents Kept in Dark Find Ray of Hope in Wrongful Adoption Suits," *Trial*, November 1993.
Anne Fish and Carol Speirs	"Biological Parents Choose Adoptive Parents: The Use of Profiles in Adoption," *Child Welfare*, March/April 1990.
Joan Hollinger	"A Failed System Is Tearing Kids Apart," *The National Law Journal*, August 9, 1993.
Marty Jones	"Adoption Agencies: Can They Service African-Americans?" *Crisis*, November/December 1992.
Rita Laws	"Adoption Subsidies: Is Your Family Eligible?" *Adoptive Families*, July/August 1994. Available from 3333 Hwy. 100 No., Minneapolis, MN 55422.
Jan Lewis	"Wrongful Adoption: Agencies Mislead Prospective Parents," *Trial*, December 1992.
Cheryl Reidy	"Adoption Fraud," *Adoptive Families*, September/October 1994.
Jolene Roehlkepartain	"Searching for Adoption Information," *Ours*, May/June 1993. Available from Adoptive Families of America, 3333 Hwy. 100 No., Minneapolis, MN 55422.
Elizabeth Rompf	"Open Adoption: What Does the 'Average Person' Think?" *Child Welfare*, May/June 1993.

Jean Seligman	"Stirring Up the Muddy Waters," *Time*, August 30, 1993.
Julie Shoop	"'Ounce of Prevention' Proposed for Adoption Law," *Trial*, December 1994.
Deborah Siegel	"Open Adoption of Infants: Adoptive Parents' Perceptions of Advantages and Disadvantages," *Social Work*, January 1993.
Gail Valdez and J. Regis McNamara	"Matching to Prevent Adoption and Disruption," *Child & Adolescent Social Work Journal*, October 1994. Available from Plenum Press, 233 Spring St., New York, NY 10013.
Beth Waggenspeck	"Damaging Images: Four Media Myths About Adoption," *Adoptive Families*, November/December 1994.

For Further Discussion

Chapter 1

1. Joss Shawyer sees the institution of adoption as a political act of aggression against women. Marvin Olasky pictures adoption as compassionate caring for a child's welfare. How are their differing views on adoption related to their fundamental differences on issues of feminism, abortion, and capitalism?

2. Charles D. Aring offers his personal experiences in an orphanage to support his argument that orphanages can be beneficial. How does his view of the orphanage experience compare with that of the North American Council on Adoptable Children? Which argument seems more appealing, and why?

Chapter 2

1. Concerned United Birthparents (CUB) suggests that most birth parents surrender their children to adoption unwillingly, due to circumstances they cannot control, or to pressure or lack of support from others. How might the membership and goals of the organization affect their description of "most birth parents"?

2. In what ways does the CUB view concur or disagree with the views of Paul Sachdev on the attitudes of birth fathers? How do the CUB and Sachdev viewpoints depict the "prevailing" view of birth parents?

3. Whose rights do Carole Anderson and Mary Beth Style believe should be protected in the adoption process? How do those beliefs affect their opinions about the "Baby Jessica" case?

4. Describe how the "Baby Jessica" case could have been handled differently at various stages (for example, at the time of the baby's surrender; when the birth parents first challenged the adoption). Whose rights should be protected at each stage?

Chapter 3

1. This chapter lists several alternatives to traditional adoption. Consider each alternative, then do the following:

   a. List arguments for and against each alternative. Note whether the arguments are based on facts, values, emotions, or other considerations.

   b. Rank the alternatives in order of preference, explaining

288

your rankings. If you do not believe an alternative should be allowed at all, explain why.

2. Many children today grow up in single-parent families. Should this fact affect decisions on whether single parents are allowed to adopt? Why or why not?

3. Elizabeth Hirschman urges that surrogate mothers should help infertile women have children, and should be allowed to charge a fee for doing so. Should decisions on whether to allow surrogate parenting revolve around the debate on charging fees for surrogacy? Why or why not?

4. Charmaine Yoest suggests that informal adoptions should be supported, in part because many black families find formal adoptions difficult. Yet she acknowledges that informal adoption is not the optimal situation for the child. Should the drawbacks of informal adoption be addressed by new policies, should formal adoption be made easier, or should another path be found? Support your answer.

Chapter 4

1. Kenneth J. Herrmann Jr. and Barbara Kasper believe that international adoptions should be discouraged, and that efforts should be made to help children within their own countries instead. Elizabeth Bartholet urges that transnational adoptions be supported and made easier. What evidence does each of their viewpoints offer to support these arguments? Which argument seems stronger? Why?

2. How do the views of the National Association of Black Social Workers, as expressed by Audrey T. Russell, and those of Rita J. Simon, Howard Altstein, and Marygold S. Melli reflect differing views of the nature of racism?

3. Judith K. McKenzie acknowledges that special needs adoptions present a formidable challenge, but believes that with intensive support, most special needs adoptions can work. Katharine Davis Fishman believes that some children are simply unable to live in a family, and are therefore unadoptable. After reading these two viewpoints, how do you think society should deal with children who may be unable to adjust to family living because they have been abused?

Chapter 5

1. Consider the pros and cons of open and sealed adoptions from the point of view of the adoptee, the adoptive parents, and the birth parents. Whose needs or wishes do you think should be paramount? Why?

2. In the past, adoption was considered the end of a process. Today, many advocates believe adoption agencies and government services should provide long-term support for adoptive families. After reading the viewpoints of the *Harvard Law Review*, Kenneth W. Watson, and Lynn G. Gabbard, what post-adoption support and services, if any, do you think adoptive families should receive? Should all adoptive families receive ongoing support, or just those with special problems? How do you think such efforts should be funded?

Organizations to Contact

The editors have compiled the following list of organizations concerned with the issues debated in this book. The descriptions are derived from materials provided by the organizations. All have publications or information available for interested readers. The list was compiled on the date of publication of the present volume; names, addresses, and phone numbers may change. Be aware that many organizations take several weeks or longer to respond to inquiries, so allow as much time as possible.

Adoptive Families of America (AFA)
3333 Hwy. 100 N.
Minneapolis, MN 55422
(612) 535-4829

AFA serves as an umbrella organization supporting adoptive parents groups. It provides problem-solving assistance and information about the challenges of adoption to members of adoptive and prospective adoptive families. It also seeks to create opportunities for successful adoptive placement and promotes the health and welfare of children without permanent homes. AFA publishes the bimonthly magazine *Adoptive Families* (formerly *Ours* magazine).

American Adoption Congress (AAC)
1000 Connecticut Ave. NW, Suite 9
Washington, DC 20036
(202) 483-3399

AAC is an educational network that promotes openness and honesty in adoption. It advocates adoption reform, including the opening of records, and seeks to develop plans for alternative models for adoption. It directs attention to the needs of adult adoptees who are searching for their birth families. AAC publishes the quarterly *Search/Support Group Directory*.

Center for Surrogate Parenting (CSP)
8383 Wilshire Blvd., Suite 750
Beverly Hills, CA 90211
(213) 655-1974
Fax: (213) 852-1310

CSP works to disseminate the latest information on the legal, moral, ethical, and psychological aspects of surrogate parenting. It publishes a newsletter on new procedures, events, and statistics concerning surrogacy.

Child Welfare League of America (CWLA)
440 First St. NW, Suite 310
Washington, DC 20001
(202) 638-2952
Fax: (202) 638-4404

CWLA, a social welfare organization concerned with setting standards for welfare and human services agencies, encourages research on all aspects of adoption. It publishes *Child Welfare: A Journal of Policy, Practice, and Program.*

Committee for Single Adoptive Parents (CSAP)
PO Box 15084
Chevy Chase, MD 20825
(202) 966-6367

CSAP is a clearinghouse for singles who have adopted or who wish to adopt a child. It supports the adoption "of adoptable children to loving families, regardless of any difference in race, creed, color, religion or national origin, or of any handicap the children may have." CSAP refers interested singles to local parent support groups and provides names of agencies that work with singles. It publishes the *Handbook for Single Adoptive Parents* and a directory.

Concerned United Birthparents (CUB)
2000 Walker St.
Des Moines, IA 50317
(800) 882-2777

CUB provides assistance to birth parents, works to open adoption records, and seeks to develop alternatives to the current adoption system. It helps women considering the placement of a child for adoption make an informed choice. It seeks to prevent unnecessary separation of families by adoption. It publishes the monthly *Concerned United Birthparents—Communication.*

Families Adopting Children Everywhere (FACE)
PO Box 28058
Northwood Station
Baltimore, MD 21239
(410) 488-2656

FACE provides support to adoptive parents and families and promotes legislation advocating children's rights. It publishes the bimonthly *FACE Facts* magazine.

Families for Private Adoption (FPA)
PO Box 6375
Washington, DC 20015
(202) 722-0338

FPA assists people considering private adoption; that is, adoption without the use of an adoption agency. In addition to providing information on adoption procedures and legal concerns, it offers referrals to doctors, lawyers, and social workers. FPA publishes the quarterly *FPA Bulletin.*

International Concerns Committee for Children (ICCC)
911 Cypress Dr.
Boulder, CO 80303
(303) 494-8333

ICCC helps those interested in adopting children from foreign countries. It acquaints prospective adoptive parents with ways to assist homeless children through sponsorship, fostering, and adoption. It publishes a quarterly newsletter, *International Concerns Committee for Children Newsletter*.

National Adoption Center (NAC)
1500 Walnut St., Suite 701
Philadelphia, PA 19102
(215) 735-9988

NAC promotes the adoption of older, disabled, and minority children and of siblings who seek to be placed together. It provides information, registration, family recruitment, and matching referral services for children and prospective adoptive parents. It publishes the semiannual *National Adoption Center Newsletter*.

National Adoption Information Clearinghouse (NAIC)
11426 Rockville Pike
Rockville, MD 20852
(301) 231-6512
Fax: (301) 984-8527

NAIC distributes publications on all aspects of adoption, including infant and intercountry adoption, the adoption of children with special needs, and pertinent state and federal laws. For research, it provides a computerized information database containing titles and abstracts of books, articles, and program reports on adoption.

National Association of Black Social Workers (NABSW)
8436 W. McNichols
Detroit, MI 48221
(313) 862-6700

NABSW seeks to support, develop, and sponsor programs and projects serving the interests of black communities. It is committed to a policy of same-race adoptions, promoting adoption of black children by black adoptive parents. NABSW publishes the annual *Black Caucus*.

National Coalition to End Racism in America's Child Care System (NCERACCS)
22075 Koths
Taylor, MI 48180
(313) 295-0257

This organization's goal is to assure that all children requiring placement outside the home, whether through foster care or adoption, are placed in the earliest available home most qualified to meet the child's needs. It believes that in foster care situations, the child should not be moved after initial placement simply to match the child's race or culture. It publishes the *Children's Voice* quarterly.

National Council for Adoption (NCFA)
1930 17th St. NW
Washington, DC 20009-6207
(202) 328-1200

Representing volunteer agencies, adoptive parents, adoptees, and birth parents, NCFA works to protect the institution of adoption and to ensure the confidentiality of all involved in the adoption process. It strives for adoption regulations that will ensure the protection of birth parents, children, and adoptive parents. Its biweekly newsletter, *Memo*, provides updates on state and federal legislative and regulatory changes affecting adoption. A new edition of its *Adoption Factbook* is forthcoming in late 1995.

National Organization for Birthfathers and Adoption Reform (NOBAR)
PO Box 50
Punta Gorda, FL 33951-0050
(813) 637-7477

NOBAR acts as an advocate for men affected by adoption, including birth fathers of adoptees, divorced fathers whose children are or may be adopted by stepfathers, single fathers, and adoptive fathers. The organization promotes social policies and laws that protect the individual rights of those involved; it also works for the unrestricted opening of adoption records for birth parents and adoptees. NOBAR publishes *Birthfathers' Advocate*, a monthly newsletter.

North American Council on Adoptable Children (NACAC)
970 Raymond Ave., Suite 106
St. Paul, MN 55114-1149
(612) 644-3036
Fax: (612) 644-9848

NACAC, an adoption advocacy organization, is composed of parents, groups, and individuals. It emphasizes special needs adoption, keeps track of adoption activities in each state, and promotes reform in adoption policies. NACAC publishes *Adoptalk* quarterly.

Resolve, Inc.
1310 Broadway
Somerville, MA 02244-1731
(617) 623-1156
Fax: (617) 623-0252

Resolve, Inc., is a nationwide information network serving the needs of men and women dealing with infertility and adoption issues. It publishes fact sheets and a quarterly national newsletter containing articles, medical information, and book reviews.

Reunite, Inc.
PO Box 694
Reynoldsburg, OH 43068
(614) 861-2584

Reunite, Inc., promotes adoption reform, encourages legislative changes, and assists in adoptee, adoptive parent, and birth parent searches when all parties have reached majority. It publishes a brochure, *Reunite*.

Annotated Bibliography of Books

Christine Adamec   *The Encyclopedia of Adoption.* New York: Facts On File, 1991. In addition to an introductory history of adoption, provides an alphabetized listing of important terms, issues, organizations, and legal decisions; nine appendixes supply information on birth rates, state social service offices, adoption agencies, and adoption-related literature.

Hal Aigner   *Adoption in America: Coming of Age.* Larkspur, CA: Paradigm Press, 1992. Relies extensively on information cited in judicial case reports of actions taken before appellate courts; eleven chapters cover topics such as the baby black market, the status and rights of unwed fathers and mothers, search and reunion activities, attacks on parental rights, and others.

Richard Barth and Marianne Berry   *Adoption and Disruption: Rates, Risks, and Responses.* New York: Aldine de Gruyter, 1988. Offers an extensive analysis of older-child adoption, reviews outcomes of placements, and considers and recommends changes in adoption policies and practices.

Elizabeth Bartholet   *Family Bonds: Adoption and the Politics of Parenting.* Boston: Houghton Mifflin, 1993. Criticizes the current adoption process; argues that discrimination by age of parents, sexual preference, race, disabilities, and country of origin should be outlawed; maintains that society must reject the cultural assumption that adoptive families are second-best to biologically based families.

J. Douglas Bates   *Gift Children: A Story of Race, Family, and Adoption in a Divided America.* New York: Ticknor & Fields, 1993. Narrates the intimate story of the white Bates family's adoption of two African-American children in the early 1970s as sisters to their two sons; traces the sociological and psychological problems this arrangement created; sees transracial adoption as "an acceptable alternative . . . if there is any hope for race relations in this nation."

David Brodzinsky and Marshall Schechter   *The Psychology of Adoption.* New York: Oxford University Press, 1990. Collection of essays summarizing psychological research on adoption adjustment, the longtime effects of adoption, adoption and identity formation, open

296

adoptions, interracial adoptions, clinical and casework issues, and social policies.

David Brodzinsky, Marshall Schechter, and Robin Henig	*Being Adopted: The Lifelong Search for Self.* New York: Doubleday, 1992. Adoptees trace how being adopted is experienced over a lifetime; they indicate how adoption affects developmental tasks and relationships at each stage of life.
Child Welfare League	*The Adoption Resource Guide: A National Directory of Licensed Agencies,* 1990. Lists public adoption programs in each state; private, licensed adoption agencies with summary charts; national child welfare organizations; and search resources.
Lois Gilman ✕	*The Adoption Resource Book: All the Things You Need to Know and Ought to Know About Creating an Adoptive Family.* New York: HarperCollins, 1992. Provides basic information about adoption, adoption agencies, home studies, independent searches for a child, open adoption, and intercountry adoptions; contains a state-by-state adoption directory and an intercountry guide to U.S. agencies.
Joseph Goldstein, Anna Freud, and Albert Solnit	*Beyond the Best Interests of the Child.* Rev. ed. with epilogue. New York: Free Press, 1979. Contends that the child's interests should "be paramount in cases involving adoption, fostering, custody, and neglect, irrespective of the rights and wrongs of the adults concerned"; recommends that the child should be represented by counsel; urges that cases involving children should be treated as emergencies and heard without delay; argues that adoption orders should be irreversible from the day of placement.
Karen Gravelle and Susan Fischer	*Where Are My Birth Parents? A Guide for Teenage Adoptees.* New York: Walker Publishing Co., 1993. Discusses how and why adopted children may try to locate and get to know their birth parents and examines possible psychological benefits and problems associated with the process.
Betty Jean Lifton	*Journey of the Adopted Self: A Quest for Wholeness.* New York: BasicBooks, 1994. An adoptee explores the struggles and journeys of adopted people; although some reviewers find its presentation passionately one-sided, it provides valuable resources for adoptees, birth parents, and adoptive parents.
Lois Melina and Sharon Kaplan Roszia	*The Open Adoption Experience.* New York: Harper Perennial, 1993. Detailed discussion of the advantages, problems, surprises, expectations,

	adjustments, and rewards of open adoption for all involved.
Ellen Paul, ed.	*The Adoption Directory*. Detroit: Gale Research, 1989. Lists state statutes on adoption, public and private adoption agencies, adoption exchanges, foreign agencies, information on independent adoptions, foster parenting, biological alternatives, and support groups.
Elinor Rosenberg	*The Adoption Life Cycle: The Children and Their Families Through the Years*. New York: Free Press, 1992. Blends current research, theory, and practical advice to provide a framework for understanding how adoption affects all members of the adoption triad at each stage in their lives.
Rita Simon, Howard Alstein, and Marygold Melli	*The Case for Transracial Adoption*. Washington: American University Press, 1994. Provides statistics on transracial and intercountry adoptions; rehearses current law regarding such adoptions; presents the case for and against transracial adoption; reviews results of recent empirical studies; makes policy recommendations; and concludes that the "best-interest-of-the-child" policy requires that the issue of race be eliminated as a determinate criterion for adoption.
Arthur Sorosky, Annette Baran, and Reuben Pannor	*The Adoption Triangle: The Effects of Sealed Records on Adoptees, Birth Parents and Adoptive Parents*. Garden City, NY: Anchor Press, 1978. This classic in the field of adoption studies takes exception to the then-current adoptive processes; argues that adoption laws should be changed to permit adult adoptees access to their original birth records.
Jean Strauss	*Birthright: A Guide to Search and Reunion for Adoptees, Birthparents and Adoptive Parents*. New York: Penguin, 1994. Proceeds from the view that seeking reunion with relatives estranged by adoption is a good thing; marshals reasoning and evidence to support her case.
Nancy Verrier	*The Primal Wound: Understanding the Adopted Child*. Baltimore: Gateway Press, 1993. This book may be ordered from Nancy Verrier, 919 Village Center, Lafayette, CA 94549.
Kenneth Watson and Miriam Reitz	*Adoption and the Family System*. New York: Guilford Press, 1992. Seeks to integrate adoption issues with family therapy; links members of the adoption triangle—adopted persons, birth parents, and adoptive parents—and their complex family systems networks; addresses adoption issues of loss, attachment, and identity for each member of the triangle.

298

Index